FUTURE LOST, FUTURES FOUND

Compiled by

**sands
lothians**
stillbirth & neonatal death society

Supporting bereaved parents in the Lothians for over 30 years
Scottish Charity No. SC 024375 Company Ltd. By guarantee

CPI Group
White Quill
The Orion Centre, 108 Beddingon Lane
Croydon, Surrey, CR0 4YY
Registered Office as above.

First published 2013 by SANDS Lothians (Stillbirth and Neo-natal Death Society)

Printed and bound by CPI White Quill Croydon

ISBN 978-0-9926998-0-2

ACKNOWLEDGEMENTS

Many parents have contributed to this book. We would like to thank them all. With them, we remember their precious babies.

In acknowledging our deepest gratitude, it has to be said that this book would not exist at all but for the vision of one person

Dorothy Maitland, Operations Manager

Our sincere thanks also to

Ian Laing, Consultant Neonatologist

Design and photographs by Jacqui Irvine B A [Hons] Painting

The book committee:

Yuill Irvine

Iris Quar

Anna Stamp

Before publication any book requires someone to do the vital yet unenviable job of checking the multitude of finer details relating to such things as grammar and spacing. We have been very fortunate to have had the services of

Anne Boyle

David Cockburn

Linda-Jane Simpson

FOREWORD

I first looked after newborn babies in the Simpson Memorial Maternity Pavilion in 1980. I was a registrar, and the medical and nursing staff was a tiny fraction of the numbers we have today. Neonatology (care of newborn babies) was in its infancy! We did not understand how aware babies were of their surroundings. Our facilities were meagre, and the techniques available to us were very limited.

The 1980s in Edinburgh brought two revolutions. The first comprised an increased sophistication in the technology that became available and our knowledge of ventilators, incubators and monitors. The second was in our developing a new gentleness with infants and their families. A counselling room was created, parent facilities were expanded, and babies began to be treated as individual dignified human beings.

Much of the stimulus which created the increased sensitivity to the compassionate needs of babies came from SANDS. Dorothy Maitland took over as Group Co-ordinator of the Lothian Branch, and built a strong relationship with senior members of the Simpson Neonatal Unit. Not only did she cause the standards of holistic care to improve in the Unit, she also willingly gave her time to teach senior staff, trainees, and both medical and nursing students. Only those who have experienced stillbirths or neonatal deaths can understand the huge burden of grief that parents carry when such tragedy strikes. SANDS has, for decades, provided a safe haven for parents under such pressures. While maintaining confidentiality, Dorothy and her excellent colleagues have used feedback from parents to educate further the staff in Lothian caring for families experiencing perinatal losses.

Thanks to SANDS, our attitudes have been revolutionised. Our bonds with parents are closer than ever before. SANDS has created a precious legacy which will never be lost.

Ian Laing

Consultant Neonatologist

CONTENTS

FATHERS' STORIES

MOTHERS AND FATHERS' STORIES

INFORMATION

INTRODUCTION

A future is lost with the death of a baby. SANDS Lothians is there at that overwhelming moment to connect parents with others who have survived a similar devastating experience.

While comparisons can be drawn between the stages of bereavement felt when any of us experiences a loss, the grief and desolation felt by parents after the often inexplicable death of their child is particularly acute and without measure. Other people, in their ignorance, often seem unable to understand or feel empathy for the grieving parent(s). In response, parent(s) then often feel the intensity of their loss is overlooked, trivialised or even dismissed, thus causing them further distress when they are already experiencing one of the most intense and profound losses anyone ever has to face.

The stories contained in this book consist of recorded conversations with parents and, in other cases, they have written down their experiences. By reading them in this collection, we hope that grieving families can see a glimmer of hope and find the courage to create a new future. It will be a hard road but SANDS Lothians, is there to help, at any time. With a true shared understanding.

When my twin daughter, Kaelen Charlotte McKenzie, died on the 9th June 1986, I honestly believed that I could never recover or be happy again. I will never forget the real physical ache that I felt. SANDS Lothians helped and encouraged me through those very dark days. I came to be very involved in helping the organisation and have now been the Operations Manager for twenty years.

My purpose has always been to help parents face a future of uncertainty with hope and courage. I want them to know that SANDS Lothians is there for them, every step of the way, for as long as it takes. I am truly proud of what SANDS Lothians offers bereaved families.

For me, the greatest tribute to Kaelen is for the organisation to continue to go from strength to strength, for many years to come. My thanks to my mum and my children, Grant, Kirsten, Megan and Robbie, who have all helped me so much by keeping Kaelen's memory a very big part of our family. I love each and every one of you so much.

SANDS Lothians COULD NEVER have been as successful today without the dedication and commitment of volunteers and staff past and present. I would like to take this opportunity to sincerely thank each and every one of you.

Dorothy Maitland
Operations Manager

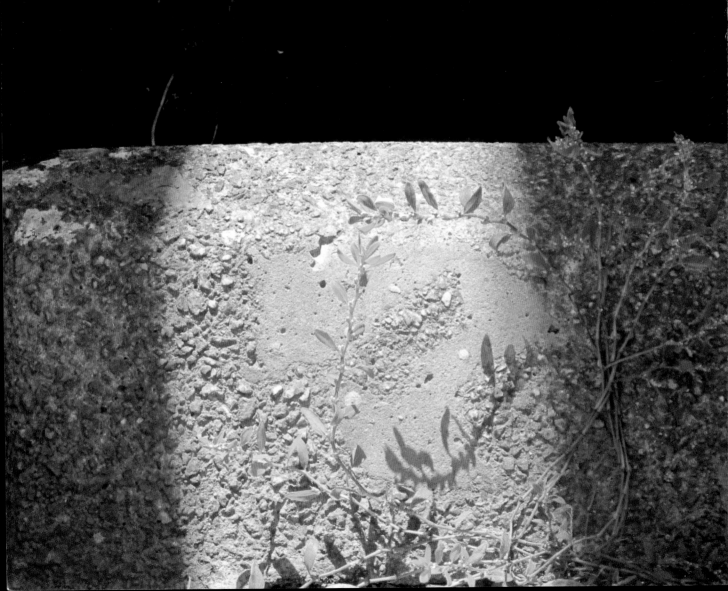

HISTORY OF SANDS LOTHIANS

"What we do for ourselves dies with us. What we do for others and the world, remains and is immortal."

Mason Albert Pike 1809-1891

In 1978 Sue was forty-plus weeks pregnant when her baby daughter was stillborn. She was unprepared for such a tragedy and left devastated. As the weeks and months passed, she found she desperately needed to speak to someone who had been through a similar experience. So she advertised in a local newspaper for anyone who had had a similar experience to call her.

The advert brought a response from other mums and Sue and they met up and found how supportive it was to talk about and share each other's experiences. They set up a small committee and did various fundraising events to put some money in the bank. They did not have regular meetings but spoke a lot to each other by telephone. This was how Edinburgh SANDS came to be founded and has since become SANDS Lothians. Its main project at that time was to provide Moses baskets to the hospitals. Edinburgh SANDS were keen that newly bereaved parents should see their baby in a Moses basket. This proved to be a wonderful idea much appreciated by bereaved parents.

In the late 1980s Jane took over. Her baby boy David died after being born prematurely. She decided to introduce monthly befriending meetings, which became a huge success. Jane also did a lot of home visits to bereaved parents, and raised funds by making Christmas cards for SANDS. During her time in office, monuments were unveiled at Rosebank Cemetery and at the Rose Garden in Mortonhall Cemetery. These proved such a comfort to parents as they had now somewhere to lay flowers in memory of their baby. Many parents did not know the resting place of their baby as they had been laid to rest in common ground in various cemeteries round the city.

In 1986 Professor Neil MacIntosh came to Edinburgh to work as Head of the Department of Child Life and Health. He was a huge influence on SANDS in Edinburgh. SANDS staff were invited to speak at medical student tutorials, thus making a great contribution to the students' learning and understanding.

In 1990 Dorothy took over as Chair. One of the first things she introduced was a separate telephone line in her house so that Edinburgh SANDS could be listed in the telephone book. This was to prove to be a great asset making it easier for parents to access help and advice from SANDS. The meetings became so big that they had to move from being held in members' houses to a church hall. The fact that on occasions fifty parents attended clearly indicated that it was a very much needed service. Dorothy also introduced memorial services throughout the year and she engaged the management at the local maternity hospital in talks about the provision of a family room.

It was at this time that Jeni became involved, in helping with the befriending. Her twin daughters Andrea and Amy had died after being born prematurely in 1987. The befriending was done in several ways, either on the telephone or by home visits and, in some cases, it required visits to psychiatric hospitals into which bereaved parents had been admitted. The profile of the work of SANDS was raised by newspaper articles, talks to health professionals and leaflets being sent out to various organisations.

Dorothy was also instrumental in the Council's allowing parents to mark their baby's grave in the Mortonhall Baby Rose Garden. When this common ground area for stillborn babies was opened, parents were initially not allowed to mark the grave. However, this was changed and it was of enormous help and comfort to parents.

SANDS Lothians are in talks with the Edinburgh City Council to landscape the Rose Garden. The roses have died due to a rose disease which makes it impossible for the roses to grow there. Talks are also on going about ways of improving the area to make it a nice tranquil place where parents can spend time visiting their baby's grave.

Between 1993 and 1995 there were huge changes. A SANDS Family Room was opened at the Simpson Memorial Maternity Pavilion on the ante-natal ward. This was jointly funded by the hospital and Edinburgh SANDS. The room was like a comfortable hotel room, giving parents the time and privacy to spend with their stillborn baby, and also for close friends and family to visit. The room proved to be a great comfort to many parents and their families, and many babies were baptised in this room too.

As the workload increased, Dorothy felt that office premises would be a necessary next step forward. SANDS were very fortunate to be able to rent the basement floor of the Red Cross Building in Great King Street Edinburgh for a token payment. The office there certainly put SANDS on the map as a more professional organisation. During this time we also took on Ruth as our bereavement counsellor. When the Red Cross eventually sold the building, we rented various offices.

Currently, we offer many services to bereaved parents at our Craiglockhart office, where we have been happily based since August 2000. SANDS now employs seven part-time staff, four of whom are bereaved parents. Our name change to SANDS Lothians reflects the fact that our parents are spread all over the Lothians.

We also rent office space at Craigsfarm, Livingston in West Lothian. Nicola co-ordinates this group, and she and Pamela run the various groups. Nicola has built up excellent relations with maternity staff in West Lothian which is proving to be extremely helpful to parents when they find themselves in one of the most difficult situations they will ever have to face. Jeni successfully completed her counselling degree, which was funded by SANDS Lothians, and is counselling there two days a week.

SANDS Lothians remains very much involved in the teaching programmes of students and medical professionals. We regularly have student midwives on placement.

SANDS Lothians continues to be responsible for many positive changes within the Lothians. At present, the Scottish Government is looking at legislation to change procedures to give every parent the chance to get their baby ashes after a cremation. SANDS Lothians was responsible for bringing to light in November 2012 the fact that some crematoria give ashes and others do not. Parents were told there would be no ashes when in fact, there were and, in some cases, these ashes were interred in the Garden of Remembrance without the parent's knowledge. SANDS

Lothians is advocating for a change in the law to be made, so that all staff – NHS, funeral directors, chaplains, crematoria staff follow the same procedure nationwide and give parents accurate information and the opportunity to make choices about what they want for their babies.

Andrea & Amy Rudge

1 December 1987

"In 1987 my twin girls, Andrea and Amy, were born prematurely and both died at birth. They are the reason I am writing this today, and a big part of why I am doing this work. They changed my career from nursing to counselling, and I thank them for the inspiration.

"I also thank my family and friends and of course SANDS Lothians for supporting me through the dark days and beyond. I used to suppress emotion and I had to learn how to share my feelings with others, but when Andrea and Amy died I wanted to tell the world about their brief time with me. I needed to give their lives a purpose and keep their memory alive.

"It has been my privilege to work with so many parents and families over the last 25 years and to hear about their precious babies. It has been an honour to be a small part of their journey to learn to live their lives again after the death of their baby. I hope the courage these parents have had to share their story will help others, who sadly find themselves in a similar position, those caring for them and those who are trying to understand.

"Andrea and Amy would be 26 if they were here today. I hope I have lived those 26 years well for them, and I know they have shown me a way forward."

Jeni Winton
West Lothian Counsellour

18

SANDS LOTHIANS' SUPPORT SERVICES

"You cannot find peace by avoiding life"

Virginia Woolf 1882-1941

BEFRIENDING AND COUNSELLING

SANDS Lothians offers two vital services to help parents cope with their loss – befriending and counselling.

All befrienders within SANDS Lothians are bereaved parents. Befriending can be done individually and in groups, and this allows parents to share their experience with others and to feel less isolated. Any parents that undergo befriending sign a befriending agreement. This allows the befriender to speak with the SANDS Lothians' counsellor about each case. This gives the befriender any necessary back up and support that they may need and, in turn, allows them to give back to the parent the best service and support possible.

If parents feel ready and at least a year or more has passed since their own loss, they can undergo befriending training. This allows them to get some insight into what is involved in helping others in this way, if and when they feel the time is right, they can go on to become befrienders themselves. Many parents find great solace in going on to help other bereaved parents and very often, this can help them find a new and positive way forward from the devastation of their own loss.

Counselling is offered by trained practitioners who are bound by professional codes of ethics and are legally required to have their own supervision from an appropriately trained counselling supervisor, all completely confidential. SANDS Lothians' counsellors offer a safe and non-judgemental space for parents to explore their difficulties, past and present. This service offers a private and confidential relationship between the counsellor and the parent.

CRAIG MILLAR COUNSELLING ROOM

The SANDS Lothians' counselling room was created to provide a private, comfortable and safe place for bereaved parents to speak to the SANDS counsellor. The counselling service is there for anyone who feels they need a little extra help, over and above befriending.

SANDS Lothians has been offering a counselling service across the Lothians since 1991 and has, to date, helped countless parents.

Their counselling room was named in memory of a little abandoned baby boy, who, to this day, remains unidentified and was found dead in a housing estate in the Craigmillar area of Edinburgh in March 2001. The baby's burned and mutilated body was found dumped on waste ground in the estate. Sadly, extensive efforts to find the baby's mother failed, so the baby was adopted by the community and taken to their hearts.

The community raised nearly £5000 to pay for the baby's funeral, burial and a memorial. They named the little boy Craig Millar and laid him to rest in a dignified manner. As many of the funeral costs were provided free of charge, there was a surplus remaining in the fund of nearly £4000. The community then decided that this sum should be donated to SANDS Lothians and the Simpson Memorial Maternity Pavilion.

The counselling room was given the backing of former Prime Minister Gordon Brown and his wife, Sarah, who themselves lost their daughter, Jennifer, at just ten days old after she suffered a brain haemorrhage. It was then officially opened in October 2002 by a local MP.

FAMILY ROOMS

A family room is a place where parents can have precious time and privacy with their baby after its birth. Family members can join the parents during these difficult but treasured hours with their baby. It gives them time to really look at their baby; time to touch him or her and count their little fingers and toes. It allows them time to be mummy and daddy and take photos of their precious new arrival.

The room is appropriately furnished along the lines of a hotel room, helping to remove the feeling of its being in a clinical environment. There is a double bed for the couple, and they can have the baby in a Moses basket or crib beside them for as long as possible. The introduction of the cold cots will be a great advantage in situations such as this.

After long discussions throughout the two years from 1993-95, SANDS Lothians furnished the first ever family room in Simpson Memorial Maternity Hospital, situated on Ward 49, the antenatal ward. The room became known as the SANDS Room. The establishment of the family room helped parents immeasurably and assisted the staff too.

Sadly, before family rooms existed, bereaved parents were often put in a room on the main labour ward and had to listen to the cries of healthy babies on the ward, while their baby lay motionless and quiet. Now, parents still have to deliver in the labour ward but are soon transferred to the SANDS Family Room. In some cases, the baby is baptised in the room.

Since the introduction of the family room in Simpsons, SANDS Lothians has been instrumental in setting up family rooms in hospitals in Edinburgh and throughout the Lothians, thus making a dreadful situation a little easier for parents and sparing them any unnecessary pain and sadness.

MEMORIAL SERVICE

Christmas is a difficult time for bereaved parents. SANDS Lothians has been holding memorial services since 1990, and, from 2002 a remembrance service has been held every year at Christmas time. It is held in a local church and parents are encouraged to take part in this meaningful service which can bring them a great deal of comfort. From recent studies, SANDS Lothians has ascertained that their memorial services have helped 87 per cent of families with the emotional aspect of their loss. SANDS Lothians' 'Lights of Love Heart' goes up in their office at the end of November along with their Christmas tree. Parents can light a candle and put a memento on the tree in memory of their baby at what is often a difficult time of year for them.

EDUCATION

SANDS Lothians' educational programmes are a very important element of their work. The organisation works closely with the medical profession and is heavily involved in teaching sessions with fourth year medical students at Edinburgh University.

Their educational work provides the students with an extremely valuable insight into the experience of perinatal death. Members of the SANDS Lothians' team attend these sessions along with a bereaved parent. The students are always very moved by the parents' experiences and get a great deal from these sessions.

SANDS Lothians also speaks at Napier University in Edinburgh to students, qualified midwives and those studying child nursing.

As part of their training, the organisation also offers student midwives placements, which allow them to gain experience in supporting bereaved parents and their families after they have experienced the death of their baby.

The team have also spoken to paediatric bereavement groups and participated in paediatric bereavement study days.

MEDICAL STUDENTS AND STUDENT MIDWIVES' COMMENTS

"So impressed with how brave the speaker was, very emotive"; "Very interesting to hear a story from a parent's perspective"; "Very helpful to hear real life experiences and lessons that can be learnt"; "Found this talk very emotive and captivating."

STUDENTS' EXPERIENCES OF SANDS

"I spent four weeks with SANDS Lothians In February to March 2012. I asked to spend time at SANDS in order to gain a better understanding of the impact of perinatal loss on women and their families. I hoped to learn what women expect from their midwives in such tragic circumstances and, most of all, how to communicate with them. During my four weeks, I got to meet a lot of women and was very grateful to each of them for sharing their experiences with me. I learned a lot from each story I heard – the general feeling was that when a woman suffers a loss, she is treated like a leper and almost hidden away. Nobody knows what to say to them and, as a result, they are often ignored.

"These women are mums and want a chance to talk about their babies and, if we don't know what to say, then that is OK – us midwives are only human! I also learned what an invaluable job the staff at SANDS do – from holding counselling services and befriending groups to helping organise funerals and finding a baby's final resting place; they truly provide an invaluable service to women and their families at the worst possible time. I felt honoured to have been welcomed by them and very grateful to everyone who shared the story of their very precious babies."
Hayley Moir

"Following Hayley's experience earlier in the year, I felt that I would really benefit from doing some work experience at SANDS as a newly qualified midwife. My training had not provided me with any experience with women and their families who were suffering or had suffered from a perinatal loss, and I knew SANDS would be a great place to learn about these experiences and to make me think about how, as a midwife, I would support families through this traumatic experience. I have been shocked, cried and laughed at my time here, I hold so much respect for everyone who works, volunteers or attends meetings with SANDS. My experience has shown me how important communication is with health professionals and families, and I will carry my knowledge and experience with me throughout my career as a midwife."
Melanie Marr

GRAVE TRACES

In the late 1980s SANDS Lothians began doing grave traces in Edinburgh and the surrounding areas, after many parents who had been long bereaved, began to contact them in search of their loved ones' graves.

They held their first meeting about this subject in their office in Great King Street, Edinburgh. The meeting was attended by more than 50 people. Also there that night was George Bell, the then Principal Officer at Mortonhall Crematorium and Cemetery. Even as early as at that meeting and with the help of his book of records, Mr Bell was able to put some parents' minds at rest and tell them the whereabouts of their babies' graves.

Anyone looking for a grave can contact SANDS Lothians. They will then be asked to sign forms giving SANDS permission to act on their behalf. SANDS will then apply for birth and death certificates or stillbirth extracts and they will cover any costs involved. The SANDS team have built up an excellent relationship over the years with cemetery and crematorium staff throughout Edinburgh. They work closely with them during traces, and together, the search for the grave begins.

To date, around 100 successful grave traces have been completed. The outcome of a search for a grave depends heavily on the availability of good and accurate records. The cemetery and crematorium staff then pass the relevant information and maps to SANDS Lothians, who in turn, can then go on to show the parents their baby's burial place and accompany them to the cemetery to show them the area where their baby rests.

SANDS Lothians then does follow-up work in this area by offering the parents free counselling, if they feel it would be of benefit to them.

Graves have been traced as far back as the 1940s. Sadly, there are times when the grave traces prove to be very difficult and sometimes cannot be found, but the team at SANDS Lothians never gives up trying to find them. The success of SANDS Lothians long-running grave trace service is something that can, often for the first time, give bereaved parents from years before - some who are still grieving - something tangible to prove that their baby existed.

Dorothy Meldrum and Bruce Meldrum's Story

At the age of 76, Dorothy (Dot) Meldrum was as sharp as a tack. She loved her computer and her mobile phone and got huge pleasure from crosswords and quizzes. She was even a lover of Facebook and a big fan of bingo and couldn't wait for people to come online so she could play the next game! Although Dot had a mental agility that would be the envy of many of us, her physical health was never quite so good.

In 2011 she was admitted into hospital following a heart attack. During this time, Dot's heart stopped completely, but happily, the resuscitation team managed to bring her back. This life-altering experience had a profound effect on Dot and after saying to her son, Tam: "I've been saved for something, son," one of the most remarkable stories began to unfold.

In 1959 Dot had suffered a stillbirth. The baby was her third child and incredibly, she was never even definitively told if it was a boy or a girl. As if that wasn't bad enough, her husband was told it was a boy and Dot was told it was a girl. Sadly, as so often was the case in those days, the baby was taken away and Dot and her husband, Jock, were just told to go home, get on with their lives and have more children... all as if nothing had happened.

Dot already had two children - Dot and Tam - and would go on to have a fourth, John. So life went on and the memories were buried, and the stiff British upper lip prevailed. But how can any parent ever forget such a traumatic experience as a stillbirth, however recently or long ago it happened? As a member of the SANDS Lothians' team says: "It is 26 years since my baby died, and, although I have four children, there should be five of them. There's always one missing."

After Dot's heart attack in 2011 and as part of her recovery, she began to see a psychologist and to confide in someone, perhaps for the first time, about the baby she had lost so long ago. One can only guess at the multitude of emotions that this must have unlocked for Dot. Perhaps having, so sadly, been made to feel she had to suppress her feelings of loss and in effect, behave like nothing had happened after such a massive bereavement, this must have brought huge relief to Dot, especially bearing in mind, that for all those years, she'd had to live with the fact that she was never sure if she was grieving for a lost son or daughter.

It was the psychologist who first made contact with SANDS Lothians in January 2012, after learning about their bereavement service for parents who had lost a child many years ago. She advised the SANDS Lothians' team that she was working with a lady who had suffered a stillbirth 52 years ago and asked if they could help find out more about this baby? After obtaining Dot Meldrum's permission, the SANDS Lothians' team began their investigation with very little to go on. Although believing that the baby was born in the Western General Hospital, they felt Seafield Crematorium was a good place to start. Remarkably, Seafield was able to confirm that there was a 'Meldrum' baby laid to rest in common ground there and the date that the funeral took place. Sadly, again, there was no indication if it was a little boy or girl.

A stillbirth extract was obtained from Register House. Worried that Mrs Meldrum would receive the extract through the post without warning, the SANDS Lothians' team wrote to her to forewarn her. As it happened, both the letter and the extract arrived through the post on the same day, but by yet another twist of fate in this remarkable story Dot opened the letter from SANDS Lothians first.

Talking fondly about their mother, her daughter, Dot, and son, Tam, recall: "Mum came on the phone to me," Tam says, "I could barely make out what she was saying, she was crying so much," he continues – I said, 'Mum, Mum, calm down, what are you trying to tell me?' He then went on to say: "Mum was eventually able to tell me that the team at SANDS Lothians had managed to trace the baby's resting place and had requested an extract from Register House of his birth. By that point, of course, I was bubbling away too! It was an incredible moment."

"We finished the call to allow us both to compose ourselves and only a few minutes later, Mum came back on the phone. It was then I heard my mum's words through her tears, 'It was a wee boy, Tam' – the extract had arrived from Register House in the same post." For the first time in 52 years, Dot Meldrum learned that she had given birth to a little boy and was at last able to name him. She named him Bruce.

Shortly after this, Dot's health took another turn for the worse. She was admitted to St John's Hospital in West Lothian and the family rallied round. "Everything happened so quickly," Tam, daughter Dot and grandson Sam recall. "We could barely believe it when the doctors told us that Mum wouldn't last the weekend. We had always wanted to take her to Seafield so she could see where Bruce had been laid to rest. This was so important to us as a family, and every member of the family, from the oldest to the youngest was involved in trying to decide what to do for the best. With the doctor's words ringing in our ears, we didn't want to take any chances. We decided, if we couldn't take Mum to Seafield, we would bring Seafield to her!"

Tam continues: "Dot, John and I piled in the car, armed with the camera and went down to the crematorium. We took loads of photos for Mum of the common ground and the memorial. Then we rushed up to get them all printed to take them to her in the hospital. Sharing the photos with Mum was one of the last things we were able to do with her before she began lapsing in and out of consciousness. Showing her where her baby boy was resting was the last meaningful thing we got to share with her; she had even managed to tell us that she was sure this was why she had been spared last year.

"Agonisingly, soon after we got the call from the hospital to say Mum's condition had changed and we should make our way in. Mum died on the 19th of February 2012. Mum always said she would go when she was ready. I'm positive that finding Bruce meant Mum felt she could let go.

"I can't even begin to say how much we will be forever grateful to SANDS Lothians for their incredible work and for working so quickly too. Mum became ill so soon after SANDS Lothians discovered all the information about Bruce. I can't imagine how awful it would have felt if we'd found Bruce after Mum died – it just doesn't bear thinking about. Finding him when we did brought such peace to Mum in the end."

On further investigation, the family found out that baby Bruce had died of a condition known as anencephaly – where the spine, brain and cranium don't form properly. During this research, it also transpired that Dot's younger brother, who had been born in January 1942, lived for three months, then died on 19th March 1942 from cardiac failure and congenital heart disease.

A SANDS Lothians' team member says: "Back in the 1950s, stillbirth was a taboo subject. What the doctors said was gospel and they were seldom questioned. It was well into the 80s and 90s before things began to change. It is so important that families be given as much information as possible from an emotional point of view but also and equally important, if a condition could be hereditary."

Dot Meldrum was only 23 years old when she had to endure the trauma of a stillbirth. The devastating effect of this event on her was barely acknowledged and she was expected to go home, take care of her other children and her husband and carry on with her life as though nothing had happened. It was another 52 years before she even knew if her lost child was a boy or a girl. Sadly, there is no doubt that many, many more elderly people alive today will be in a very similar position.

But this is just one of these stories. This is the story of a little baby boy born on the 18th June 1959, unnamed and lost to his family for 52 years. But Bruce Meldrum was never forgotten. Thanks to the hard work and determination of his family, SANDS Lothians and the resolute love of his mother in her final months, he was given a name and his resting place was established.

After over five decades of not knowing, Bruce's mum was given the peace of seeing her baby's resting place before she died. She even managed to choose where she wanted the dedication plaque to go. In her absence, the inscription was chosen by her loving family and poignantly reads: 'Bruce Meldrum, born 18th June 1959 – Found at last 2012.'

MOTHERS' STORIES

"What though the radiance that was once so bright,
be now forever taken from my sight.
Though nothing can bring back the hour of splendour in the grass,
glory in the flower;
we will grieve not,
rather find strength in what remains behind."

William Wordsworth 1770-1850

Lilly Berwick

"Lilly was my third pregnancy. I have a daughter, Hannah, who's eight years old and a son Liam, who's five.

"We found out I was pregnant in September 2010 and everything seemed to be going fine. We had the 12-week scan on the 21st of December, an early Christmas surprise! Again, everything was fine, which was such a relief, as I'd had a fall in the heavy snow we had had in November.

"On the 18th of January, I had a midwife appointment as that was me at my 16-week milestone. I was really looking forward to hearing the heartbeat! My mum came with me, along with my son. The midwife took my obs which were fine, then felt my fundus (the part of my uterus that could be palpated abdominally) but was having trouble getting a proper trace. She just said it was very faint, so she wanted me to go to the hospital, to be on the safe side. At this point, most people would be worried, but this happened with my eldest daughter so I assumed everything would be fine.

"When we arrived, I was taken into a treatment room. They put me on a monitor to check my pulse. The midwife wasn't happy, so she sent us down to the scan room for further checks. At that point, I knew something was wrong. I told my mum to get hold of my husband.

"He met us down at reception and my mum went to pick up my daughter from school. We were sitting in the waiting room and my heart sank when they called my name. At first, I refused to go in. Looking back, I realise I knew something was wrong and I just didn't want it confirmed as then it would make it painfully real. The lady we saw asked for my details and keyed them in. The screen came up and we saw the baby. She measured the baby at this point and asked, 'How many weeks did you say you were?' 'Sixteen,' I replied, at which point my husband squeezed my hand (he was watching the screen from a different angle). She turned the monitor round and then turned up the volume. Then she said the dreadful words, 'I am so sorry, sweetheart.'

"I remember screaming from the roof tops and sobbing, sobbing to the point where there were no tears left for me to cry. She had to have it confirmed by another lady, which just prolonged the agony, as part of me was hoping I would hear a heartbeat.

"We were taken into the family room to be told by the consultant that I would need to give birth to the baby. Both my husband and I were not happy about this, as I had had my eldest daughter by emergency caesarean section and my son by a planned section. The thought of going through a natural birth in such very sad circumstances, was something I dreaded. The consultant looked up from her notes and said to us, 'I understand, but you need your womb to be empty.' I wanted to slap her, how dare she? The midwife came back with a tablet and told me to come back on the Friday morning, the 21st January, at 10am.

"The Wednesday and Thursday were two unbearably long days but having said that, I can't really remember anything about them. My mum came with me on the Friday, as my husband couldn't manage. We were shown into a side room and the midwife introduced herself. She was really lovely. She was shocked and angry that nobody had given us any information on the options available to us with regard to the baby burial or cremation. This added to an already terribly difficult time as I then had to phone my husband to discuss our options.

"The tablets were given to me around 11am and our daughter, whom we named Lilly, was born at 2.30pm. She was completely perfect. I spent a couple of hours with her, giving her lots of kisses and cuddles. The hospital took some photos. I don't think I would have coped with any part of this painful experience without my mum being there. It was so special to be able to share and have those special moments with my mum and her granddaughter. I was discharged at 8pm.

"I will never forget seeing my husband's face when I came home and while showing him the pictures, he said, 'Just perfect.' I hated leaving Lilly, but kept cuddling the SIMBA (Simpsons Memory Box Appeal) blanket to bring me some comfort.

"She was laid to rest on the 8th of February at Loaninghill Cemetery. I think having the service and seeing my husband carry the coffin made it all the more real and brought so many more feelings to the surface. It was so lovely to share that day with close friends and family who were, and always have been, a massive support to us both.

"The post-mortem took 16 weeks to come back and the results showed my baby was a girl and the cord was round her neck twice. That was the only indication as to what had caused her death.

"In January 2012, in the run up to Lilly's first anniversary, I joined the SANDS West Lothian group after my friend Heather, who was always there for me with a shoulder to cry on when I needed it, found the group in the local newspaper. My husband has been my rock through all this, and I don't know where I would be without him. The shared sad loss of our daughter has brought us closer and made us even stronger. He gave me a lot of encouragement to attend the meeting. It was the best thing I ever did and I did it at just the right time.

"When I first went and heard the other parents' stories, I thought my loss was only at 16 weeks where all theirs were further on, but the team at SANDS completely reassured me that it was fine and, since then, the meetings and the help I have got through SANDS have brought me a lot of comfort and support. I was amazed at how many people were there. They had all lost a baby too and understood how I was feeling. They know exactly what to say at the right time, when you need it the most. This was such a comfort as often family and friends try to say the right thing but can unwittingly make things worse.

"The ladies at the meeting and myself all share something in common and a title, 'Angel Mummys'. I have formed friendships with these fantastic ladies that will last a lifetime and I can't thank SANDS Lothians enough."

Lilly

I love my little Lilly, I always will
the pain isn't fading like they said it will,
how can they understand
they didn't lose a child.
I miss your tiny toes and nose
I feel your essence as I hold your blanket close,
it is the memories now that I cherish the most
how can anyone understand?
How do they know?
Every day a tear will flow.
They don't know how I feel.
In my heart I hold you close and tight,
I can't hold you and kiss you goodnight
The heartache and the pain feels fresh and new,
Because inside my tummy you once grew.

It's now been over a year
since I kissed you goodbye
I imagine you are a butterfly in the sky
When it rains I look for a rainbow
I find you each day in all that I do,
when it's dark I look for your star
Every time there is a breeze I know you're not far
I love you right up to the moon and back.
Sweet dreams
Mummy and Daddy x

Sara Brash

"Our son Cameron was around three years old when I became pregnant again. With Cameron, my pregnancy had been relatively easy, but this time I had morning sickness from day one right the way through, which made me so tired. It was a long nine months, but all the scans and medical check-ups reported that the baby was doing fine despite how I was feeling. I was seven days overdue and at that completely fed-up stage, when I finally went into labour.

"It was a Monday morning around 9am, and I slowly progressed throughout the day at home. I suppose, in hindsight, there had been less movement than during previous days, but I didn't really think much of it as I was too busy thinking about the labour and what was to come. However, I do remember saying on the phone to one of the midwives at the hospital that there didn't seem to be as much movement, but she assured me that it was quite normal during labour.

"I sent Cameron off to his grandparents, and Duncan, my husband, came home from work. We phoned the hospital regularly throughout the day, but because the contractions were only about ten minutes apart, they kept telling us to wait at home as this hospital's policy is to only admit patients when contractions are around five minutes apart. The contractions started to get closer together throughout the night so we finally made our way to the hospital about 5am.

"By the time we got there, I'd been in labour for 18 hours. For a long time afterwards, I used to think about that walk across the deserted hospital car park – it was the last time we were happy. Despite what was ahead, we had that giddy feeling of anticipation. I remember Duncan joking that he could just make a bolt for the car and come back later when it was all over. We went into triage, had an initial assessment, and then the midwife strapped me into the heart monitor machine.

"I began to feel a little concerned as she could only find my heartbeat, but she reassured us that there must be something wrong with the machine and she went off to get another one. She came back a few minutes later with a second midwife and started hooking me up to the new machine. I know how temperamental these machines can be and, of course, they had to keep stopping every time I had a contraction so I wasn't overly worried.

"However, then both of the midwives began to act more frantically. Everything seemed to slow down and I recall that I could see people talking but couldn't hear anything. The room was really small and I remember suddenly being really aware of my surroundings, I looked up, and the room was suddenly full of a sea of blue uniformed midwives, about eight of them. I just couldn't fit together all the information, couldn't piece together all the little pieces of the jigsaw in my mind: where had they all come from, why were they crying, why are they all looking at me?

"I remember asking myself if I should be comforting them because they all seemed so upset and then I remember looking over at Duncan and he was leaning against the wall, holding his head in a really strange way, his hands over his ears as if he was trying to block something out.

"The next thing I remember was the midwife holding my hand and stroking it. She kept repeating over and over, 'Anna, do you understand what we're telling you?' Her words echoed in my head for years. It was like my brain was treacle and the pieces of the puzzle were coming together incredibly slowly, but as they did, my world collapsed. I suddenly felt like I'd been hit by a train. It was this sudden overwhelming, all consuming, and emotional punch. I would become so familiar with that horrendous feeling of delayed realisation over the following months, those ten seconds of 'normality' then BAM – reality hits as you realise that your baby is dead.

"Nobody could pinpoint the exact time our baby died, but it must have been a few hours earlier as there was no discussion over emergency delivery. A consultant called Sara Cooper came in to check me over. She was very kind. She recognised quite quickly that I had not realised that I still needed to give birth. It gradually dawned on me how far I still had to go and what lay ahead. They told me they would make me as comfortable as possible as the drugs now, obviously, wouldn't affect the baby.

"I don't know if it was the shock, but the drugs didn't work properly. Duncan was really struggling as he thought they would give me a caesarean section and it would all be over quickly. But they insisted that, because I was in good health and the baby was no longer a factor, there was no reason to take the risk of a caesarean.

"The hospital called my mum – like a mature 35 year old, I just wanted my mum! She came all the way up from North Berwick. She had been told that the baby had died, but she had not been told that it had not yet been delivered. Later she told me how shocked she had been when she walked into the room and saw that I had not delivered yet. She stayed with me and Duncan throughout the labour.

"Under the circumstances, the labour was as normal as it could be, but the hopelessness and the thought of not hearing my baby cry at the end was just dreadful. About five hours later, our baby was born. It was such a terrible time, there were people coming in and out all the time. During a normal labour, everything is so carefully monitored and controlled but when your baby dies, they just let it happen.

"It was all so clinical, like a medical procedure. As a result, the final minutes were very brutal. I found out later that the end of labour with a stillbirth can be quite fast and abrupt.

"Someone once explained to me that it's your body realising what's happened and it tries to discharge the stillborn to protect you and to stop you getting blood poisoning from your baby.

"I hate the term 'stillbirth' as it conjures up images of tranquillity and angels playing harps but it's nothing like that; it's all the hardship and pain of labour with none of the joy at the end, only devastation. I felt so sorry for my mum having to sit and watch everything. I think she would have left the room if the last five minutes hadn't been so dramatic with everything happening so fast. The doctors and midwives were all running in and out of the room as of course they were only concerned about my health. At some point during everything, there was a change of midwives and in walked Sara Davies. We were fortunate that she had a lot of experience in this area.

"Duncan and I were totally devastated by what had happened, and we were struggling to make sense of the important decisions we faced, such as whether or not we wanted to hold our baby. I remember initially being horrified at this thought as I didn't know what to expect, but the midwife was very supportive and talked everything through with us. She helped us realise how important these decisions would be in the years to come. Looking back, I was so glad to have her there and keep us focused, as at the time I just wanted to run out of the hospital. Naively, I thought I could just have the baby, be home by 2 o'clock and just put the whole thing behind me.

"After all the trauma and drama of the birth, the midwife was so calm. She checked my baby over, wrapped her in a white blanket and put her in my arms. Everything stopped. Here was my little baby. She was warm and pink and just looked like she was sleeping. She was totally perfect, a beautiful colour, with her little eyes shut. You would never know it was anything other than a sleeping baby. It was so surreal and utterly terrifying. I was scared to even touch her in case my finger went through her skin. Surprisingly, everything about her was very robust. I remember someone asking me if I wanted to wash her and my first thoughts were 'God, no, I'll break her!' This was the first time in my life I'd seen a dead body, and her body terrified me.

"Left up to me, I don't think I would have had the courage to pick her up myself, which is a horrible feeling as a mum. I have beaten myself up over that for years. It was so vital to have a good midwife with us at the time, to do the important things and make us aware of how precious this time is, and that if we didn't make the most of it, we would regret it for the rest of our lives.

"The whole situation was so far outside anything we had ever experienced before, that our normal coping mechanisms deserted us. The Anna that I had always been: confident, assured, always knowing my own mind, had disappeared [and I was] transformed into a gibbering wreck who couldn't function and who was terrified of a tiny baby.

"Looking back, I am so glad we spent that time with her. I didn't wash her, but I wish now I'd done everything. I wish I'd dressed her and gone for a walk with her but you just don't think straight at the time or have enough courage. I've heard about one girl who'd taken her baby for a walk round the hospital in a pram. To some people that might seem strange or upsetting, but I would say, do it, absolutely, do as much as you can with your baby, build as many memories as you can.

"There were so many questions, so many decisions, and so many people explaining so many things. We were asked about photographs, handprints, clothing and post-mortems. People kept appearing with yet more forms to be filled in and signed, and that's when it all got too much. I just wanted everyone to go away so I could process a little and cry, but I had to deal with the paperwork if I wanted to go home.

"One of the easiest decisions we made that day was naming our baby. We both agreed immediately. Both the midwife and the consultant who had been such an enormous part of the day were both called Sara. We had been staring at their name badges all morning. We had a list of names in Duncan's wallet, but when he suggested Sara, it just seemed perfect. A member of SANDS Lothians' team told me they feel that it's so important that women are led at this time. They need people to help guide them and tell them what they can do and what's allowed as they almost feel they have to do everything they're told.

"What she says is so true because I remember that I felt I had to ask permission to see Sara again later that morning, I felt as if she'd become the hospital's property, but she was mine. Sara was really big when she was born; she was 8.2lbs, robust and well developed so there was no problem about her deteriorating. We could have done a lot more with her, but we were so lost ourselves at the time and everything was so frightening and overwhelming.

"The second time she was brought into the room we just sat and held her for ages and stared at her. It was probably only about twenty minutes, but it felt so peaceful. The midwife then came in to get her. As she walked out the door with her for the last time, I thought my heart was going to explode. I just wanted to hold my baby and take her home. When the door shut, it was like I'd been cut off from her, a line had been drawn – that was it, my responsibility to my baby was gone.

"I remember clearly an overwhelming feeling of panic as we drove away from the hospital. I had no idea where Sara would spend the night or what they would do with her. Where would she lie, would she be cold? I can map every second of my son's life from the day he was born, but four hours after her birth, I had no idea where my daughter was. I remember driving past the hospital a few days later wondering if she was still there; it haunted me. I felt such a coward; I should have been braver and asked more questions. We could have spent more time with her the next day.

"I remember the midwife suggesting that we buy her something to wear and take it to the hospital. A few days later I stood in a shop, surrounded by pink babygros, and I just couldn't bring myself to buy anything, I wasn't brave enough. I was terrified that the sales assistant would ask who it was for. To this day, I have no idea what she was wearing in her little white coffin. I didn't even want to go to the funeral, and I didn't want anyone else to go. I just wanted to shut off my mind. I wanted to lock down my life, it was all too much.

"Poor Duncan had to deal with everything. He had to make sure that everyone was told, he had to get rid of all the baby things we had bought, sort all the death certificates, arrange the funeral and make sure that Cameron's life kept going. I just went into meltdown. I felt like a child, and Duncan did everything for me.

"The day of Sara's death is very vivid as is the day of her funeral, but I have no memory of the weeks in between. I have no memory of meeting people for the first time. Thanks to Duncan, I never had to tell anyone. Her funeral was held at Mortonhall. I genuinely did not want to go as I had no ability to control my feelings. Both sets of our parents were there, and we asked a family friend, Rev John Lindsay, to take a small service. We went to see him a few days before to discuss the arrangements. We were quite adamant that there was to be no mention of God or speeches about how things happen for the best.

"Looking back, it does seem a bit of an odd request to a minister, but at the time, he didn't question it. I spoke to him years later about it, and he told me that, in his entire life serving God, Sara's funeral was the hardest thing he has ever had to do, and it affected him for a long time after.

"We had agreed to a post-mortem but, not uncommonly, it gave no answers. There were no cord problems and there was nothing wrong with her, physically. She was fully developed and a good weight. The bottom line was that Sara suffocated, but how or why she suffocated we will never know. I can't believe in this day and age, with all the advances in technology and medicine, that is all we get.

"I tortured myself for years. Perhaps if I'd been stronger on the phone to the hospital, stressing the reduced movement, insisting I was coming in, things may have been different. In America, for example, you go in to hospital as soon as you go into labour, but because of our poorly funded maternity services, this is not an option. Perhaps if I had had a late scan or if Sara had been monitored sooner they would have known something was wrong and they could have got her out quicker. Ironically, because I kept good health, exercised, ate well and don't smoke, my pregnancy and labour were classified as low risk and therefore, resulted in no intervention.

"It is so frustrating, even now. I remain convinced Sara's death could have been prevented. I don't blame the hospital in any way, I blame the system. I don't think you should be allowed to go over 40 weeks, especially when you are aged 35, and doctors should always listen to a mother's gut instinct if they think something is wrong.

"I think being a strong, together person before this event made my reaction to it worse. It made me doubt and worry about every aspect of myself, and I began to be scared of myself. I'd never had any difficult emotional challenges to face in my life then, suddenly, this horrendous event happened that I had no control over. I couldn't change it or turn the clocks back. I couldn't even understand it, and I certainly couldn't make it better. I was so lost. That's what is so awful about death, it's so final. It's not like a disease that you can try and reverse.

"I struggled to cope with even the little things. Duncan used to lay my clothes out for me because I couldn't even think what to wear each day. We used to sit on a Sunday and draw up a plan for the week coming and what I would do each day. I was like a child that needed everything done for them. Duncan took seven weeks off work. For him to do that, shows the magnitude of how much it hit him too, as he had not had a day off sick since I met him. When Duncan returned to work we seemed to part ways in our grieving process. Up until that point we were on the same page, but returning to work gave Duncan some sort of normality back into his life and allowed him to be distracted from the way he was feeling.

"I was treading water and barely getting through each day. I had always had the ability to draw a line under an event and move on with life without looking back. But this time, I wasn't able to manage this. The more I tried to block out the enormity of everything and underplay it all to myself and others, the more haunted I became by it. I just buried it deeper and deeper so I did not have to deal with it. This became easier when the GP prescribed me antidepressants, which in my opinion, just numbs your mind so you don't have to process things.

"As the weeks went by, I just went round acting as if nothing had happened, with my brain fogged. I went back to work full time after three months. This seemed particularly cruel, as I had arranged to take the year off and return to work part time. To be fair, I could have taken longer as I was officially on 'maternity leave' but it seemed pointless to stay at home as I had no baby and I wasn't sick – it was an awful feeling.

"As the new year began, we decided we'd have another baby. I thought that would solve everything and it would make me feel better. I stopped taking the medication; it was January so not the greatest timing. It's such a miserable month anyway, and I remember thinking, 'What have I done?' as I began to cry all the time. My job is very public as I manage people and am the front runner of a team. I was under so much pressure to be professional and hold it all together. I just couldn't keep it up. Into February, and cracks started to appear.

"The grief began to manifest itself in strange ways. I began to get paranoid about my health, and I convinced myself that I had cancer and that's why Sara had died, to spare her. My mouth broke out into ulcers so I thought I had mouth cancer. Then I got shooting pains in my legs so, of course, I instantly thought I had a DVT. I obsessively researched everything on the internet late at night and became convinced I only had three months to live. I became fixated with death and having an accident. My skin dulled and my hair began to fall out, my whole being deteriorated.

"I would lie at night for hours, irrationally thinking about everything and going over and over the events of Sara's death. Duncan started to get frustrated with me and, in as gentle a way as he could, told me I would have to start pulling myself together. My mum suggested that I should get help. Even Cameron started saying, 'Mummy's crying all the time'. I started to feel like I was letting everyone down. I kept trying to give myself a good shake: 'What's the matter with you? You're a gibbering wreck - come on!' I was so frustrated with myself.

"I was surrounded by a lot of people who really cared and were so sorry for what had happened, but because I had put the shutters down early on, no one dared really ever ask how I was. I stopped going out and meeting friends and slowly my world became very small. I had buried everything so deep that I could not ask for help. Fortunately, one of my friends, Mands, had been waiting in the wings, watching events and biding her time. She clearly was not buying any of my 'I am fine' acts. I'd catch her staring at me. I don't know why I never asked her for help, but I passed an offhand remark one day and she pounced on the opportunity.

"At last I opened up and everything came out, including all my dreadful fears about cancer and all my health worries. Mands told me that she had expected us to sit, talk and cry, but in fact the things I was telling her were way beyond her ability to help me. She realised how scared I was and that I needed more than a friendly chat. She did not know if these thoughts were normal, but she would find someone that did. The next day, Mands phoned the SANDS Lothians' office. I found out after that in fact my mum had actually done the same thing the week before.

"Mands told me about the SANDS group meetings that night and I remember thinking, oh no, it will be a bunch of people sitting around crying, feeling sorry for themselves and it would be like I'd have to stand up and say, 'I'm Anna and I'm a mess!' — I concluded it wouldn't be the sort of thing for me. Out of curiosity more than anything, I decided maybe I'll go and see what the office was like. I sat outside in the car, and I saw the light on in the office.

I watched people go in, but again, decided it wasn't for me. I told Mands the next day that I'd been down but wasn't brave enough to go in, but I would maybe try next month.

"Luckily, she read between the lines of what I was saying and phoned SANDS Lothians to make an appointment. Mands realised I'd gone past the self-help stage and just couldn't push the door open myself. I needed help. She made the appointment and told me she would be picking me up and taking me!

"I remember the first meeting so vividly. I couldn't speak, I couldn't even say Sara's name out loud. I'd pushed everything so far down. I remember at one point the befriender told me she'd had to have an MRI scan because she was convinced she'd had cancer after one of her twins died, and I suddenly felt such relief to meet someone who'd had all the anxieties I had. I asked her, had people not thought she was crazy? Perhaps these were normal fears after all and I wasn't losing my mind. Here was someone who had had the same fears twenty years ago and she was still alive!

"That one conversation made such a huge difference to me. I remember going home that night and for the first time in weeks, I felt a sense of peace and for the first time in months, I slept. Gradually, it became clear that I had been displacing my grief in other ways – my hair falling out was a definite sign of stress. I was deluding myself about the enormity of my loss. Looking back, I was clearly suffering from post-traumatic stress, although that was never mentioned by the doctors. Perhaps I also had post-natal depression, even though I didn't have my baby. Whatever the case, I definitely had deep depression as the result of a traumatic event, and I needed to deal with it before it ate me alive.

"Looking back, there was very little help after it happened. The GPs never came near me and the midwife and health visitors that came to visit me just cried all the time. Everyone's very sorry for you, but nobody seems to know how to help. The SANDS Lothians' befriender was the first person who was matter of fact and didn't just try to comfort me with a well-meaning 'there there'.

"She was so knowledgeable about stillbirth and the different ways parents dealt with things. She told me about the history of stillbirth in this country, and how it used to be received. She told me how the families never got to see their babies and about all the laws that had been changed and improvements that had been made over the past 40 years. This aspect really engaged me and really helped me start to get some perspective.

"She was the first person to treat me like a parent. She was also the first person to dare suggest that this was not just about me and my loss. Many people suffered loss when Sara died: grandparents, cousins, friends, aunties and uncles. If I wanted to make Sara real, I would need to share her with others. I felt a very strong bond with my befriender and started to visit her regularly.

"Slowly I could feel things improving. I also started going to the monthly meetings. I felt I had been such a coward. There were parents there whose babies had died only weeks before, and they would share their stories, speaking so proudly of their babies. Over the months since she died, I had spoken so little about Sara. These days, I feel so much pride in her and can talk about her all day when given the chance!

"I got so much out of the meetings. Never had I felt such affiliation with a group of strangers. We would sit and chat late into the night in the SANDS' offices. I used to come out of the meetings elevated, buzzing inside as my hopes and fears were shared by others. My most prominent memory of these meetings was the humour and laughter.

"Duncan used to tease me that he thought it was a group of people sitting about crying. That was so far from the truth. Yes, there were tears, but the laughter was more prominent. I used to think that people would be shocked if they could hear us – Scottish humour. The guilt of laughing was shared by all the parents at the meeting so the relief to laugh out loud amongst 'friends' felt so amazing.

"As the summer went by, I felt more balanced and began to open up to close friends. However, although I was pretending otherwise, I knew I was pregnant again. Working with my befriender over the months, I had finally reached the stage where I was ready to talk about Sara, and I desperately wanted to tell people about her and show everyone her pictures, but I knew people would want to focus on the new baby. I suppose I also did not want people to think, 'Thank goodness, new baby - she'll be fine now,' as that was far from the truth.

"I got lots of support, care and medical attention from the NHS with my third pregnancy with the same consultant and a whole array of specialists. Part of me couldn't help cynically wondering where they'd all been a year ago. I was told that the baby was a girl, and I remember being floored as I suddenly realized that the new baby wasn't Sara and I just wanted Sara. Everything else was the same; it was almost a year to the day. I lived from one appointment to another. There was no enjoyment or peace about this new baby.

"The last month of pregnancy, I began to go downhill again. All the good work that I had achieved over the summer began to fade. The impending doom began to take over as I was convinced the same thing would happen again. On reflection, it wasn't a good thing to get pregnant again so quickly. My rationale went to pieces as I was convinced that I had suffocated Sara in my sleep. As a result, I would not lie down and spent the nights sitting upright on the sofa. The tiredness and stress began to take its toll once more.

"The birth of our third child, Kirsty, fell a month after the first anniversary of Sara's death. Because of my mental health, the consultant agreed to induce me at thirty-seven weeks. The labour was just horrendous. I panicked immediately and went to pieces. I couldn't cope. At our request, Sara Davies kindly agreed to be our midwife again, but even she didn't appreciate how psychologically weak I was until about half way through. I think everyone in the labour ward was terrified something would go wrong again so they filled the room with experts, and the atmosphere was tense and clinical. She was even delivered by a doctor instead of a midwife.

"When Kirsty was born, the irrational anxieties that had returned over the last month of pregnancy became worse. Duncan thought that a new baby would be the start of the old Anna coming back, but instead it seemed to make things worse. Kirsty was sleeping all the time because she was born early, but I was convinced there was something wrong with her brain.

"I went to the doctor one morning, distraught that my baby was sleeping all the time. He must have thought I was crazy as he had a room full of women complaining that their babies wouldn't sleep! Then a few weeks later, I made another appointment and told him, 'She won't smile – all the babies out there are smiling'. It was just one irrational worry after another. The doctor was concerned so suggested medication again.

"To compound matters, my dad died seven weeks after Kirsty was born. It came completely out of the blue, he had a heart attack. The events of my dad's death were very traumatic and because of how quickly I seemed to be going downhill again, I got really scared for myself. But SANDS Lothians came to the rescue once more. They realised that after another baby the SANDS Lothians' offices and meetings can often be logistically difficult to visit as you cannot take your baby in case it distresses someone else. Instead, they put me in touch with another parent who had gone through a similar experience and who lived close by to me.

"Nicky had a different attitude to me. She was all about facing her fears, as opposed to my approach of running away. She had a huge positive influence on me. I didn't want to go back on medication, and I realised that I needed to sort myself out and reclaim my life once and for all. Nicky prescribes to the 'religion' of running, and her enthusiasm for it is very persuasive. So one wet December morning, I bought myself a cool pair of running shoes, hired a huge treadmill, and I began to run. It was my saving grace then and all these years since.

"I started getting up very early, five mornings a week to run. It's wonderful, and when I finish I am buzzing. It is time when I can think, process and start the day with endorphins flowing. Very quickly, my health came back and things began to settle down. There is no doubt that mental health can really be helped with exercise. I returned to work quite quickly after Kirsty was born. This was a conscious decision as I felt the discipline of work would be good for me. I also accepted a promotion while on maternity leave so went back to a new job.

"Work became a great healer. The new job was extremely tough and had long hours attached to it, but the promotion gave me complete control over an array of projects and people. It was very challenging but rewarding which helped distance myself from the failure I would always feel surrounding Sara. Although I could not control life events, work I could control and make a difference. It's also a great distraction when things are not going so well in your head.

"About three years after Sara had died, I came back to SANDS Lothians. SANDS Lothians is a terrific place to return to as everyone knows you, knows your story and there is no pussyfooting round why you are there. Things were getting difficult again, and I could feel the dark clouds looming. But this time it felt different. I'd finally come to terms with what had happened and realised that my old life and the old Anna were gone.

"I used this time to finally 'draw a line under it'. I accepted that life would never return to the way it was, I would never be the person I once was, but this new Anna wasn't so bad (apart from the obsessive tidiness!). The large number of friends that I had once had did not need to return, and I let go the disappointment of how few friends came near during those difficult years.

"I had created a safe reality that I was comfortable with. I had a small group of fantastic friends who had been there for us both, a very supportive family, an amazing career but, most important, I had three kids and a husband that I am enormously proud of. Three years later, my session with my befriender showed me that I was finally grieving for myself and what I had personally lost that day. It was closure of sorts.

"Duncan was terrific as well during this time as I finally felt we were back on the same page and we would talk late into the night talking about it. At last, I could treasure the nice memories, and it became so important to me to celebrate my daughter. We framed a photo of Sara and put it up in the living room for all to see. We got a plaque put up at Mortonhall. I became more in control of how I dealt with Sara, and I wasn't just conforming because I felt I should. I was finally able to acknowledge my own needs and emotions. We decided to tell Cameron about his little sister and, in a way, this helped Duncan too – dads deal with their grief so differently.

"I finally let myself begin to move on. I gradually came out of the safe little world I had created in Colinton Village. I joined the SANDS Lothians' Committee, which allowed me to maintain the connection with SANDS Lothians which was vital to me and to help ensure the charity's survival.

"There are so many pieces of advice I could pass on to the families and friends of bereaved parents, but the main one is to make the baby real by acknowledging their existence. Don't think you are doing them any favours or sparing difficult memories by not mentioning it. For example, one of the hardest things I find is when people ask me how many children I have. I always want to say three, but sometimes, I want to spare feelings so I say two, then I'm wracked with guilt for the rest of the afternoon.

"Family and friends can help with this by having photos up, mentioning them in conversation, including them when counting grandchildren and using their names when telling stories. There is nothing worse for a parent [than] to have their baby referred to as the 'the one you lost'. You did not misplace her, she died. She has a name, so use it.

"There are often no answers after the death of a baby so this acknowledgment that it happened and treasuring and marking the fact that a baby existed, albeit for a short time, is so important. One of my good friends, for example, got a star named after Sara. I was overwhelmed by this gesture.

"I think Duncan and I have become very cautious and over-protective parents. If the children get sick, I always have a sense of doom and find it difficult to get perspective. I will never be the person I was before Sara died and will never get over her death. Time is no healer, but what time does do is allow you to control your emotions rather than be controlled by them. You build a front to the world and grieve privately, in your own way. Compared to those very dark days, I have come far. The dark clouds still come at times but they never last quite as long.

"The death of a baby can change the whole course of your life. For example, I have a job that I would never have had if she had not died and consequently, we would not be living in the splendid house we have. I know a whole array of amazing people that I would never have met. I am more compassionate than before and understand that bad things can happen to good people and how brave these people are to just get up in the morning.

"I have come such a long way in the healing process, and although I still relive the events of Sara's death through in my head about four or five times a day, I don't get absorbed in the grief of losing Sara anymore.

"One of my biggest regrets was struggling to enjoy Kirsty as a baby. It was hard to bond with her as I was sure she was going to die, so I distanced myself from her. I will always have terrible guilt over that. Guilt is one of the hardest things to come to terms with, and it can eat you up. It is a terrible emotion, but you often question everything you did.

"I remember asking Duncan if he ever blamed me for Sara's death and it was clear from his expression that the thought had never crossed his mind, but I definitely blamed myself. You have to learn to forgive yourself. At last, I am no longer at war with myself.

"I was on the SANDS Lothians' Committee for a while before becoming chair. It's so important to me that SANDS Lothians continues to exist so that the next bereaved parent who comes along will be protected from unnecessary grief and pain and be guided through the heartbreaking decisions and the difficult weeks, months and years that follow the death of a baby.

"SANDS Lothians are Sara to me. She's real here, everyone knows her, and it's a place of comfort and safety for me. I try to make light of my situation and play down the enormity of it when asked. My wonderful friend, Mands, once called me 'The Great Pretender'. Right from the start, I have appeared full of composure and togetherness. Scratch the surface, and even she was shocked at what was there. If you appear fine, people will think you are fine. What I have learned is although this approach may be admirable, it's not very clever."

Asked what advice she would pass on to others, Anna says: "Find one person – the right person, even a paid person or a professional service like SANDS Lothians, but someone that you can really talk to again and again and again. A person who has the ability to understand what you're going through and that you don't feel you have to apologise for taking up their time or phoning them late at night. But most of all, more than anything, you must try and find a way to let it go and forgive yourself."

Eve Lowrie Burns

Taking a deep breath, Ros begins: "Four and a half years ago, on 24th December 2007, I was 32 weeks pregnant. We'd had the usual Sunday before Christmas when we have a big family get together. I had been very good that year and bought everything beforehand so I'd be organised and we were all set for Christmas.

"Normally when I got up in the morning, the baby would have been kicking about but on the morning of Christmas Eve, nothing seemed to be happening. I did think that was very strange, but just carried on with everything because it was such a busy day, being the day before Christmas. There were presents to sort, deliveries to be made and I'd arranged to meet friends for lunch. However, in my heart of hearts, I still thought – there's something not right here. I returned home with my three older children, Emily, 13, Tom, 10 and Beth, 19 months and phoned the hospital. The nurse I spoke to said I was probably stressed, busy and just needed to sit down and have a cup of tea. I insisted no, something's very wrong and I'm coming straight in.

"I drove myself up to the hospital, and when I got there it was very quiet and I was taken in straight away. They strapped me up to the monitors, and I continued to have that terrible gut feeling that there was something wrong, perhaps I'd resigned myself to the fact that bad news was coming.

"I remember thinking, how am I going to tell everyone? We had lots of children at the house – our children and lots of nephews – how could I ruin their Christmas too? My son, Tom, had asked for another baby sister for Christmas. It broke me knowing he had got his wish, but she had died. I felt detached from what was really happening, and it was easier thinking about everyone else rather than me."

With her heart breaking, Ros continues: "The nurse didn't say anything at that point but she got the ultrasound technician in, and it was then that I heard the dreadful news that my baby had died. I had to phone my partner, Paddy, who had to get someone to look after the children so that he could come in. He also had to break the news to our children.

"By this point, it was around 7pm on Christmas Eve. When he arrived, they induced me. They had given me the option of going home, having Christmas and Boxing Day and then coming back in to have her, but I thought: how on earth could I do that? How could I go home and cook Christmas dinner, knowing my baby was dead inside me? No, she had to be born that evening; she couldn't be born on Christmas Day. After a four-hour labour, my beautiful baby girl was born at ten to 12 on Christmas Eve. She was 4lb and perfect, just perfect. We called her Eve.

"The next morning I drove myself home. Paddy had his car so we ended up having two cars at the hospital. I just remember thinking – that was a bizarre thing to have to do. I was on automatic pilot. I had to go on – I had three children at home, and it was Christmas Day. I hadn't even wrapped the presents as I was going to do that the day before. Paddy had told the children what had happened, as Emily and Tom were old enough to know that something awful must have happened, me leaving them, on Christmas Eve."

Ros continues: "I didn't agree to a post-mortem, I just didn't want her being touched. I know most stillbirths are unexplained; it's like a cot death in the womb. However, they did all the other tests and they showed that she had been absolutely fine. All they could tell me was 'it was just one of those things'.

"During my pregnancy, I was tested for diabetes, and the result was negative, but I have always had this doubt in my mind as to whether or not that would have had anything to do with what happened later. I suppose I'm just looking for reasons and clues and an answer to the 'why'. The pregnancy had been fine up until 20 weeks when we'd also had to have a Down's syndrome test, but this too, came back clear.

"My previous pregnancies had all been fine, but perhaps I was a bit more stressed about this one. I was a bit older too, at 39, but I'd been an older mum with Beth, and everything had gone smoothly with her. These were just some of my many concerns and questions when all the test results came back. I was told my age would have had no bearing on what had happened.

"When I look back again to the morning it happened, I just felt that there was something different. My whole stomach had changed shape and my baby wasn't moving, she was obviously just lying. Maybe I should have gone in earlier in the morning but, again, I was told it would have made no difference. I do remember that she did some somersaults as I was going to sleep the previous night and I often wonder if something had happened then, but I suppose I'll never know."

"We had a little funeral for Eve on January the 14th at Mortonhall." Ros continues: "I'm quite a private person and I couldn't bear having a lot of people there, so it was just the five of us. I didn't want to have to worry about other people. I carried Eve's little coffin in, and I'm so glad I did. We each laid a rose on her coffin, and Paddy and I each wrote a poem that was read out. She was cremated and she rests in the little Rose Garden. She has a plaque there too but it took me a year to go and see it – it was all so hard."

For my little Eve

For 32 weeks you were part of me
I worried every step of the way
The hopes and dreams that were for you and me
Kept me going to that fateful day

You were to be the little sister
To be the final one
To play with your brother and sisters
And to have all the fun

The day then came, you lay quietly inside me
I just knew you were no more
There was nothing left for me to do
But to simply let you go

My whole body aches to hold you
To feed you, to comfort you
To do all the Mummy things
That the joy of a baby brings

Be at peace, baby Eve
You will never suffer pain, nor anger or fear
Be at peace, baby Eve
The one that I can never hold dear

Love Mum x
14 January 2008

Ros continues: "In the months after losing Eve, I went back to the gym and back to work. I only took three months off which, in hindsight, was a big mistake, I should have taken longer off. I was a senior finance manager, and I had previously run a large department. When I went back, I had the job of setting up a governance and risk team, and I just remember wading through a pile of papers and thinking – I just can't be bothered with this, it means nothing.

"I then had this wild idea that if I gave up my job and my career it would take some stress off me and we could try and have another baby. Sadly, that didn't happen, so then I felt left with no career, no baby, no nothing. Perhaps it hadn't been the brightest thing to do!

"At that point, it was just a month before Eve's first anniversary and my favourite aunty was dying too, so it was a terrible time. I just felt we had to get away. We live in a little village and I just couldn't bear being there at Christmas because everyone gets involved in carol singing on Christmas Eve. It's so lovely and beautiful but would have been too much for me at that time and I didn't want to ruin everyone else's Christmas.

"So we went skiing, and I hate skiing! I decided to throw myself off the top of a mountain to keep me occupied and keep my mind off everything. I was stuck in the beginners group and, strangely, everyone else seemed to have something they were running away from. Without spilling out all our life stories, we got great comfort from each other – it was really very therapeutic. I've never seen those people again but, at the time, it was just what I needed. We've actually been away every year since, although we are thinking about staying at home this year for the first time."

Ros continues: "Going back to work, I felt if I just slotted back into my old routine everything would be OK and go back to normal – I was so wrong. I was in a very male-dominated industry, so it was almost as if they didn't know what to say. My boss said nothing, he completely ignored the fact that I had lost a baby. Even when I left, he didn't even say goodbye, and I'd worked there for 20 years. I suppose he just had no idea how to deal with it.

"I went back to work at the end of March. By September, I'd handed my notice in and I left in November.

"The loss of Eve was completely life changing," Ros adds: "Last year when Beth went into Primary 1, I started to beat myself up a lot for leaving work; after all, I had really enjoyed it. It gave me confidence, independence and an identity. I thought about going back again but after beating myself up a bit more, I decided not to, as I felt I didn't fit into that environment any longer. I wanted to do something more giving and worthwhile. I was grieving for my baby, but I was grieving for myself too and the person I once was. A part of me was dead.

"I'd also had a couple of miscarriages, too, so I started re-evaluating everything. I started working with the Good Food project, which is part of the Cyrenians, twice a week, delivering food to homeless and vulnerable people throughout the Lothians and the team I work with are the most wonderful people. It has really helped me, to help others.

"Beth also knows all about her little sister now. I waited until she was 3 years old to take her up to Mortonhall. It was a beautiful day and there were flowers everywhere. She kept running around calling, 'Baby Eve, Baby Eve – where are you?' As my heart broke for her, she suddenly turned to me and said, 'Mummy, maybe she's turned into flowers.' It took my breath away. Her words were so beautiful. It was Beth's way of making sense of things and the way she said it was so gorgeous. Eve wasn't there and she knew she wasn't coming back, she couldn't see her but she could see flowers everywhere. 'Maybe she has, darling,' I replied, 'maybe she has.' I don't ever want to forget that moment.

"I'm going to get her plaque changed to include Beth's words and I got a tattoo on my arm with all the children's initials, Eve's name and the words 'Maybe she turned into flowers'. Beth continues to talk about her sister. We'd bought a six-seater car before Eve was born and someone once asked why we had a car with six seats and straight away, Beth said, 'that's Mummy's seat, that's Daddy's seat, Em and Tom in the back, that's Beth's seat and that's Baby Eve's'.

"Paddy and I tried to have more children," Ros says. "One of the miscarriages I'd had was in between Beth and Eve and the other was after Eve. By that time I was 40. I'd given myself 18 months to become pregnant again but there came a point in time when we would have to stop trying. This time came with great sadness but a little relief too as slowly, I began to move on.

"The first time I heard about SANDS Lothians was through a lovely lady that lives in the village. After I lost Eve, she'd written me a letter saying she'd lost two babies herself. She'd heard what had happened to me and told me how helpful she'd found SANDS. She had offered to come with me to some meetings and she was a great support to me.

"The next time I saw her, I remember looking at her and thinking about the babies she'd lost and being surprised at how normal she looked! At the time, I found it hard to believe I'd ever be normal again as my life had fallen apart. We're still in touch to this day.

"One of the other things I remember so clearly about that terrible time was, one day I'd ventured out of the house for a pint of milk and one of the mums in the village crossed the road to avoid me. We had been due within days of each other and she was still pregnant. Her crossing the road and the fact that she still had her baby, made me so angry. Another mum stated, 'At least you have your other kids,' as if they were throw-away toys! It was so helpful to go to SANDS and realise my feelings were completely normal.

"The first meeting I went to, I just sat in the corner crying and listening to other people talking. No one made me feel I had to speak until I was ready. I went to the meetings in Edinburgh for a good few months then I tried to set up something in my own area. I'd done my befriending training, but perhaps it was a bit soon for me to do it off my own bat then, but I feel ready to try again now. It would be another way to move forward.

"I also do fundraiser's for SANDS Lothians now, and my village friends have raised quite a lot. We've managed to make enough money for a cold cot."

Ros reflects: "I feel it would really have helped to have another baby. I feel the family's not complete. I feel I've let Paddy down by not having another child, although he says he's happy. He is a stiff upper lip man and doesn't talk about things, but when Eve died, he took a month off work, which, for a workaholic, is a long time! He deals with things in his own way, but there is no doubt losing a child can put a toll on a relationship. Personally, I still feel I'm 'filling' my life. I need to be very busy; keeping busy is good for me; I like routine and it keeps me going."

When asked what advice she can give others, Ros says: "The pain will ease. I used to wake up in the morning crying because I didn't want to wake up at all, and I could barely get out of bed. Now I am beginning to live life more fully. I am training to do a 'Tough Mudder' to raise more money for SANDS Lothians; it's like an army assault course. It gives me a great focus, and I will be pushing my own boundaries."

And for those not quite as sporty as Ros, she says: "Give yourself time and allow yourself to grieve. Think about yourself first and [do] not worry about upsetting or scaring others. Know you're not going to be the same person you once were. I have a pre-Eve and post-Eve 'me'. I am starting to accept the new me as I am, and I am slowly getting there. Our life experiences make us who we are; we adapt and have to move on, but this can take time."

Ending, Ros says: "Most of all, speak to someone. Go to SANDS and talk about your baby and never feel guilty. For me, Christmas has gradually got a bit easier, you learn to live with the big gaping hole and I can ski now…sort of!"

Shortly after bravely telling her story, Ros has gone on to become a befriender in the SANDS Lothians' Edinburgh office and now works there every Monday, where she helps to support other bereaved parents.

Lewis Deed 26 April 1991

Tracy begins: "Lewis was due on the 16th of May 1991, but two weeks before my due date I had to go to the doctor's. My blood pressure was high, so they sent me to hospital.

"When I got there I was closely monitored, but my blood pressure was not going down. I told my husband at the time to go home as our other son, Ian, was only 16 months old. I was then taken for a scan and never thought anything was wrong so wasn't overly worried. The nurse went away to get a doctor and they both had a look at the scan. I was then sent back to my room with nothing further said.

"The doctor then came into my room and asked where my husband was. I said I'd sent him home to look after our son. I asked what was wrong and then I heard the excruciating diagnosis as he told me, 'Your baby has Spina Bifida and fluid on the brain and won't live long after the birth'."

Tracy says: "I felt like I'd been hit by a train. The dreadful reality that now overshadowed what had been the pending exciting arrival of my baby was horrendous. The shock I felt was overwhelming. I kept thinking – I'm going to have a baby that's going to die. How could I even begin to come to terms with that?

"I walked along the corridor to phone my husband. I told him to come back to the hospital as the baby was going to die. He came straight in with my mum and all I could do was sit on the bed in my room, staring at the wall. I remember the arrival of a nurse who just seemed to blurt out in a matter of fact way that my baby was handicapped; she then seemed to stop herself, and muttered, 'I'm sorry'.

"Then the consultant arrived and simply said, 'Well, dear, you have had a good weep now.' He told me to go home and come back in two weeks when they would induce me. I'd have the baby, and then I could go home. It just seemed so cold and matter of fact."

Tracy continues: "I insisted that I wanted to stay and have a caesarean section, so it could all be over. However, it was agreed that I should be induced and have a vaginal delivery and that we should get started.

"My mum went home to look after Ian, our son. A few hours later, I was moved to a delivery room and the emotional and physical pain inside was just incredible. In the room next to me I could hear someone else in labour, but my labour had stopped. I was then told just to get a goodnight's sleep – easier said than done!!

"The next morning, the midwife came in, and she was so lovely. They induced me again and then offered me an epidural. I couldn't stop crying as I felt like such a failure. When Lewis was ready to be born, I was terrified. I had visions of a monster with a big head, and I hadn't expected him to be born alive. I asked them to take him away as I couldn't bring myself to see him. However, he was born alive, and he was truly lovely.

"I asked to see him. My beautiful son Lewis had been born at 6.10pm; he was 5lb 8oz and tiny. They had packed his back as his Spina Bifida was very severe."

Tracy goes on: "We were moved to a side room in Ward 52, the maternity ward. Lewis was so frail, but he was on morphine and was very comfortable. I just held him in my arms, but he kept stopping and starting breathing. It was heartbreaking. At one point I put him in his Moses basket as I had to go to the toilet. I was praying he would be gone when I got back as it was all so hard to watch.

"When I returned to the room, my husband said they thought he'd gone, so immediately I panicked and got back into bed with him.

"The midwife at the time was due to go off her nightshift at 6am, and by this time it was 12 noon. She never left our side. Our doctor was wonderful too. He had to keep checking Lewis's heartbeat and was so gentle with him. He encouraged us to cuddle him as much as possible.

"Lewis passed away at 1.50pm in my arms. My mum and dad came to see him, and they brought Ian with them, so for a few minutes, Ian and his brother were together."

Tracy says: "I left the hospital with my husband, my mum and the midwife holding my hand. I will never forget her touch, it brought me such comfort."

Tracy continues: "After leaving the hospital, I became really over protective of Ian so I wrote him a letter. He only read it a few days ago at the age of 23!"

Dear Son

Although just now you are far too young to read this, I am writing it so in the future it may explain why at times I will be over protective of you and to tell you why I love you so much and the reason you are an only child. We did not intend it to be that way in the beginning but it happened.

You are the firstborn. What proud parents we were when we brought you home from the hospital. We both wanted to cuddle you and to push the pram. A happy healthy little boy you were. People would say, and still do, what a cute little boy and I would burst with pride.

You were only twelve months old when I found out I was pregnant again. What a shock. We had not planned it that way. Your dad was out of work and money was scarce and we knew it would be so difficult with two. When we came to terms with it, we knew we would manage somehow. It would be a good playmate for you and I began to imagine what it would be like. The two of you running around plotting mischief. Two of you with sticky hands and dirty faces splashing around the bath.

Your dad was so good. Taking you out when I was tired, bathing you, putting you to bed and reading you a story. So I knew he would be just as good with the new baby. He used to pat my stomach and tell me he was starting to look forward to being a dad again. He even bought me a beautiful maternity dress, even though I knew we couldn't afford it. That's the kind of man he is. We looked to the future as a family.

Then all of a sudden things went wrong. We went for a routine check-up only to be told that the baby had Spina Bifida and would be stillborn. We could not believe it. Two weeks left of the pregnancy and now this. We could not take it in at first. Why us? Our friends had all had healthy babies. This must be a big mistake, we thought. Then I went into labour and your little brother was born. A tiny frail 5lb he was. He was so beautiful. From the front he looked absolutely perfect. So dark. He had a tiny button nose. He was lovely. He was born alive, we were told, though, it was only a matter of time. There was no hope for him, so you were brought in to see him with Granny and Granddad. You then went home and your little brother lived for two days. Then we came home from the hospital and you were the one who helped us to cope. It was as if you sensed our loss. You would come up and cuddle us without being asked. We even took you to the funeral. We have a photo of your brother and you know his name.

Now we have moved to a new area and you are growing into a lovely little boy. We have taken the decision not to have any more children. We have you. We know at times you must miss not having anyone to play with. You see, watching the pain and suffering your little brother went through was enough. We know at times we can be too over protective of you and you get frustrated with us. We are so glad we have you. We want you to be happy and we are learning to treat you normally but you will always be very special to us. You are the one that has helped us cope with our grief and will keep on doing so.

From your mum and dad.

Tracy goes on: "I am now divorced from Lewis's dad, and it was a very difficult and messy time. Up until three years ago, Ian lived seven days with each parent but I was so happy when he eventually decided to come and live with me full time. He is now at university studying computer science. I completely dote on him and he is the apple of my eye. He is so precious to me.

"I know he's 23, but I still iron his clothes and lay out his socks! I make sure he has juice on the bus and I text when he's late home and still wait up for him to come in. I'm pleased to say though that I stopped sewing his gloves together and threading them through his blazer when he was 18! When Ian finally read my letter to him, he laughed and said it all makes sense now!!

"I remarried two years ago to a wonderful man called Kenny. We've actually known each other for 12 years and I am now very happy.

"In February 2012 I had to endure the heartache of losing my dad who had been suffering with dementia. He was 62, a pure diamond and my rock, through all the heartache with Lewis and my subsequent divorce. I recently wrote Lewis a poem for his birthday."

For Lewis – Born Friday 26th April 1991

Your face just so perfect
Your hands were so small
So little time
To take in it all

Your birth such a pleasure
And yet tinged with pain
You entered this world
With nothing to gain

You were not born to live
To be tall or be short
A brilliant scholar
Or great at sport

You had a time limit
How long we never knew
To spend just two days
The hours were so few

And yet you're so precious
In my thoughts, yes, each day
Although I did know
On earth not to stay

I look at your picture
A lock of your hair in the drawer
My own private thoughts
In my mind I do store

I think of you, son
You gave me so much
Asked for nowt in return
Just that gentle touch

Yes I do love you
I wish I could say
Happy Birthday dear Lewis
It's your birthday today.

"Over the last few years, I've gone on to teach keep-fit classes," Tracy says. "The midwife who was so wonderful when Lewis died is now a mum herself, and she sometimes comes to my class! When I see her, I remember the kindness she showed me at the most heartbreaking time of my life, and I will never forget that.

"I became aware of SANDS Lothians through the hospital after Lewis was born, but I didn't get involved with them until five years ago, when one of the lady's who now works with them came to work with me at my then place of work at the time.

"I went along to one of their meetings and had never felt such peace about being able to talk about Lewis and not feel awkward.

"I then decided to get involved in fundraising for them. Lewis would have been 21 in 2012, so I wanted to do something special and decided to run a half marathon. I have ended up doing four this year and I am doing the full one next year. I have to thank my friends and family for all the incredible support I have had. Without the friends I have made in the fitness world, this would never have happened. They'll know who they are!

"It has helped so much to do fundraising for SANDS Lothians to honour my lovely little boy's memory.

"At the end of one of the marathons, I received the Oliver Ward shield from SANDS Lothians for individual fundraising efforts in the 2012 Edinburgh Marathon."

"For a grandparent who finds themselves in the middle of such devastating heartbreak, be strong for your wife, your child and your surviving grandchildren. The advice I would give to other grandparents is to be open and talk. Don't try to be the strongest or try to block the reality out but allow yourself to grieve too – it's the whole family's loss. It's OK to cry and get the tears out. I certainly did.

"In sad situations such as these, people often think 'why me' but perhaps, after learning more about stillbirth, they should think - why *not* me, why *not* us? Sadly, it happens to so many people but it's not spoken about much. It's almost a taboo topic that is not openly discussed, so few people are aware of how often it happens. After it happened to LeeAnn, people started to open up and tell me of their own experiences. Friends of ours that I'd known for years told me they'd lost a baby – something I had never been aware of as they had never talked about it.

"Go to SANDS group meetings if it helps. We got a huge amount of support from our village and our local community. The love of these people that we had known for many years helped us through, they were so incredibly supportive to us. They restored our faith in human nature.

"I know everyone is different and perhaps some grandparents find it hard to give support because they may have strong views about lifestyle while pregnant and may feel, in some way, their child is to blame. Criticism like that never helps — inevitably, the bereaved mother already blames herself, even if she has done nothing wrong."

John McKeown, father to LeeAnn McKeown, grandfather to Kaidyn and Jamie Cunningham McKeown

Emily Diamond

"We had been trying for a baby for a little while, but in the run up to our wedding decided that we would wait. I didn't really fancy walking up the aisle suffering from morning sickness or not fitting into my dress properly. However, when we got a positive test a fortnight before the big day, we were both very excited and incredibly happy.

"At first everything went really well. I had quite bad morning sickness (morning and evening), but I knew it would all be worth it. I had a small bleed at 10 weeks, but was reassured that this was perfectly normal. They gave me a scan and I'll never forget the moment when we saw the flickering heartbeat. It was the most amazing thing I had ever seen. Martin and I left the scan room grinning like idiots.

"Everything went well again until we went for our 20-week Fetal Anomaly Scan. The sonographer was taking a long time. I started to worry about the baby. After approximately 15 minutes, she told us there was a problem with the machine and we would have to move to another machine. We were offered the chance to come back at another time. We decided to complete the scan at that time.

"After waiting for another machine to become free, we moved to another area to complete the scan. She then told us she would have to lean quite heavily to get a clear picture because it was an older machine. She leaned so heavily that I was left bruised, but I had seen that flickering heartbeat again, so I was relieved to know that things were OK.

"The next day I was at the swimming pool with my class when a strange feeling came over me. I felt really hot, but put it down to the temperature at the pool. Then suddenly, [I] felt a release of pressure and there was water

66

rushing down my leg. I was so embarrassed that I tried to cover it up. I phoned my midwife, but was reassured that the baby must have moved and pressed down on my bladder. That made me even more embarrassed – a grown woman wetting herself in public!

"The next day I had another bleed. I was visiting a relative when it happened and I just ran out. I wanted to get to my husband and to the hospital. I kept telling myself that it would be fine, just like the last time, but I had a really bad feeling. At the hospital, the doctor performed an internal exam and a swab was taken. The doctor told me that my cervix was tightly closed, but they were concerned about my blood pressure. They didn't know why I was bleeding, so they decided to keep me in overnight. I raised my concern about passing a lot of water suddenly the day before, but that I had been told that the baby was probably pushing down on my bladder. We were reassured that this would be the case as we could hear baby's heartbeat and my cervix was closed.

"The next morning I was feeling much calmer and my blood pressure had returned to normal. I raised my concern about the scan and was told the sonographer was a professional and that all essential checks had been done. I asked if another scan would be done to find out more about the bleeding and was told that it wasn't necessary as I had had a scan a few days ago. At 3pm I was told that I could go home.

"The following evening I had another bleed, so I phoned the labour ward sister, who told me to come straight in. The midwife on duty commented that there were signs of an infection and I was admitted to the ward. I asked about test results from my previous admission and was told they would be available the next day. At about 3am, I told one of the midwives that I was very worried about the cause of the bleeding. I was told 'Mother Nature is cruel!' and left alone.

"At that point, I felt like my world had been turned upside down. Was she trying to tell me something that nobody else dared? I cried for what felt like a long time before another midwife came and reassured me that things would be fine. She let me listen to the baby's heartbeat to reassure me.

"In the morning, I asked again about test results from the previous admission and was told that it was the weekend and I was not classed as an emergency, so they were not available yet. The day passed without incident and I got to listen to my baby's heartbeat several times. Each time I heard it, I became calmer and more convinced that everything would be ok.

"I buzzed for help during the night. When one of the auxiliaries came, I explained that I was having cramp-like pains in my lower abdomen and lower back. I suggested that it felt like really painful trapped wind, but that I wasn't sure. I was given some peppermint oil in hot water to sip. I was discharged the next morning.

"Three days later, I had a glucose tolerance test carried out in [the] antenatal day bed unit. Again, I asked about test results from my previous admissions and was told they were all clear. I raised concerns about a strange sensation I had when going to the toilet. I said I thought it might be piles, but was concerned that it was something else as they seemed to be in the wrong place. I was not checked over, but handed a prescription for suppositories signed by a doctor I never met. I telephoned for my results later that day and was given the readings and told they were 'unusually high'.

"The next day I received a phone call in the morning to say they were very concerned about my sugar levels and asked me to come in to the diabetic clinic that day. I was told I had gestational diabetes and went home to search for information on the internet. I hate needles, but I tested my blood and injected myself with insulin because I needed to keep my sugar levels in check for my baby to stay healthy.

"Two days later, on the 5th June 2011, I was tidying the house for my family visiting later that day. I put on some music to help motivate me and the baby started moving a lot. I joked with my husband that the baby was dancing. He put his hand on my bump and agreed there was a lot of movement. Later that afternoon I felt the deep throbbing spasms in my back again. Martin got me a hot water bottle. I must have looked bad because my family left so I could rest. Within a few minutes, I felt more pain and the need to go to the toilet. When I went to the bathroom, I felt more pain, and the lumps I had been told were piles were hanging out. The next thing I knew I was in the car heading towards the hospital. Martin says he knew something was really wrong when I let out a scream. He says he has never heard a noise like it.

"When we got to the hospital, we headed to A&E because we thought the pain was from the piles. I stood at the reception desk trying not to cry. When I was told to take a seat, I put my head on the desk and told the receptionist that I couldn't sit. A nurse with very soft hands came through the door and led me to a curtained bay. Martin was asked to wait outside while she took a look. I knew things were bad when she ran out of the bay shouting for help.

"I was lifted onto the bed and wheeled to Resus. They told me it was a precaution, and it would give them more room to move around. They gave me gas to breathe, and time started to become an abstract concept. I thought everything happened in a few minutes, but I later found out it was much longer. Lots of people came into the room. I was introduced to them, but I couldn't really keep track. I remember the surgical team coming in and thinking that this was getting serious. I kept asking for Martin, and, eventually, they brought him in. He says he overheard them talking about 'getting ready to deliver', but I was completely unaware.

"It came as a total shock when one of the doctors told me that the baby was about to be born. I told her that couldn't happen because it was too early at only 22 weeks and 3 days, and that the baby wouldn't survive. She nodded and told me I was right, but there was no choice. The lumps I had been told were piles were actually the baby's leg, which had descended. She had to tell me several times before my brain could even start to compute.

I remember Martin holding my hand and looking into my eyes. I kept telling him I was sorry, and he told me that it wasn't my fault. A few minutes later, our baby was born.

"They whisked the baby away, but there was nothing they could do. We were asked if we wanted to see the baby. We both agreed immediately and they brought over this tiny little bundle. I remember asking if the baby was a boy or a girl. I joked that Martin and I had a bet on it. They told us she was a girl, and I said I'd lost the bet. It seems crazy now acting like that, but I was in shock.

"Soon after that, we were moved to the labour ward. I was angry that they tucked the baby under the covers for the move, but later realised it was to stop other people moving around the hospital from staring.

"When we got to the labour suite, I delivered the placenta and then phoned my mum to tell her what had happened. I remember being very calm on the phone. Over the next hour, my mum, dad and sister arrived at the hospital. Martin's mum arrived a little later as she had further to travel. We took lots of photographs and everyone had cuddles. The midwife told us she was going to organise a family room. She asked us if we had a name, and we both replied, 'Emily', at the same time. Sometime later, Martin went to check when we'd be moved.

"After the visiting hours on the main ward, we were moved to the family room. While we sat cradling our baby, we could hear all the other newborns on the ward crying. If there was any piece of my heart not yet broken, then that noise finished me off. We spent the night holding each other, holding Emily and trying to get our heads around what had just happened. Martin paced the room for hours.

"The next morning, the midwife on duty did a very good job of talking us through the information she had, helped us fill in the necessary forms and explained everything that would happen. We asked her to weigh Emily and we were told she was 400g. Our families came to visit again and have another cuddle. It broke my heart to see my gran holding our tiny baby.

"The people at the funeral service we chose were very good. They arranged Emily's funeral without lots of fuss. We were allowed to put a teddy and a pink rose into the coffin with her. I went with my mum the day before the funeral to see the coffin. We sat and talked to Emily for a while. We weren't rushed by the staff, who were very supportive and kind.

"On the day of the funeral our parents, siblings and my gran came to our house in their brightly coloured tops. Everyone was handed a different coloured rose. We wanted a rainbow of colour to celebrate the brief life our Emily had, and the huge impact she had made on our lives. When we got to the crematorium, my legs felt like jelly, but Martin guided me in.

"I was so proud of Martin and my sister, Pamela, for standing up in front of everyone and speaking. Martin spoke about Emily and how she would always be with us, and Pamela did a beautiful reading."

Little snowdrop

*The world may never notice
If a snowdrop doesn't bloom,
or even pause to wonder
If the petals fall too soon.*

*But every life that ever forms,
or ever comes to be,
Touches the world in some small way
for all eternity.*

*The little one we longed for
was swiftly here and gone.
But the love that was then planted
is a light that still shines on.*

*And though our arms are empty,
our hearts know what to do.
For every beating of our hearts
says that we love you.*
Author unknown

"Over the next few weeks and months we found out that I had an infection called Strep G. The signs had been missed when I first presented at the hospital with bleeds. We have been told that the waters I felt at 20 weeks had been my waters breaking.

"It took a long time to come to terms with what happened and to deal with all of the emotions including the guilt and the anger. We have been told that some of the systems in the hospital have been changed as a result of our complaint, and I can only hope that the changes that have been implemented save others from going through what we did. Our beautiful Emily may only have been with us for a short time, but she will always be a part of our lives."

Lara Docherty

"In July 2010, my husband David and I got married," Lianne Docherty begins. "We were keen to start a family soon after. When it happened quicker than expected in the November, we were over the moon. We told our parents and they were delighted because it was the first grandchild on both sides. We decided not to tell anyone else until after the 12-week scan. Mum always said that the weekend we told her was the best weekend of her life because the day after we gave her our good news, my sister got engaged. It was a weekend of huge celebrations.

"Throughout the pregnancy everything was fine. The 12-week scan went well, and I didn't suffer much morning sickness. Our first scan was on Hogmanay, so it was a great way to end one year and start a new one. After that scan was fine, we decided to tell the rest of our friends and family our good news, and they were all delighted.

"Once I'd had my 20-week scan, I felt I was on the home stretch. I started to look at baby things and began buying bits and pieces – I couldn't help myself, I was so excited about the new arrival. I was doing everything right, never smoking, not drinking, and eating all the right things.

"Once people knew how far on I was, they started asking me if I could feel the baby move. I must admit, I was conscious of the fact that I didn't really feel much movement but never having been pregnant before, I didn't have anything to compare it with. People said everybody's pregnancy is different, but I did start to feel a bit anxious.

"I spoke to the midwife about my concerns and was sent for a scan at 25 weeks. I was told my placenta was at the front and that was acting as a cushion then as politely as possible, the lady said there was a bit extra of me too! The baby had to kick against both the placenta and me before I would feel anything so that calmed me down a little. I started to relax more as we'd now had three scans and everything was fine.

"We excitedly carried on with all the preparation for the new addition to our family. The nursery was done, and all our plans were made. Then came the weekend of our local gala. It was a really busy weekend with a lot to do. I was very tired when I got home as I had walked a lot more than normal.

"That evening, we went to friends for dinner. I was aware of the fact that I hadn't felt much baby movement that day, but I was really tired and you get told when you're tired your baby's tired. On the Sunday, I still felt that something wasn't right, but, as I'd had three scans and I'd been told at each one all was fine, I tried not to worry.

"However, by the Monday, I decided that I needed some more reassurance. This time, because I was coming up to 34 weeks, I was sent straight to the hospital to have a trace of the baby's heartbeat done. David came with me – but not for a second did he think anything was wrong, just that I was overly worried.

"As we were driving to the hospital, I suddenly had an awful thought. What would happen if something was wrong and we had to do this drive back home again and everything has changed? It was a 'what if' that niggled persistently at the back of my mind.

"When we arrived at the hospital, we sat in the waiting room for a little while, then got taken into the room to have the baby's heart trace done. They picked up my heartbeat, at which point I think it hit my husband that something could be wrong. I then had to have another scan and, soon after that, a doctor came into the room and told me the worst thing I will ever hear in my life. My baby had died. Our much loved, and much wanted first child, had died. There was no heartbeat. I became completely numb.

"You would think I'd burst into tears and be hysterical, but there was nothing. I was in total shock. Our whole life and our dreams had gone. It had all been taken away from us. My world had stopped turning."

Lianne continues: "My mum and dad were in Tenerife at the time, and they organised flights home straight away to be with us. They were distraught about losing their grandchild, but Mum just wanted to be with me. David's parents live in the north of Scotland and got the bus down immediately. My sister also came straight to the hospital to be with us.

"As I was 34 weeks, Mum had thought it would be safe to go on a little break before the baby came. It was awful having to tell family and friends the terrible news.

"I knew I would have to deliver the baby, but I don't think this had dawned on David. I think he believed I would have a caesarean section. None of us had experienced anything like this before and couldn't really understand why I had to go through labour. Looking back, it would really have helped to have all that explained in more detail at the time.

"It wasn't until later the next day, when David asked the midwife to explain things more fully, that we began to understand a bit better. I had been sent home from the hospital having been given the tablets you take to start getting ready for labour and then told to go back two days later. It would really have helped to have someone to talk to during that time.

"Those two days were dreadful. Luckily, I had friends and family with me, but what if someone was alone with no support? People could end up taking drastic action and harming themselves, and no one would know until they didn't turn up for their next appointment.

"I'd never been through labour before but am familiar with the stock answer people give, 'you'll forget all the pain because you'll have your beautiful baby at the end of it'. Try doing it knowing you're giving birth to a dead baby.

"I was put in a family room where I stayed all the time. My midwife said she was there only for me, but she often had to leave. I know it's all down to money and resources, but it was so busy that day; she often had to go and tend to others. David came with me, as did my mum and dad, but none of us knew what to expect. There was so much waiting and uncertainty as to what was happening. We had been told to go in at 9am, but nothing happened until after 12. The sitting and waiting until then, was so hard. Eventually, I was given tablets at 12.30, but my labour didn't start until 7.30 that evening. Our beautiful Lara was born at 1.30 the next morning, weighing 4lb 7oz.

"I had been taken to the delivery room for the birth. I'd been told that they would make it as pain free as possible as of course by now, the drugs won't affect the baby. I think my labour went a lot quicker than had been expected. I'd been prepared for an epidural, but something wasn't right, and I kept telling them that I felt really uncomfortable. When they examined me, it was too late, I was already crowning. I had to carry on without an epidural and relying on just gas and air.

"Earlier on, when I was still reeling from the terrible news that my baby had died, it had been so hard to make any of the important decisions about what to do after she was born. Did we want to see her? Did we want to dress her? I wish I had been able to speak about all this more and take time to reach the right choices, but I felt the only time it was discussed in depth was when I was completely spaced out from all the drugs, and I couldn't take anything in.

"As it happened, we got to see her straight away, then they took her away and dressed her. Again, looking back, I would have liked to dress her myself. I saw her when they lifted her up, but I never really saw her little body properly. When I next saw her, she was all dressed up and cosy; if I could change that part, I would.

"I ended up feeling a bit stupid. I had put a few clothes in my bag for her but, if I'd been able to think things through a bit more I would have taken a blanket to wrap her in. Everything seemed so strange, I almost felt like I had to ask permission to dress her in the clothes we'd brought.

"Lara's arrival came with a sense of relief. Like any proud new mum, I wanted to shout from the rooftops that my baby had been born, she was our little girl. Our daughter. I don't think David really knew what to expect until he saw her. He hadn't realised that he would actually get a baby to hold.

"After her arrival, the time we then got together in the family room was so precious and so important. We were able to take photos of her with David and I, and then photos with all the family. It wasn't how it should have been, of course, but we were so glad that we got that time with her. It is something we will treasure forever."

Lianne reflects: "I can't imagine how we would have coped if we'd said no to photos. It's so important to have them. After we had to say goodbye to Lara at the hospital, the photos were the one thing that David could focus on to help him deal with his grief. He made them all into a book about Lara's little life – her scan pictures, the photos when she was born and the photos of her little coffin and funeral.

"Like any other proud parents who would get out an album of photos of their new baby, it was nice to be able to show her off when people came to visit. She may have died, but she was our baby and she was perfect.

"We'd given Lara the last of our kisses and cuddles and said goodbye to her in the family room. We just wanted to go home to try and come to terms with our loss. However, we were then told we couldn't go home yet because we had to wait around again to speak to a doctor about a post-mortem. We were so frustrated, and David was ready to walk out. It was more precious time wasted that we could have spent with Lara.

"In the end, the post-mortem showed nothing. I found that really hard to come to terms with. I needed answers. I needed a reason as to why my baby had died.

"The consultant who talked us through the results was very nice but simply said those horrible words that so many parents hear, 'It was just one of those things.' Apparently, the cord was round her neck when she was born, but they couldn't confirm that would have been the cause of her death.

"I had such mixed feelings after the post-mortem. In a way, I was glad she was perfect and there weren't any problems that could affect any future pregnancies, but, at the same time, I couldn't cope with there being no reason at all. If she was perfect, how could her heart be beating one day and not the next? Of course, I tortured myself. Was it because I walked too much that day? Did I do too much gardening a few weeks before? Did I eat something I shouldn't? I was in such turmoil that I listed all my questions for the consultant to try and find a way to put my mind at rest. It was so hard to get the thoughts out of my head. It was my body, and I felt I must have done something wrong. I just wanted Lara. The pain and emptiness were unbearable.

"Her funeral service was lovely, and there ended up being a lot of people there. We have such lovely friends and family. You wonder how you get through things this difficult but you just do; something takes over and you do it for your baby. David had to find the strength to carry the coffin from the funeral parlour to the funeral car. I was asked to hold the cords, which I did. I was Lara's mummy, and I wanted to settle her in her final resting place. After the funeral, we got a beautiful little headstone for her grave.

"It was only a year ago that Lara was born, so it's still very raw," Lianne says. "Sometimes I still can't believe it's happened. So many of my dreams and plans have been taken away. I lost my future with my firstborn.

"I remember one of the people at the hospital saying, 'We'll see you back soon.' I know she was probably right and people often go on to have another child quite quickly, but it was the last thing I wanted to hear at the time. When David went to register her death, he was also told, 'Don't worry, you'll be back soon with a birth certificate.' I know people mean well, but these are horrible things to hear when you're in the depths of despair.

"As it happens, I did get pregnant again quickly – only three months later. I was delighted but tortured at the same time! I knew the months ahead would be so hard. I no longer knew who I was. I couldn't shake the feeling that I must be a bad person for this to happen to me. I didn't know how I would cope when my husband went back to work. I couldn't face the simplest of things, like driving and going to the supermarket, things I'd done without a second thought before.

"I asked the doctor for some help, but they couldn't suggest anything, and all they offered me were antidepressants. However, one of my mum's friends had mentioned SANDS Lothians, and that's the first time I heard about them. I eventually plucked up the courage to phone and was all ready to leave a message as it was after 5pm but got the shock of my life when someone answered!

"I started going to meetings and had befriending and counselling. I got counselling through my work, too, as a teacher, which all helped.

"When I became pregnant again, I felt that I had a bit of a future again. However, my second pregnancy was eight months of utter hell and worry! All the joy had been taken away, and it was a really difficult time. I couldn't tell anybody, apart from my mum and dad. I almost became detached and shut it out of my mind in case something happened. The nursery was still as it was in preparation for Lara, but the door had remained shut. I didn't dare look at any new baby clothes or toys.

"All the scans throughout my second pregnancy were fine, and they kept a close eye on me. I was told that I could deliver at 37 weeks so that helped too. Towards the end of my pregnancy, I was getting scans every fortnight and then, for the last month, they did heart traces three times a week. The placenta wasn't at the front this time, so I could feel more movement, but there were still days I phoned the midwife in a panic. It was the same midwife I'd had before, and she was really wonderful."

Lianne goes on: "This time, I finished work early. When I was quiet and calm, I could feel the baby moving, but if I'd had a hectic day at work and was tired, I couldn't feel anything. I had to take a break to concentrate on the baby. Literally, I did nothing. When I'd been pregnant with Lara, I'd gone to yoga classes. I made friends with lots of other people that were expecting babies too. Then, of course, they went on to have healthy babies and I didn't. I lost all those friends as it was just far too hard for me to stay in touch with them.

"I remember on one occasion, I had managed to go to one of the baby's first birthday parties, and all I could think of was Lara should be here. She was never mentioned, and, in a way, that was worse. She may not have been alive, but she was still my baby. I just couldn't risk putting myself through anything like that again with the new baby, so I did my best to avoid putting myself in similar situations.

"All through my pregnancy with Eilidh, I was worried about her getting here safely, now I worry about anything happening to her now that she's here! She was supposed to be delivered at 37 weeks, but that would have taken us to about two days before Lara had been born, so it was agreed I could go at 36 weeks.

"Luckily, she was born on the 1st of June. It would almost have been unbearable for Eilidh to be born a year to the day that Lara died, and I didn't want to still be pregnant at Lara's first anniversary. I opted for a caesarean section, another labour would have brought back too many memories."

Looking back, Lianne says: "Sometimes, during my second pregnancy, when I'd had to go back to the hospital for check-ups, I had to walk past the family room again. It was heartbreaking. I was so worried that it would be occupied and I would see the light on. One day it did say 'occupied.' I felt sick. I knew exactly what they were going through. I just wanted to go in and offer them some words of comfort, but I was pretty certain the last thing they'd want to see was a pregnant woman. I felt so desperately sad for them.

"I really hope that through SANDS Lothians' work and sharing my experience with other bereaved parents, we've all made it a little easier for others that may suffer or have suffered the same terrible loss. It's the little things that make a difference, and the mistakes that need to be avoided …

"A month or so after we lost Lara, I got a phone call asking why she hadn't been for her hearing test yet. I was driving along the M6 at the time, so luckily, David took the call. I heard him saying, 'She was stillborn in June' and

I burst into tears. This incident and how it could have happened was looked into, and we received an apology but it was a terrible experience, and not one I would want anyone else to go through.

"The joy of pregnancy has been taken away from me completely. Even if I go on to have 20 successful pregnancies, they will never be without fear. I still find it hard to look at anyone else who is pregnant, but at least now, I can do it without bursting into tears. However, it's still something I find really difficult.

"I also found understanding my husband's grieving process difficult," says Lianne. "There is no doubt men and women handle things like this so differently. I just couldn't understand how he could go and play sport or watch the television or cheer on his football team, as he had done before, but counselling helped me understand my feelings and emotions. It helped me understand that people grieve so differently, and men and women react in diverse ways. It was harder for my husband to talk about his feelings, but he dealt with his grief in a way that was right for him.

"Men can also be more delayed with their grief as they try to stay strong for us. There were certainly times when I wished he would have just broken down and cried, showing me he was feeling the pain too. My feelings were so raw and every day, I wore my heart on my sleeve; yet his way of coping seemed poles apart from mine.

"Then I remember, one day, he'd been watched *Harry Potter,* and one of the little characters in it, 'Dobby', had died, and the way it was held and cradled, reminded him of holding Lara. He got so upset that he just wanted cuddles with Eilidh and just to see that, to see he was feeling what I was feeling, helped me a lot. He did confide in me later, telling me that he had his bad days, but kept them to himself. It's almost as if they wait until we're stronger and then they let go."

Lianne continues: "David and I knew each other about three years before we were married. Lara's original due date was on our first wedding anniversary. We went through so much in our first year of marriage. I look back at my wedding photos and know I'll never be as happy as I was on that day. Having said that, and now that Eilidh is here, I'm happier than I ever thought I'd be again, but I know I'm a different person now. I'll never again be the person I was on my wedding day. Everything I ever wanted all came together and then my life fell apart."

Asked what advice she would give to others, Lianne says: "During the early stages of grief, talk to people who have a shared experience, who understand and who can genuinely say, 'I know how you feel', and you know they mean it. Go to SANDS Lothians' group meetings; you'll never be judged and you can talk when you're ready. You can talk to people who are further on than you are and who can help you with difficult milestones like anniversaries and Christmas.

"When you're having one of those days where no one else understands, you know you can pick up the phone to one of your SANDS friends and simply talk through the difficult times. I have two daughters and I wish, more than anything, they were both here, but we'll never forget Lara.

"We made a lovely area in the garden with a rose bush and windmills to remember her. Everything changes when you lose a baby, but going on to help others is such a comfort and a good way to process your grief. I am gradually moving forward and finding my new 'normal'. It's a different normal, but it's a normal I am slowly coming to terms with."

Matthew Douglas Findlay

Corinna begins: "I knew from the outset that falling pregnant naturally might be difficult for me because I had PCOS – polycystic ovarian syndrome and bicornate uterus which meant that it was split in two, resulting in less space for a baby to grow.

"In 2005 I fell pregnant but had a miscarriage, and in 2006 the same thing happened again, but both were early losses. On December the 3rd 2006, I got a positive pregnancy result and at last, everything progressed well. All my scans were good, giving no cause for concern; the only worry was my bicornate uterus, which we knew about and we were prepared for, should I go into premature labour. I knew the chances of going to full term were slim, and it may be more difficult if the baby was breach, but we were ready for all of that.

"My due date was 10th August 2007 and on the 6th July, when I was 35 weeks pregnant, I finished work. I went out for a little while with friends but, when I got home, I didn't feel quite right, but just put it down to finishing work and being a bit nervous about the baby coming. Then at about two o'clock in the morning my waters broke. We went straight to the hospital. My labour hadn't started, but I was kept in and put on antibiotics to stop any infection.

"Nothing happened on the Saturday then on the Sunday 8th July around 2.30pm, I remember sitting in the car in the car park with my husband, Dougie, listening to the radio, when I suddenly got a really sharp pain. We went back into the hospital but nothing else happened. Then around 4pm I got another pain and was put on the monitor.

"My labour then started pretty quickly, going from two little pains to pain all the time. I was still on the main ward, and they brought in a portable scanner to see if the baby was breach or not. The scan showed that he was, and after I was examined they told me I was 5-6 centimetres dilated.

"There was a sudden rush to get me into theatre for a caesarean section. They were trying to do a spinal but it wasn't working. Everything had happened so quickly and with such urgency that when Dougie came into theatre in his scrubs, someone thought he was one of the medical team and asked him to do something!

"The baby was coming. I was put onto my back and suddenly his little foot came out first. Dougie remembers this so clearly but I was oblivious to everything as I was on gas and air. Our beautiful baby boy was born at 7.24pm and I remember lying there thinking he hasn't cried, why has he not cried? However, I also remember that he was whisked away to intensive care almost immediately as he was so early.

"Sadly, soon after this, Dougie and I had this sixth-sense feeling that something wasn't right. We still can't explain it to this day; it was just an overwhelming feeling of dread. Soon after Matthew was born, I was taken back to the ward, and we just sat waiting and hoping we'd see our baby soon.

"Around 8.45pm, the doctor and midwife came in and I could see by their faces that something wasn't right. Our hearts shattered as we were told that Matthew had died at 8.38pm."

Corinna bravely goes on: "We found out after a post-mortem that Matthew had congenital laryngeal stenosis which is a very rare condition where the upper airways don't develop properly, which meant that he couldn't breathe for himself, but they couldn't intubate him either. They had been trying for 74 minutes to save him.

"Afterwards, the doctors investigated the condition extensively for us and found that there had only been 35 reported cases in the whole world. If they had been able to find out Matthew was suffering from this beforehand, they could have done a caesarean section and before they cut the umbilical cord, they would have done a tracheotomy on the baby to help him breathe and then they would have cut the cord. They would then bring specialists in to operate.

"This gave us some comfort for future pregnancies, should the same thing happen again. It wasn't a genetic condition and none of the reported cases had been born to the same mum, so we were hopeful it wouldn't happen again.

"We gave Matthew the full name Matthew Douglas Findlay, after his dad. This hadn't been our original plan, but we felt, given the circumstance, it was the right thing to do.

"We spent the Sunday and Monday with our son and then, heartbreakingly, the time came when we had to leave our baby behind and return home. The following Saturday we went to see him again at the funeral parlour and we saw him dressed in his little outfit, in his tiny coffin.

"We then had his funeral on the 17th of July. He was cremated at Warriston but we buried his ashes in the Mortonhall Rose Garden on the 25th October 2007. We still visit at birthdays and Christmas and I sometimes take Matthew's brother and sister, Daniel and Natasha, who were born a few years later."

Corinna reflects: "What I went through with Matthew was so hard as it was my first pregnancy. I used to feel Matthew kick but after my other pregnancies, I realised it really hadn't been that much but because it was my first I had nothing to compare it with at the time.

"After Matthew died, we got photos taken at the hospital. It was the first dead body I'd ever had to cope with and we weren't sure what to do. However, I so clearly remember in the room there was a little poster up on the wall that said, 'It's better to have a photo that you don't want, than to want a photo you can't get' and that made up our minds: we wanted photos of our precious son.

"I fell pregnant again four months after Matthew died, and I had a little boy in June 2008. He was seven weeks early but again, we had planned for possible prematurity. He was a healthy baby, and we got him home two weeks later. Understandably, I had been very anxious during this pregnancy, but after I'd had an MRI scan and was reassured nothing was wrong, I managed to relax a bit.

"With Daniel my waters broke first and then he was born five days later. I managed to stay calm through it all. Then soon after, I became pregnant again and my little girl, Natasha, was born in July 2009. I hadn't had an MRI scan with Natasha as they said the disadvantages outweighed the advantages.

"Again, my waters broke first, then I went into labour. I know I was in denial a little as I was so scared to give birth to her. Her birth was a bit more intense. I felt at least if she was inside me she was safe. She was about two and a half weeks early, so she stayed in the longest! She was born safe and well, and it was such a relief.

"We refer to Matthew as a 'special brother' to Daniel and Natasha who are now four and three years old, rather than a 'big brother'. They see him as a star in the sky but they are at the stage where they see there are lots of stars in the sky, so we now tell them that's all his friends. They understand and know a lot, even at a young age.

"Sometimes they ask difficult questions – usually when I'm driving! One day Daniel asked me why we couldn't just dig Matthew up and bring him home. I couldn't find the right words to answer him. I tried hard to keep my focus on the road as the tears filled my eyes. The simple logic of a child.

"We found Matthew's first birthday very difficult. We try and call it a birthday rather than an anniversary, we want to celebrate rather than mourn. I almost live Matthew's milestones as Daniel hits them too. My pregnancies were all the same time of year so it was hard not to compare each one to the last."

Corinna says: "I found out about SANDS Lothians through my doctor a few weeks after Matthew died. Dougie took a while off work because he just couldn't face going back. We spent a long time grieving and reflecting on everything, and it helped us to work through our feelings together.

"When Dougie first went back to work, it knocked me a bit as it meant I was then on my own. Matthew had been our first child and the first grandchild on both sides so there had been a lot on our shoulders, and a lot of grief for us both to handle when we lost him."

Corinna continues: "In the early days, we both came to SANDS for a one-to-one session, and we were then encouraged to come to meetings. Although Dougie's not been back, I still come nearly every month. I often come home after the meetings and talk with Dougie for hours about the things shared in the group, and that helps him too."

Asked what advice she can give to others, Corinna says: "Don't expect too much of yourself. Take everything a day at a time, and do what's right for you. Take time for yourselves as a couple to share your grief together. Try not to put your grief on hold as it will hit you later, take the time to deal with it.

"I have just qualified as a befriender for SANDS. I completed the two-day training course, so now I can go on to help others. I was going to do it a little while ago but I hit a bit of a bad spell again with my own emotions and I wondered if I was ready. However, I felt that I've had so much support that I wanted to give something back and be able to help others. I decided that I've walked the walk and I can now help others on their journey too."

Nathan Douglas Harrower

Helen begins: "When my husband and I married, he already had two children from a previous relationship, so I had step-children. Then I fell pregnant with my first child. Nathan and I was absolutely delighted.

"From day one, basically from the minute I saw that blue line on the pregnancy test, I had a baby. My pregnancy was fantastic. I loved being pregnant and was thrilled with every movement my baby made. I had no morning sickness, and I blossomed throughout my pregnancy. It was probably the healthiest I'd ever been in my life.

"There was not one unhealthy thing that crossed my lips because I was looking after my baby. I got my first scan and everything was perfect. When I got my bloods taken, one set came back that required further checking. I had to get another scan done and some more tests. I was under 20 weeks at this time. I did feel anxious at this point but was reassured that my baby was fine.

"I got to my due date on 14th August, but there was no sign of the baby coming. The family had done a sweepstake about the day the baby would be born and the sex it would be. There was about £50 in the jar but as the days went by no one was winning!

"We went to see the midwife who said I'd have to be induced, but when I went in for the antenatal appointment, they did a sweep of my membranes to try and start me off. It was a Friday so they thought I may start over the weekend but if not, they'd induce me on the Monday.

"Nothing happened over the weekend and the baby was still very lively and moving about. Before I'd left work, my colleague used to say she would always sit opposite me at meetings because she just loved watching my tummy move about. She said she would see me flinching as my baby had his own little football match inside. He was such an active baby.

"I went in very early on the Monday and remember saying to my mum, 'Next time I see you, I'll have my baby!' I'd phoned everyone really early in the morning to let them know I was going in as everyone was frantically waiting for this baby to come. It was my dad's birthday on the day I went in and he said, 'Don't worry; you have 24 hours to have this baby, so it's born on my birthday!'

Helen continues: "When I arrived, they gave me a scan. It showed that I had no water left so they told me I'd have to stay in, otherwise they would have induced me, then send me home while things progressed. I was then given a room and settled in.

"When I got the first inducement drug, the baby didn't like it – he reacted badly straight away. I was then moved from that room to another room where I could be more closely monitored. I had the big brown straps on but still nothing was happening. I told my husband just to go home and have a sleep, and I was told to get some rest too.

"People were checking me regularly. My baby's heartbeat was fine and he was still moving about. All was well. The next morning, the 24th my husband came back in about 6.30am. The doctors came in and asked me if it was OK to bring a student in. I said that was fine but not a big group. I didn't mind one or two coming in with my doctor. So in traipsed about a dozen people all standing staring at me.

"I remember feeling angry that nobody seemed to respect what I wanted. The doctor marched in, looked at my notes and then turned to his students and said, 'Nothing's happening, who wants to break the waters?' Although I had no water left the sack hadn't actually broken so it would still need to be broken, but I didn't want this done by a student! Another consultant came in and must have realised how uneasy I felt, so she did it and gave me some reassurance after everyone else had left.

"Breaking the waters was pretty painful. The consultant had warned me that she'd have to go quite far up but I just said, 'Well, this is going to have to come out, so just carry on and do what you need to do'. Although I was excited, I was beginning to get a bit anxious.

"I then got the drug that goes into your hand to induce you. I was told once that was injected labour could start very rapidly and be quite intensive. We then spoke about my choice of pain relief. I'd decided I would have the epidural so I could still be awake and aware, and they talked me through how it would work. I was still being monitored when all of a sudden the baby did a massive movement. It's hard to explain how dramatic it was, but it almost bucked my whole body off the bed.

"The consultant suddenly said, 'We need to deliver now'. The baby's heartbeat had dropped sharply. I remember being wheeled through as they were telling me what was happening. They had to give me an emergency caesarean section and deliver the baby immediately. I was asking if my baby was all right, and they just said he was in a bit of distress and had to come out. They didn't even wait for me to have the epidural; they just gave me gas to knock me out as quickly as possible.

"All I remember is them telling me to count 1, 2, … as they pasted over my stomach with the iodine. Someone else said they had to put a catheter in at the same time. I asked where my husband was and I remember hearing 'I'm here' and then that was it. After that, I only remember black, then blackness again when I was waking up. I came to with a jolt and first thing I could say was: 'Where's my baby?' That was when my world as I knew it changed forever.

"When I woke up, I was aware of pain. I went to touch my stomach and was stopped. There were people all around me gowned up and I heard someone saying, 'Helen, you've got a baby, your baby's here and then my husband said, 'We've got a son'. Then through floods of tears I said, 'We've got Nathan' and I felt so happy because I had my son. I said to my husband that I couldn't see – I think my anaesthetist panicked at that point until he realised I just needed my glasses. I put them on and realised my arm was wet. I couldn't understand why but it was my husband's tears.

"In a daze, I asked why was I so wet? Then someone else said, 'Your mum's here', again, confused, I asked, 'Why's my mum here? I haven't even seen my baby yet.' Then one of the doctors came along and said the dreaded words, 'Helen, your baby's not very well'. I asked what they meant. They said there was a bit of a problem, my baby had been distressed and didn't get a lot of oxygen.

"I remember taking this man's hand and saying, 'Are you my baby's doctor – are you Nathan's doctor?' He said yes and I said, 'I know you'll make Nathan better for me, so just go and make him better because I want to hold him'. He told me it would be a while before I could hold him because of my own operation. I said I didn't care about me; I just wanted to see my baby. I must have zonked out again as the next time I woke up I was in a different room.

"Everyone was there, my husband, Mum, Dad and my sister. I was high as a kite. I kept saying to Mum, 'I've got my son, Mum'. I remember her saying, 'I know, darling, but he's not very well'. I said, 'What do you mean he's not very well?' I just couldn't take anything in.

"After they'd all left, the consultant who delivered Nathan came in, and I could see she was visibly upset. I was obviously away with it, because I kept saying that Nathan was going to be fine and told everyone to stop worrying.

I was busy reassuring everyone else. I was told that it was really important that I went through to see him and I exclaimed that of course I wanted to see him!

"They wheeled me through in my hospital bed to the neonatal room. I asked if I could walk, but I wasn't allowed. They got my bed as close to Nathan's cot as they could and that was the first time I saw him. He just looked so beautiful. He was surrounded by pipes and the ventilator, but he had a little hat on and I remember thinking he was really big. I looked at his arms and hands, his little face and feet and toes. I adored him already. They took a Polaroid photo for me. I was told I had to go back to my room. Before I left, I asked if he was getting better, but nobody said yes or no, they just said he was doing ok for now.

"Later my consultant and Nathan's doctor came to see me. They told me my little boy was seriously ill. I asked what they meant by that – was I going to have a very disabled child? They told me he wasn't going to have a very good chance of surviving and, at the moment, the machine was breathing for him. When they said those words, that's when I realised how bad it was.

"I think I just numbly told them to go on, to tell me what they had to tell me. They said he had suffered a lack of oxygen during the birth and when he was delivered, part of the cord was very discoloured and looked like it hadn't been working properly. They then explained that when Nathan was born he was only just alive when they got him out. They resuscitated him to get him breathing as much as they could, but within the critical first five minutes of his life, he didn't make the big dramatic good response to the treatment that the doctors had hoped for. He had to be resuscitated, ventilated and rushed to neonatal. Even his dad hadn't been able to hold him.

"The enormity of what they were saying gradually sank in. I then said, 'I need off this bed because I need to be with my son.' They said they couldn't do that and adamantly, I said, 'You will take me off this bed or I will get my husband to take me through. If I have to walk through I will, but I have to get off this bed and get to my baby'.

"They got me a wheelchair; I was still getting treatment myself, but none of that mattered. All I could think about was Nathan. We went through and sat with Nathan for a long, long time. It was where I needed to be. I couldn't hold him at that time, but I had to be with him."

Helen painfully recalls: "I had a room in the labour ward and I could hear all the other babies crying. Through the night, I couldn't hold back my own tears as I think everything began to sink in. I was in a room on my own, with only a little Polaroid photo of my baby, and I just thought, this isn't how it should be, it was all so wrong.

"Later, my mum came back in and my husband and I went along to see Nathan and we were able to speak to the chaplain. I said I'd like him to christen Nathan. We were all there when Nathan was christened and we made my sister, Julie, his godmother. We were able to hold him for the first time, but it was hard to cuddle him properly because of all the machines."

Helen goes on: "I asked if he was getting any better and they said no, but they then said they had to do more tests. By this time, he couldn't even swallow properly, and they had to suction him to get rid of his saliva.

"I remember the gurgling noise so well, and at one point told the nurse that I would do it. The consultant then asked to speak to us both. I asked Mum if she would stay with Nathan. From the moment, I was fully aware of what was happening; he was never on his own; there was always someone there who loved him.

"We went into the doctor's room and no holds barred and without dressing it up, he said, 'I'm very sorry to tell you, but we need your permission to switch off the ventilator'. I just screamed, 'No! No way, there must be something you can do. My baby's 8lbs 4oz, he's a big boy, he's not premature, you have to make him better.'

"Devastatingly, the doctor then said there was nothing more he could do, they'd done everything they could since he was born. Again, in desperation, I said, 'I don't believe that. What part of me do you need to make him better? Tell me which bit and I'll give you it.' He just repeated his words, 'There's nothing; we just can't do anything else. He can't breathe or do anything on his own.'

"I just caved in completely. I remember holding my husband's hand and saying that this just couldn't be right. The doctor went on to tell us that he needed one of us to give permission. I remember saying that before I gave him my permission, I had to go and speak to my son. I went to Nathan, sat beside him and forced out the most painful of words: 'I'm so sorry, darling, you've done everything you should have done, but we just can't be together and I'm sorry for what I'm about to do, but I have to let you go.'

"When I returned, I told the doctor, if my son's machine had to be switched off, he had to promise me that he'd do it when I was there and that I wanted to hold my baby with no tubes while he's still alive. I then went back through to my room, and I had to tell my family. I said they all had to come and say goodbye first, then we would say goodbye.

"Everyone was crying. They'd all taken photos to have precious memories of Nathan, and then they all wanted to give me a cuddle before I went through as I was distraught.

"They put my husband and I in the family room at the neonatal ward. They brought Nathan through. He was still in his little cot but still attached to the ventilator. They undid everything there and then, and the doctor gave him to me, and at last I could hold my baby properly. We took some photos. It was so hard, but we just had to. Then my husband held him for a little while, then gave him back to me.

"I was cuddling him close, but I knew he was slipping away. I said, 'It's alright, darling, don't be afraid, Mummy's here with you. It's OK to go, just let go, you'll be fine, my granddad's waiting for you, and he'll look after you until Mummy gets there.'

"One tear fell from Nathan's eye and gradually he stopped breathing. He only lived for about four or five minutes off the ventilator. I knew he was away, and I was just howling, rocking him and holding him, talking to him and comforting him, singing to him. He had to be pronounced dead. At a time I wouldn't have wanted anyone else in the room, I had to call the doctor. I was allowed to still hold him while the doctor checked him then said, 'Yes, he's away.'

"When he said it again, it made it even more real. It was so awful. My beautiful son was pronounced dead at 17:26 on the 25th of August 2004. That's the day I class as having with him because the day he was born, I was still so spaced out. In a way I feel quite lucky because my baby was alive and I got to feel him nice and warm – they get cold so quickly.

"I remember saying to his dad, pass his blanket over because he's getting cold. I knew I still needed to care for Nathan and look after him. Whilst I was holding Nathan, his dad told me we looked beautiful. I was still cuddling him and singing to him as mother and son, and he was dressed in the little outfit I'd bought, to take him home as all parents do, but that wasn't to be the case for us. He was gone.

"I sat with him for quite a while. I put his little hat back on, and he looked nice and cosy. I remember telling him, 'I'll need to put your mitts on because you'll scratch yourself.' I had such a short time to love and care for him.

"When we decided we were ready, we were to phone for one of the midwives to come through. His dad was ready a lot sooner than I was. It was one of the hardest things I've ever had to do – walking out of that room without him, knowing I'd never see him again.

"When the midwife came in she asked if I'd like some photos. She took the three of us together even though Nathan had passed. I'm so glad we got those photos of us all as a family, and then we got some of Nathan on his own."

Helen bravely goes on: "I was then wheeled back to my room, and I knew I'd have to see my family. They were all still sitting there, and I just told them Nathan was away. They had waited all this time for us to come back.

"That evening, my husband said he couldn't stay with me as he couldn't cope and needed some time to himself. My sister stayed with me that night, refusing to leave me and for that I am forever grateful. I was kept in for a few days after that. I wanted to go home but wasn't allowed. That night my sister and I were looking out of the window in my room and noticed one big star in the sky – my sister said, 'that'll be Nathan' then the pair of us dissolved into tears.

"That night my milk started to come in and it was so painful. The doctors decided to try and stop my milk so they bound me up – that was supposed to stop it and it did. But every time a baby cried, my breasts were agony. Through the night there was a baby crying – it was a horrible cry, I was convinced it was Nathan. The nurse came in and told us it was a withdrawal baby, a baby that had been born addicted. I yelled 'to drugs!!' I just screamed: 'My baby's just died and there's someone through there that's a junkie and her baby's alive!'

"I just went crazy and told them to take the baby off her that she didn't deserve it. Every year I think of that baby, it would have been the same age as Nathan, and I don't know if it was a boy or a girl, but it had a cry like I'd never heard before and never want to hear again; it was awful. That's the only time I've ever said someone doesn't deserve their baby, but I was beside myself with grief. Even now, eight years on, I haven't moved on, I just go on."

Helen says: "They did a post-mortem, which showed there was a problem with the cord and the placenta. Something happened that cut the oxygen supply off and when it came back that's when he did the big jolt, it was him suddenly getting a gush of oxygen. The induction drug hadn't caused any problems. There was nothing wrong with him apart from the fact that he wasn't getting enough oxygen all the way through the pregnancy. If he had survived, he would have had some form of disability, but they couldn't ever say how severe.

"You replay it all over in your head, all the time with all the ifs, buts and maybes. When the time came, I didn't want to go home, the nursery was all done and I'd only made the cot up the night before I came in, but I had to go home. I walked out of that hospital with a memory box and a shawl when everyone else was walking out with their baby."

Helen continues: "I decided I wanted a private funeral. I didn't want any flowers or cards, I wanted nothing. We didn't know where to start with funeral arrangements but went to a funeral director in Edinburgh and told them that our baby had died. We decided we wanted to cremate Nathan. I couldn't bury him in a hole in the ground.

"We had three cars, and we all left from my house. The hearse was already at Mortonhall waiting for us. The nearer we got, I kept saying, 'I can't do this, I can't do this.' We had to wait a minute outside as there was a funeral already there, but that short wait allowed me to compose myself.

"My consultant and four midwives were there. When I saw them, I just started to cry, it was so nice. There were only about 20 people there. In the paper we'd put no flowers, only donations to the neo-natal unit.

"After the funeral, when it was time to go back and collect Nathan's ashes, we went straight to Mortonhall. We'd phoned beforehand to say we were coming in and were told that was fine. In the lead up to collecting his ashes, we'd been trying to decide where we were going to put them, and if we were going to have a plaque or put his name in the baby book. So we went in and I asked when we could get his ashes. The lady said, 'You're not going to get any ashes'. I said, 'What do you mean we're not going to get any ashes?' She said, 'You won't get any ashes from a baby.'

"Dumbstruck, I told her the undertaker had told me that I would get his ashes back, and, when the reality of what she had just said hit me, I completely crumbled. I felt like I'd lost him all over again. She phoned the undertaker there and then, in front of us, with me crying in the background, and she tore strips off him and told him to never again ever tell bereaved parents that they will get ashes from a baby. That undertaker sent us a single white rose the next day.

"Nathan had died once, and it was like he'd died all over again. Now, the rules are different with regard to getting ashes back, but I've never come to terms with that. Every time I go to the chapel, I always feel so guilty. It was devastating. It took me a long time to deal with that and a lot of counselling. Nathan's name is in the baby book in the chapel of remembrance at Mortonhall. It's a tiny bit of comfort for me."

Helen says: "After the funeral, every bit of me felt numb. I didn't know what to do with myself. I felt stupid and useless and empty. You've cared for your baby for nine months, and they're no longer in your tummy, but they're not in your arms either, and you're never going to see them again.

"Nathan's death had a major impact on my husband and me. In the first few months we were inseparable, almost behaving like one being, then we just drifted apart. He seemed to move on sooner than I did, and I was still dealing with raw grief. It was a dreadful time. I felt such a failure. I'd been the rebel all my life and now my baby had died. I felt I'd let everyone down. I didn't want to talk to anyone or see anyone. I prayed every night that I wouldn't wake up in the morning. I just wanted the pain to stop.

"My sister was amazing. She came round every morning to get me out of my bed. She told me it was time to get up and made me tea and toast every day. She was a total life saver. After about two or three weeks, my husband phoned SANDS UK who told us about SANDS Lothians. I thought he would tell them I was a lunatic but he just told me that he didn't know how to help me. We were so up and down with each other at that time; it was all so fraught.

"The first day I came to SANDS Lothians I met two befrienders. We had a cup of tea and I told them my story. It helped so much and after that, I came to every meeting and also had counselling, one-to-one. In fact, I've used all of SANDS services!

"Speaking years later, one of the SANDS Lothians' team told me that I used to come to meetings but never took my coat off, and one day I just came in and straight away took my coat off. I became more involved and helped with events and fundraising. It was somewhere I was allowed to talk about Nathan to other people without feeling bad or that I would upset my friends and family."

Helen goes on: "I had my second son, Owen, in 2006 and while I was expecting him, I came to pregnancy support meetings. It was such a different pregnancy. Everything I could have had, I had: oedema, diabetes, Nathan never had enough water and Owen had too much. Every day, I was checking he was moving. There was a huge difference in the way I felt seeing that blue line again for the second time, and my first thoughts were 'Here we go again, now come on, baby, let's do it this time'.

"I wanted to know this time if it was a girl or boy, I needed to prepare myself. Secretly, in my heart, I wanted a boy. Having Owen was a big positive step for me. When he was a baby I was so wrapped up in him, he was my world. However, the older he gets, the more I realise, everything Owen's done so far, all his milestones, Nathan should have done all those things too.

"Owen knows about his big brother, he's always been part of his life. In his child-like way, he often comes out with the difficult, blunt questions only a child can ask, but they are actually quite therapeutic for me. One day, when I wanted to celebrate Nathan's birthday, Owen said, 'Will he be having a birthday in heaven? If you're dead, Mummy, do you not come back? Do you want him to come back? Would he come back as a baby or as my big brother?' and then after all these questions, Owen would just skip off and carry on playing.

"My husband and I separated in 2008 as our relationship was never the same after the loss of Nathan. Even eight years on, the loss of Nathan is still devastating but getting involved with SANDS Lothians has been so therapeutic. I spoke at the memorial service last year and felt very honoured to do that. I read 'Tiny Angels'. I have written things in the past for Nathan, but I thought it may be a bit hard to read them for the first time. Reading at the service was a real turning point for me."

One of Helen's poems:

For Nathan

Time is not my healer
I long to hold you every day
My heart and body aches
Let my tears be your strength

No matter where I am my
Love and thoughts are for you
My Nathan, my son
My beautiful boy
Be strong, feel love as
Mummy loves you, my son

Love Mummy

"I saw a different side to how hard they work at SANDS and the endless effort that goes into getting funding, organising events, generating support and keeping the services going for bereaved parents. It's so close to my heart now and I have such a passion for working here. If I have a bad day, I don't have to explain myself. We can feel normal again here and there is a lot of laughter."

Looking back, Helen reflects: "Little things carry special meaning for me. I have a special tree in the garden for Nathan, my sister bought a star for him after seeing the star in the sky from my hospital room in those early dark days, and I get great comfort from seeing rainbows.

"I remember so clearly one time, in the early days, when I had a terrible dark day and felt I just couldn't go on, I phoned my mum to see if she could come round, and I asked her to keep talking to me on the phone as she got closer. Then I heard someone at my door but could hardly bear to open it. When I gradually pulled the door open, nobody was there but my letter box was rattling. As I looked out, there was a massive rainbow arch. Still on the other end of the phone, Mum said, 'Who's at your door?' I replied, 'A rainbow! A rainbow's at my door!' I have no idea who tapped my door, maybe it was a little gift from Nathan."

Asked how she feels now, Helen says: "Working within SANDS has helped me greatly in so many ways. If newly bereaved parents come in and in the depths of their grief ask me if things will ever get better, it is wonderful to be able to say to them, 'Yes, you'll be able to go on. I used to stand where you are asking exactly the same thing but yes, one day, you'll be able to smile again'."

Lyla Haslin

"We found out in March 2010 that we were expecting, and our due date was 14th December 2010. Although my partner, Tim Haslin, had three boys from a previous marriage, this was my first child.

"I had a good pregnancy, problem free, apart from the usual heartburn and some swelling. I had a suspected low lying placenta at 20 weeks, but it had moved by 36 weeks.

"My baby didn't come on my due date, so on 22nd December, I was booked in for induction of labour on 28th December, exactly two weeks after my due date.

"Everything seemed fine, and I went in on the Tuesday morning to be induced. When we got there, we were taken onto the ward, given a bed and told the midwife would be along to do some checks shortly. When she arrived, she listened for my baby's heartbeat, but she couldn't find it. I wasn't concerned at this point, still thinking that everything was fine. The midwife called her colleague to say the baby was misbehaving and could she try and find the heartbeat. Sadly, she couldn't find it either. We were then moved along the ward to the scan room. After a short wait, we were scanned and then heard the awful words, 'I'm sorry, there is no fetal heartbeat'.

"Devastation and utter disbelief don't even begin to describe how we felt. All I could think about was my mum and dad at home, waiting to hear the good news. I had to call my mum there and then. Hearing her cries will haunt me forever.

"Shortly after the first scan, we were scanned again by a more senior person to confirm what had happened. We were then taken to a room and informed about what would happen next. I don't remember much of this but I do remember that I just wanted it all to be over and done with, as soon as possible. I was desperate to get out of hospital.

"My parents came up immediately as did my brother and his wife. We all tried our best to comfort each other. Although I was heartbroken, all I could think about was getting pregnant again. It was strange, I felt so incredibly sad, but I knew I wouldn't get angry and I wouldn't blame anyone. I couldn't change what had happened and wouldn't torture myself further with 'whys' and 'what ifs'. I was given a tablet to end the pregnancy and told to wait half an hour after taking it to make sure there were no reactions to it and asked to return two days later to deliver the baby.

"We went home and sobbed our hearts out and tried to get our heads around what had happened. I started getting pains about 5pm the following day which got progressively worse. We called the hospital and went up around 1am. We were taken straight to the labour ward where I was examined and was found to be 6cms dilated. I was given gas and air, diamorphine and shortly after that, an epidural. The regular contractions stopped, so I was put on a drip to try and start them again.

"The midwives were so incredibly nice, especially one who stayed with us most of the time, and who at 11.19am on 30th December 2010, helped us deliver our beautiful, perfect, sleeping angel, Lyla, the most gorgeous little bundle we had ever seen. Lyla weighed 8lb 7oz and was 48cms long. She had lots of dark hair and a cute little button nose. She looked just like her mummy. We washed and dressed her and took lots of pictures.

"My parents, gran, sister in law, aunt and Tim's mum and her husband, came to see us. We spent some time together then everyone left and Tim and I spent the rest of the day with our precious daughter. We left around 9pm. We returned the following day after buying a little pink fleece outfit, which we dressed Lyla in and then we spent more treasured time with her.

"With its being Christmas and because of the heavy snowfall that year, it was about a fortnight later that Lyla was laid to rest beside her great-granda, my mum's dad. After a beautiful service conducted by a family friend, we released lots of pink balloons at the graveyard. We will send her balloons to heaven every year on her birthday.

"At the time of writing this, I am due to have Lyla's little sister in about seven weeks and I know Lyla is watching over us."

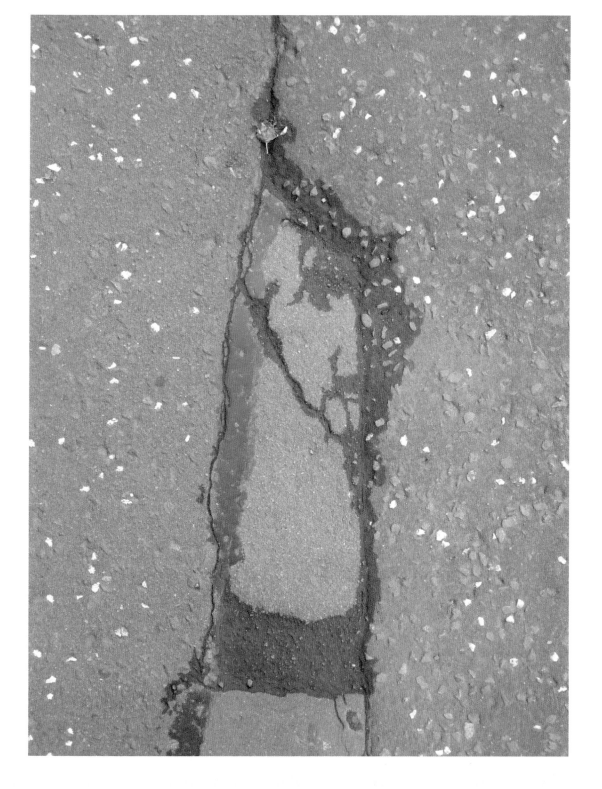

Haydon John James Kennan

Helen begins: "I was diagnosed with endometriosis when I was quite young. It was so bad that they put me through a mock menopause to try and shut down my system and then restart it in the hope that it would re-programme itself, so from early on, there was always a question mark over whether or not I would be able to have children.

"During my first marriage, I didn't conceive at all. Then I went on to meet my husband, Jim, and amazingly, we fell pregnant with our first baby in October 2007. We went for a scan and were told that our baby was fully developed, but it had passed away.

"It was estimated that our baby was around 20 weeks, but he hadn't developed beyond the size of a 12-week baby. We named him Euan but I was advised not to see him as I might have found it too distressing. I didn't have to go through labour because the baby was so small, but I was given a D&C.

"I fell pregnant again around October 2008 but sadly, I lost that baby too, but it was an early loss this time, at about nine weeks. Then I became pregnant again in January 2011 and before I even had time to confirm it with the doctors, I knew I'd lost it. Jim and I feared we would lose this baby again so we decided not to tell anyone about our third loss.

"While all this was going on, I'd had to start using a diabetic insulin pump. My blood sugars were perfect for conceiving, so we tried again, but this time decided it would be our last try. We went on holiday, but I hadn't been feeling great. I was craving a lot of meat which was unusual as I don't eat much meat. When we came home from that trip away, I found out I was pregnant again but my insulin pump had malfunctioned, so I was lucky to still be carrying the baby. I'd ended up spending the whole night in hospital with an insulin overdose. Against all the odds, the baby was still there.

"We desperately hoped we'd get to the 20-week stage as that was the furthest we'd got before and we felt, if we could just get past that point, it would be plain sailing. We did, but by the time I was 22 weeks, they started to find problems with my baby. They noticed he had an enlarged heart and had two holes in it.

"The 20-week scan had also showed that the baby had a large nuchal fold at the back of his neck which indicated there was a possibility that he could have Down's syndrome, over and above his heart problems. I have a close cousin with Down's so that aspect of my baby's problems didn't faze me at all. He was my baby and I'd love him just the way he was."

Helen continues: "As time passed, the doctors started noticing more and more things which began to cause them concern, and at that point my health started to deteriorate too. I have kidney reflux which I have had since a child and that started to give me problems again. I was on medication to try and keep my blood pressure down because it was becoming raised as a result of my kidneys not functioning. I was fighting pre-eclampsia from 23 weeks. I was getting scanned every second week because of all the difficulties and at 25 weeks I was told I was having a boy.

"I had actually been told it was unlikely that I'd be able to carry boys because of my history, but I was having a son. My first loss was a boy and they were fairly certain the others had been too, and I'd just had a feeling myself that I'd been carrying boys.

"We were understandably very anxious when we found out it was another boy, but soon after being told we were having a son, we chose to go for a 4D scan which we paid for privately. The first image I had of my beautiful son in my womb, he was busy picking his nose, so Jim and I decided we'd have our hands full with this one!

"Very soon after this, I was admitted to hospital as my kidneys had started to really struggle and my next scan showed my normally extremely active baby just wanting to sleep. I was admitted to the high dependency unit and put on various drips and medication, including steroid injections to help Haydon's lungs to mature because they knew he would most likely be arriving soon. I spent the next two weeks in hospital.

"By this point, I wasn't worried about me; my only thoughts were for my baby. I told the doctor that if it reached the stage of their having to choose between saving me or my baby, I told them they must save my baby – I would die for my baby. However, they told me that wasn't their policy. I desperately wanted to keep my son safe for as long as I possibly could.

"At 30 weeks, I was getting the doppler scan and echo x-rays every day to check on him. One day his heart rate appeared different and there were lots of shadows and vibrations. I instinctively knew that morning that something was different. It was just a gut feeling but I knew something was wrong.

"I phoned Jim at his work and told him I thought we were going to have our baby that day. I had started to feel dizzy and quite unwell myself and all I could think about were words my doctor had previously said – that often with kidney problems, you don't know you're ill until you start feeling poorly and once you feel poorly, it's critical.

"After one of my scans, I was escorted back up to the ward, which in itself was unusual, but they wouldn't let me walk up on my own. Once I was reattached to all the monitors, the doctor came in and told me I would be having my baby that day. My kidneys were failing and they had to get him out. They had no choice, and they didn't have much time. Preparations were made for an emergency caesarean section and, during the build up to it, I kept talking to my belly, telling Hayden that he better come out screaming!

"When I went to theatre, my beautiful boy did come out screaming. They quickly showed him to us before rushing him away. We had a gorgeous chubby, pink, screaming baby boy. They whisked him away as he was having difficulty breathing. They managed to ventilate him, but it took them seven minutes to do so. He was then taken to the neonatal unit because he was ten weeks early."

Helen goes on: "Every day there was a development. With every hour that passed he was getting stronger. They got him off the ventilator the first day and he was on CPAP for the second, but he hated this with a vengeance. This obviously motivated him and by day three, he was off CPAP and breathing pretty much on his own. He lost weight to begin with but gradually began to thrive and at 5½ weeks we got him home.

"Because he'd been in hospital for so long, the first week we got him home we'd asked people to let us have time with him on his own so we could have him to ourselves for a while, but in that first week I had him at the doctors three times.

"He would scream and go bright red when he was doing the toilet or had wind. The pains in his tummy were excruciating for him, and he had difficulty feeding because he was so uncomfortable. The doctors said it was colic, but I knew it wasn't. I'd worked with children for 20 years and I knew this wasn't normal. Later they would wonder if it was Hirschprung's disease, a condition where the bowel hasn't formed properly and one that was common in children with Down's.

"My health visitor tried to show us baby massage to help ease his pain, and we bought herbal remedies to try and help him but nothing worked. Haydon was exhausted and he even started to struggle with his breathing again which became a huge concern for us.

"On the tenth day that he was home, we went to our beds once we managed to settle Haydon for the night and he seemed comfortable. The neo-natal unit had lent us a sleep apnoea mat. They didn't think we'd need it, but since he had had so much monitoring in hospital, they felt it would give us peace of mind and a little reassurance.

"Through the night the alarm went off twice. We were nervous wrecks but he seemed OK. I got him up for his 4.30am feed, but he was so tired and clearly struggling. I phoned NHS 24 but they decided not to send an ambulance because he was still breathing and there wasn't an obvious emergency. They then contacted my GP who rang us at 8am to see how Haydon was. I told her he was just the same, lying limp in my arms, hungry but not feeding. She came over and phoned an ambulance straight away, and he was rushed into the local specialist children's hospital.

"He was diagnosed with bronchiolitis. They had taken an x-ray of his chest which showed patchy areas that indicated an infection. He was put on CPAP as soon as he was admitted to the high dependency ward and was rarely off CPAP after this. We had small periods of time each day where the doctors tried to wean him off it, but he struggled with this for a long time.

"He was put in an incubator to have a few days of isolation and treated with antibiotics. He then appeared to get a little better and was moved from the incubator back into a cot. They then told us the infection had come back and once more he was put back on CPAP, which again, he hated. He then started having episodes where he'd stop breathing, and they'd have to resuscitate him. They had to do this 36 times. It was devastating.

"Haydon had numerous physical and neurological tests to try to work out if he had a form of epilepsy. I was certain, however, that these episodes were more linked to stress and anxiety as it seemed that whenever he got a fright that's when they would be worse.

"The respiratory team and the cardiology team were both working with him, but no one could work out what was wrong with him. They thought it might be one of the holes in his heart that could be causing the problems so they decided to send him to another hospital a few miles away that specialised in heart surgery. He would spend nearly seven weeks in that hospital.

"They had to ventilate Haydon to get him across to the hospital as he was still having episodes where he would stop breathing and it was too dangerous to travel without doing so. They ventilated him and got a central line into his neck for his medications and antibiotics then put him in a travel pod for the journey. It was then a race against time to get him to the hospital. Jim and I travelled as quickly as we could by taxi and train, and we got there at the same time, which was amazing since he was blue lighted across.

"Our poor son had been through so much in his short life. He had needed several blood transfusions, canulas in his hands and his feet which, after a while, caused the veins in his hands and feet to collapse, and then they had to start using his head. It was all so hard for us to watch.

"Before we had moved hospitals he'd developed MRSA, which is a hospital infection, so when we arrived at the specialist heart hospital he had to be placed in isolation. The nurses and I tried to keep him stimulated as much as possible. He was a 3½ month old baby, but even with his Down's it hadn't really impacted on his development. Despite all his problems, he'd already started to hit milestones we didn't think he'd reach.

"He was given heart surgery the day after he arrived, but the doctor's first words to us were, 'It's not looking good for your boy, is it?' That was the first time anyone had said to us that they didn't think he'd make it. All the time we were told he would grow out of these issues and it was all just immaturity. As much as his journey was a struggle, not once had we thought we may lose him.

"Within a week later, he'd had a lot of tests. He had tracheobronchomalacia, which meant his windpipe and lungs would collapse in on themselves whenever the ventilator was taken out. Then he would suffocate in his own skin.

"They discovered that he did have Hirschsprung's disease. Also, because he had so much ventilation from birth he'd developed chronic lung disease; he had pulmonary hypertension and the two holes in his heart. Although they'd managed to fix one, it had caused a shunt of pressure onto the other.

"A week after his surgery, his MRSA infection had cleared so he was given the all clear to be moved onto the main ward. We were still in intensive care, but at least we were with other families.

"One of the doctors came in to see Haydon after he'd had a look over his notes, and they thought at first they may have been able to put a trachea in until he was old enough to support his own breathing. They thought the Down's syndrome may have caused poor muscle tone and that may have been why he was floppy at times.

"I asked the doctor what the results of his test were and what they were going to be able to do for him. Then came the crushing reply – 'Nothing, we can't do anything'. I was sitting on my own on a ward, surrounded by families, when I was given the devastating news that there was no more they could do to help my boy.

"Jim had been at work, but he came straight to the hospital, as did one of my friends. Next day, the respiratory and cardiology teams all met up for a discussion about Haydon, along with his surgeons, and then they met with us. Every doctor said that he couldn't be helped. They started to speak to us about making decisions for him and considering letting him go. We were adamant that we weren't making that decision for him. If Haydon wanted to go, it would be his choice.

"Then there was talk of sending us to a hospice as we may get a few more weeks with him. We were told that, there, we could walk him in his pram, bath him and do family things. They had a policy of no ventilation and if we were to go there we would have to remove his ventilation tube, and we knew that he would deteriorate rapidly as soon as that happened. So we decided the hospice wasn't for us.

"We knew we may still have a bit of time with him but we decided to get things moving just in case. My mum came through that night with her family's christening robe. It was 65 years old and had been worn by every member of our family. Haydon wore it too when he was christened on the Thursday morning by the hospital chaplain.

"We stayed overnight with him in the hospital room because he had been deteriorating all day and we wanted to stay with him. I was lying in a camp bed parallel to him. He'd always been such a monkey trying to pull all his feeding tubes out. He never tried to pull his breathing tube out, but he had a good go at all the other tubes.

"For some reason, that night, I suddenly sat bolt upright in my camp bed, and I just had this feeling that Haydon needed me, that happened quite a lot, just a gut instinct. I turned to look at him, and this time he had both hands on his ventilator tube trying to pull it out.

"My poor little boy had had enough. There seemed to be no more fight left in him. His lungs were in such a bad way by this time, it almost seemed as if he started to have panic attacks as his lungs were so sore and he wanted the tubes out. Normally, I would be able to calm him and comfort him, but even I couldn't manage to do that, that night. Both Jim and I then agreed that if I wasn't able to comfort him, then no-one and nothing could.

"The doctors gave us the choice to give him pain relief medication to sedate him if we wanted them to, as he was in so much discomfort. Haydon was looking at Jim intently and we both knew he was telling us he'd had enough. However, we also knew that if he had the medication then that would be it – he wouldn't regain consciousness after that. It was a horrible choice. Eventually, we made the decision to have him sedated. He was in distress, the machines were going haywire, his heart rate and oxygen saturation were all dropping and he was in a lot of pain. He was really struggling, so we made the agonising decision to have him sedated, knowing this would be our time to say goodbye.

"He started to relax and the doctors told us that now was the time to speak to him if there was anything we wanted to say. We were told that he would fall into a deep sleep, that he may still hear us but this would be the last time he'd be responsive. We got him out of his cot, while he was still ventilated. They had a chair for me to sit on, and I held him in my arms.

"All through my pregnancy he had always responded to one song in particular. It was a little sad song called *Blackbird* by Alter Bridge, and I couldn't understand why he liked it so much, but I could always feel him moving around to it. When we had him home, whenever he heard it he would react to it. The song was such a depressing song but I'm sure he was telling us – that was his song.

"When we listened to the lyrics, *really* listened to them, it was his story, it was *Haydon's Song*. We had it played to him as I held him in my arms. I held him close to my chest so he would feel like he was back in my tummy listening to his song and to my heartbeat keeping him safe and sound for the last moments of his life.

"The doctors told us that even with all the medication, he was still quite distressed. They said they could give him a little more but if they did, we would be approaching the time that we'd have to let him go. We asked if we could take everything off his face and remove the last of the tubes.

"We looked away as they did this as we didn't want to see the tubes coming out. When we looked back, he was glowing, just like a little angel wrapped up in a fluffy white blanket and at such peace. He hung on for about another hour. He was determined he wasn't going, but slowly, our precious, much loved boy slipped away.

"It was Good Friday, the day he died, which brought its own set of problems when we tried to get him home. All the funeral directors were on holiday, and we had a bit of a struggle trying to find someone who could get him home during the holidays. In the four months Haydon had been with us, Jim and I had only been home for the ten days that we had our baby home. The thought of going back home without him was almost too much to bear. We needed him brought home, we needed him close by.

"We had his funeral a week later on Friday the 13th – he certainly picked his days! Right up to the last minute, he was still playing his cheeky tricks. His little coffin, which we like to call his 'forever bed' wasn't ready for him and needed transported up from Newcastle. He was finally laid to rest in it, and it was a replica of his bedroom. We had an animal safari train going round his room so we got the exact same thing on his coffin. It was white wood but all hand-painted with his name on it. We had his song at his funeral, along with a slide show of his photos put together as the story of his life. It was a chance for everyone to get to know him properly. He was such a special little boy.

"He was laid to rest at a cemetery just up from our house. We recently reached another milestone when his headstone was finally put in place. Again, true to form, the dates got muddled up but thankfully, they corrected them. I'm sure that was our boy still being a little monkey – he liked to keep us on our toes!

"I am a very spiritual person and if I didn't have my beliefs, I don't know how I would cope. The first few months after he died I just didn't want to be here anymore. Poor Jim was trying his hardest to support me and at the same time deal with his own grief. He also had the job of dealing with all the practical things, paperwork, finances and worst of all, clearing out Haydon's room. We've reached a deadlock on that one just now – we just can't bear to part with anything else.

"It was so hard coming home after leaving the hospital and seeing all the clothes he'd been wearing that morning before he went in. His used bottles, his dirty bibs, his Moses basket – nothing had moved. We could still picture him in our minds in our home.

"It's hard enough losing him but even harder to know he suffered. It got so bad at times we struggled to see any benefits of having him – there was no pleasure for him. We tortured ourselves. We were told nothing would have changed the outcome; he was just born with all these problems. I had to watch my son suffer and go through so many resuscitations. Nothing could ever have prepared me for that."

Helen continues: "Haydon was almost forced into having to tell us how he was feeling. His communication skills seemed to develop very quickly; we could tell from his expressions what he was feeling. There were six serious issues listed on his death certificate, most people only have one.

"He was a little warrior – a real fighter. We nicknamed him our miniature superhero. He could only wear babygros to allow for all the monitors and tubes and we got him an extra special little Superman babygro and told him he was our tiny superhero.

"Luckily, we had made little hand and foot casts during slightly happier times at the hospital as a gift for Daddy as he'd had a sickness bug and couldn't visit Haydon until his bug had passed. Thankfully, we now had these as such precious mementos. I've set up a charity fund in memory of Haydon and I work with another child bereavement charity and the specialist heart hospital to provide hand and foot moulds to go in the memory boxes as keepsakes for other parents.

"It helped me to do that too, it was almost a distraction for me. I've tried so hard to keep the lid on all my grief; I feel if I let it out I won't be able to cope – at times, I still feel like that even now."

Helen says: "I first heard about SANDS Lothians when a friend of a friend lost her son and she'd used their services and suggested I go. In the early days, I don't know what I would have done without them. The befriender assigned to me just seemed to instinctively know when I was having a rock-bottom day and would phone me. It took me a while to leave the house to go into the office but I eventually did it and I got great support. My GP had initially thought SANDS might not be the right place for me because Haydon was beyond neo-natal but there was nowhere else for me to go. I know now that others who have lost slightly older children attend SANDS.

"I am still waiting to have my treatment for post-traumatic stress [disorder] through the mental health team, as I am constantly replaying images in my head and having flashbacks. I also play over the lung clearing suctions and physiotherapy to clear his chest, as well as his blood tests, blood transfusions, his canulas and his resuscitations. The images replay all day, every day, particularly the resuscitations and his little hands and feet being so bruised from all the treatment. I am so frustrated to still be waiting for this. I used to be so strong, and now I can barely get myself out of bed. I feel let down by the system, and I feel like I am stuck in limbo. I am still battling so many demons.

"My doctor is wonderful. I tried to struggle through for about three months, but I just wasn't coping and Jim was frightened to leave me, and I just wanted to die. It took me a while to see my GP, but I was completely honest with her and I just said – you need to help me because I don't want to be here.

"Despite all of this, I've made myself a promise that, once I'm feeling better and I'm back on my feet, I want to help others and perhaps set up a SANDS group in Midlothian.

"Jim and I share the same memories, we've grown stronger together and if either of us are replaying a memory, it's only the other who really understands. We had Haydon together, we shared him together and we lost him together, and we are still very much together. We are still strong.

"I can't, or perhaps more to the point, won't have more children – I was too ill. We could make a choice to try again, but there would be no guarantee that we would have a live birth. We decided never to put another baby through that again. We may foster or adopt some time in the future, but at the moment we don't know. Right now, the only baby we want is Haydon.

"Some days, I cope better than others, but every day is different. I'm not even back at work yet, mainly because of the nature of my work. I work in child protection."

Asked what advice she can give to others, Helen says: "Seek out people who have been through something similar. The best support comes from those who just know. It's a lonely grief. Talk about your child, talk about your experience. My baby was here, we are his parents, and he will always be our child. We still have a duty of care to him in the form of tending to his grave and remembering his birthdays and anniversaries.

"The best support comes from those happy to listen. They understand. Don't forget the fathers either – it's their loss too. Online communities can be a huge help – you get great strength from others, even if they are total strangers, the shared experience brings you together.

"Even financially, you may well run into difficulties. When we had Haydon, we got our family allowance then when he died, I was given a notice period as they were stopping our money. So I am now in a position where I am unable, mentally or emotionally, to go back to work, but I have no wages. Not only have we lost our son, we have lost all financial security. Our savings cushion was intended to bring up our baby, but that money has now paid for a funeral and a coffin and there's next to nothing left."

Helen reflects: "You grieve for the person you once were. I used to be strong, confident and outgoing, now I can barely walk down the street. We should be doing more with our lives, but we don't know how to. It is the awkward grief, a grief that no one wants to talk about. The grief that everyone thinks you'll get over, but it's not something we'll ever get over, we just learn to wear a better mask to help others feel comfortable with our grief, when we're not even comfortable with it ourselves.

"Since losing my son, my whole world has changed. His loss has caused a ripple effect and now I have a lot of different friends and sources of support, compared to the friends and life I once had. The grief of losing your child impacts on every aspect of your life, and in particular, friendships, because no one knows what to say or how to support, so they drift away.

"Our Haydon, our gorgeous, precious little boy, is buried with his teddy, his bear and his favourite sheep rattle. Family put letters and jewellery into his coffin, and my dad gave him money for the ferryman. He's still wrapped up in his favourite white blanket, and we buried him in his Superman babygro. Haydon was, and always will be, our miniature superhero."

Paul Lawson

3 October 1992

Jordan Lawson

27 September 1993

Joan begins: "I don't like the word 'stillborn'; I prefer 'born asleep'. My son Paul was born asleep twenty years ago. It was three weeks before his due date when I had a show, and I started to panic. At the time, my husband was working, so I got my son Aaron dressed, and I went into hospital. Instinctively, I took my hospital bag with me.

"When I got to the hospital, they started to monitor my baby's heartbeat, and it was then that the midwife couldn't find anything. The feeling of dread grew in the pit of my stomach. I had to wait for the specialist to come in, and I was then sent for a more extensive scan and even twenty years down the line, the words that were then spoken still ring in my ears, 'I'm sorry, Mrs Lawson, but your baby's dead.' Those are words I will never forget.

"My husband at the time was, by that point, at my side and in shock. He said, 'Just take him out, get him out', but the medical staff explained that they couldn't do that, and I would have to go through labour. I was 37 weeks. All the way through labour I kept thinking, maybe they've made a mistake; they've just looked at the monitor wrongly but sadly, there was no mistake. My little boy, Paul, was born asleep on the 3rd of October 1992."

Joan continues: "I fell pregnant again quite quickly after Paul died. This time with a daughter we would call Jordan. Paul had been quite small so when I was pregnant with Jordan, they did extra growth scans, but that was the only extra monitoring I had."

Looking back and reflecting on how her next two pregnancies were monitored, Joan feels let down and says: "If they'd done the scans on Jordon that they went on to do on my next two daughters, Niamh and Blair, I'm certain they would have found out what was wrong with Jordan.

"I went into labour with Jordan. This time a week early, and again went into hospital. They monitored my contractions and my progress and devastatingly, once again, they couldn't find a heartbeat. In my heart of hearts, I just knew something was wrong, but all I could think was not again, please, not again. How could another of my babies die? I'd done everything right, eaten all the right things, gone to all my appointments and my husband hadn't let me lift even the lightest of bags. It just couldn't be happening again and once more, I had to go through labour knowing my child wouldn't be alive at the end of it."

Joan continues, bravely: "Paul's post-mortem results came back completely clear. There was nothing wrong with him. I read something years ago that likened a stillbirth to a cot death in the womb. That's what happened to Paul; he was perfectly healthy; he just passed away in my womb.

"Fairly soon after Jordan was born, the doctor explained that they thought there was something wrong with her as her ears were lower down than normal and there was something wrong with her jaw-line. They thought it may be something to do with her urinary tract, but it wasn't until her post-mortem that we found out for certain. Her results showed that she only had one kidney and it was too small. It wasn't flushing out her system properly. It wasn't classed as any syndrome, it was simply that her kidneys hadn't developed properly."

Joan says: "In hindsight, I still can't help but feel that, if they'd done the scans that I went on to have with my next two pregnancies, where they scan the babies' internal organs too, they would have picked up that Jordan was suffering from this condition, and it would at least have prepared me a little for the outcome. She had died when I went into labour, it was just too much for her little body to cope with."

Joan goes on: "The minister that did both Paul and Jordan's funerals was the minister that married my husband and I. She had also christened my eldest son and was at the birth of both Paul and Jordan. She helped me and my family so much. She helped me through the most horrendous heartbreak of two labours where I knew my baby had died."

Joan reflects: "Looking back, one of the hardest things that still gets to me are the 'what ifs' that I play in my head surrounding Jordan's death. If only they'd done one scan to check her internal organs, could things have been different? I was told afterwards that because there was nothing wrong with Paul, there was nothing for them to look for in Jordan. I know this was all twenty years ago but even to this day, the turmoil I have surrounding the monitoring of my pregnancy with Jordan still haunts me. I hope it's changed now for other parents, and they don't have to torture themselves like I do.

"I was told after Jordan's post-mortem, that even if she'd survived the labour she wouldn't have lived for long. She would have needed a kidney transplant as her system would have been weakened so much. However, I would rather have gone through her dying after being born, if it had meant that I could at least have got to know her for a few minutes.

"I lost both my babies within a year. One of the things the hospital had said to me was that if I felt ready, a good way to get over the death of a baby was to have another one. I did desperately want another baby, not to fill the gaping hole that was now in my life, that could never be filled, but I just had such a need to cradle a living baby.

"At one point, shortly after Jordan was born, there was a lady on the same ward. I think she'd had a stillbirth or lost a baby in the past, and she'd just had a healthy little boy and she let me hold him. I have no idea to this day who she was, but I would love to thank her."

Joan says: "Because I was told there was something wrong with Jordan, her death was almost a little easier to cope with. I knew she wasn't well and had she lived, she would have had a struggle. I got to hold Paul but not Jordan.

"I was told that when she was born, she had a little film over her face which they had been frightened to take off her in case it affected her skin. I got to see her but not to hold her. She had beautiful pink hands and long fingers. I wish, so much, that I had held her.

"At her funeral, my husband carried her coffin out to the funeral car, so in a sense, even he got to hold her. That day we left from my mum's house. The funeral directors brought Jordan into the house, and I remember saying that I wanted to be left alone with her, just to have a few minutes with my daughter. However, my mum and husband wouldn't let me, and I know it was simply out of worry for me. The night before the funeral I'd woken up with a raging high temperature, and we'd had to get the doctor out in the morning. The doctor had asked was there any where I had to be that day and I told him it was my daughter's funeral. He was so worried about me that he asked if I really had to be there and quite firmly I told him, there is no way anyone was stopping me going to my daughter's funeral.

"At Paul's funeral, I was on automatic pilot. It was almost as if I was organising someone else's baby's funeral. During his funeral, I went to put a rose in his grave beside him and as I walked away, my husband had to catch me as I physically collapsed. Even if I felt ill, nothing was going to stop me going to Jordan's funeral.

Joan continues: "After Paul and Jordan died, I got Polaroid photos and the negatives for both of them. There were no memory boxes at the time, but I do have their footprints and their little hospital bands."

Joan reflects: "There is no doubt that the death of a baby affects the whole family. When I went into hospital to have Paul, my son Aaron was a year and nine months old. I told him that Mummy was going into hospital to get a little brother or sister for him.

"The morning after Paul was born, my uncle came to pick me up. He took me back to my mum's house where she had been looking after Aaron and even though he was still so young, he just seemed to know that something was wrong. He just seemed to sense it. Then when I went into hospital to have Jordan, and Aaron was so excited again about having a baby brother or sister, when I came home for a second time without a baby, all I could think was, I'd done it to him again. He thought he was getting a brother or sister and again, he didn't. How could I even begin to explain that to a little boy?

"I think this was one of the main reasons I got counselling through SANDS. When my son was around five or six years old, he had started to have trouble at school. He was trying to hurt himself and burn himself on the radiator, so we had been trying to get him some help. He kept saying, 'Why did I survive and Paul and Jordan died?'

"We managed to get him some counselling. In the first five years of his life he had lost a brother, a sister and his papa whom he'd been so close to. Initially, I don't think his counsellors thought it was anything to do with all these losses, but as Aaron began to open up, it became clear that this was the root of his problems. He's now 21, but he doesn't talk about that time much, so I'm not sure what he remembers. When he'd seen his counsellor, they told me he was a very sensitive boy, and he was feeling my distress, so that's what prompted me to go and see the counsellor at SANDS to help work through my grief.

"I had around ten sessions but even after the first session I felt such a weight had been lifted off my shoulders. Before I had my counselling, I always felt that I *had* to go to Mortonhall on their birthdays and again at Christmas. I felt I couldn't and mustn't miss any of these dates and in time, through counselling, I gradually felt released from this ritual. I was helped to see that I could remember Paul and Jordan always, anywhere and anytime.

"My husband and I stayed married for 21 years, splitting up in 2007. We went on to have two more daughters, Niamh in 1995 and Blair in 1996. My pregnancy with Niamh was terrifying, but I was monitored closely and the baby was scanned to check her kidneys were working properly. Because Paul was three weeks early, they started me off three weeks early with both girls. In the week before Niamh was born, I went into the hospital daily for regular tests, checks and scans to ensure everything was OK. It put my mind at rest a little bit.

"The day before Niamh was born they did another scan which showed she was breach. At that point, they thought I would have to have a caesarean section, but I didn't want one. I was scanned the morning of the day she was born to check how she was lying, but I knew she'd turned overnight as she'd woken me up! I was three days in labour, but I managed a natural delivery in the end, and I did the same with Blair."

Joan says: "I remember after Niamh was born my husband went to the payphone to call our family and give them the good news. Beside him was a man on the phone telling his family his baby had been stillborn. Having been through it, I know my husband then felt guilty that we were now so happy. It was a surreal moment."

Looking to the future, Joan says: "I would love to be a midwife but I would also like to do counselling too, so that I could help others. I had started to do my Access to Nursing course but it was such a heavy intense course that I didn't have the time for all the studying.

"Since having Paul and Jordan, I've seen things from the other side and I know how much it would have helped me to have a midwife present who had been through what I was going through. It allows for a special understanding and greater empathy. Maybe this is something that happens now but I'm sure it would help to have special midwives to deal with these heartbreakingly difficult births."

Asked what advice she can give to other long-ago bereaved, Joan says: "The grief and the hurt does get easier, but it's always there; it never leaves you completely. When I first lost Paul and Jordan, there was a big hole in my life for a long time afterwards. I could never even sit with my hand on my stomach. It was too hard. It took a long time for me to move on.

"When Niamh and Blair were born, my grieving process started all over again. Different anxieties would creep in and I would panic if they went quiet. I would be so relieved when they started crying again!"

Joan recommends to others: "Get involved with SANDS, get counselling or go to meetings, it will help even if your loss was a long time ago. Even just join their Facebook page and talk to others, it will help you and you can also help comfort others.

"When time passes, and others feel you should be 'over it', through SANDS, you can chat with others who really understand what you're going through and that you will never be 'over it'. Even the kindness of strangers can bring so much comfort. Any parent out there who has suffered a loss whether it was yesterday, two years ago or twenty years ago, talk to somebody."

Luke Mallon

25 May 2007

"Luke was born on May, 25th 2007 and died in the early hours of 31st May 2007 after a massive cerebral haemorrhage.

"In May, 2006 I returned to the UK from Spain after 3½ years as my marriage had broken up. My husband at the time, David, loved his life in Spain but I was miserable and our marriage had suffered hugely due to my desire to return to the UK combined with the stress and strain of six years of fertility treatment.

"After our third attempt at IVF in Spain, my consultant diagnosed me with 'empty follicle syndrome' and advised that 'normal' IVF treatment wouldn't work for me. He suggested for the condition a revolutionary new treatment, which was very costly and very invasive. After much soul searching, I decided that I just couldn't put myself through any more heartache and decided to resign myself to the fact that I would never be a mum.

"In hindsight, I think the reason David and I split was purely due to the fact that I was so heartbroken that I couldn't give him the child that he so desperately wanted, and I was sub-consciously pushing him away. I went into self-destruct mode after a few months of trying to come to terms with the decision and left behind my life in Spain, as well as my husband, to start a new life.

"I mention this aspect of the story as I believe that it has a huge bearing on what happened next and is hugely significant with respect to the events that followed.

"Prior to leaving Spain, I had been seeing a nutritionist who had also been using kinesiology on me to try to assist my body to conceive naturally. I was slightly sceptical but would have tried anything at this point! She was a Swedish lady and very passionate about complementary therapies and she was hugely supportive to me, so I did become more positive towards her approach. She was convinced my body needed to be balanced.

"I finished the course about two months after returning to the UK and couldn't get anymore as it wasn't available within the UK. A few months later, my cycle changed completely and, as I had been told I would go through the menopause early, I assumed that was what was happening, so I visited the doctor to get checked out. The doctor assured me that my hormone levels were normal and that I wasn't going through the menopause at all. I dismissed it and forgot all about it.

"A few months after my marriage broke up and I returned to the UK, I met Phil through work. Things were fairly casual as I was still reeling from my marriage break up as well as coming to terms with not being able to have children. In the December of 2006, only six months after meeting Phil, I discovered (by accident) that I was pregnant. I was in total shock! I couldn't make any sense of it, but I was overjoyed at the same time.

"I had suffered from recurring urine infections for about eight weeks and eventually the doctor asked me to do a pregnancy test as he had a hunch that I was pregnant (he only admitted that after I confirmed the test was positive). I initially laughed at him, but he was defiant and told me to do the test that evening and go in to see him the next day. I think it was the one and only time I ever did a test without expecting to see a positive result. I almost collapsed! I then had to break the news to Phil and then my friends and family, who were overjoyed for us!

"I could relax and enjoy the fact that I was finally going to have a baby after all the heartache and suffering I had endured. I say relax, but I never really relaxed as I was terrified something was going to go wrong. Whether that was some kind of sixth sense, or just because of the road I'd travelled to get here, I suppose I'll never know.

"I had a fairly straightforward pregnancy, health-wise. I was admitted to hospital with unexplained bleeding at 23 weeks and had recurring urine infections throughout my pregnancy, but other than that, I kept well. I was even still going to the gym three times a week!

"I suppose life was quite hard during my pregnancy as work was extremely busy and stressful, and I didn't get a great deal of support. We were going through a huge merger and everyone was dealing with massive workloads and huge amounts of issues. Aside from that, Phil and I were having to set up home together in preparation for our precious little bundle, so it wasn't plain sailing.

"I had been suffering from swollen ankles and had put on a fair bit of weight all of a sudden from about 24 weeks, but everyone, including myself, put that down to the fact that I hadn't been showing at all up until that point, so my body was just finally starting to adjust.

"I had been feeling quite tired and sluggish and had the occasional headache but didn't think anything of it. At my last midwife appointment, my blood pressure had apparently been slightly elevated, but the midwife just dismissed this as me being a tad stressed. I really wish she'd called me back to check it again and things may have been so different.

"One day at about 27 weeks, I went to work and felt absolutely awful. I told my manager I was going home and even phoned my mum to come and pick me up from the train station as I didn't feel fit to drive. My mum's face said it all when she clapped eyes on me. I hadn't seen her for a couple of weeks and she couldn't believe how awful I looked. She took me straight down to the doctor's surgery and they confirmed my blood pressure was sky high. I was put on medication after being diagnosed with pregnancy induced hypertension and, after a few days of being in hospital, they had it under control and I was discharged and put on bed rest.

"I lounged around for two weeks, only ever going out to attend my day bed appointment where normally all was OK. However, less than 24 hours after my last day bed appointment at 29 weeks, I started to feel so ill again. I couldn't quite put my finger on it, but I just knew something wasn't right. I sheepishly called the hospital and said, It might be nothing but I just don't feel right'. They told me to come in straight away and get checked, which is what I did.

"I was immediately diagnosed with pre-eclampsia and it turned out that my blood results the previous day had shown my platelet count had dropped significantly and they suspected I'd be back.

"They tried for 24 hours to stabilise my blood pressure but it was all over the place at times. It wasn't until the next day when my blood results changed dramatically that they decided to give me my first steroid injection to strengthen the baby's lungs and they gently told me that delivery was imminent.

"They couldn't deliver me at St John's as I was less than 34 weeks gestation, so they transferred me by ambulance to Simpsons. I had been told by my consultant before I left that I would have a caesarean section as soon as I got there as time was of the essence. However, on arrival, the junior doctor told me that the consultant now in charge of my case had decided to try inducing me first.

"In hindsight, I should have forced the issue as my consultant at St John's had been quite clear on the path we needed to take. I had only had one steroid injection at this point so, by inducing me, it would buy me a bit of time, assuming my condition and the baby's was stable.

"After several attempts to induce me failed, I was moved to the high dependency ward as my blood results had deteriorated slightly. There had been a bit of a scare just prior to moving me as the medical team weren't happy with the baby's heart trace. It was dismissed, and I had no reason to question it.

"Very early on the Friday morning, three days after being diagnosed with pre-eclampsia, my consultant came to tell me that they had run out of time and that they had to perform an emergency caesarean section. Up until this point, I think I was blocking out all my emotions as the fear and the reality suddenly washed over me:'It's too early for the baby to come out,' I sobbed, but my consultant was so lovely and compassionate and gave me a huge hug.

"Luke was delivered that morning by emergency caesarean section at 29 weeks and 5 days gestation with Phil just making the delivery on time. I don't even remember much about the delivery, and Luke was taken away instantly where he was placed on a ventilator by the neo-natal team.

"Phil got to see him briefly before they took him away, and he told me they were really pleased with his Apgar score, which is the very first test given to a newborn to quickly evaluate their physical condition and to determine if there is any immediate need for extra medical or emergency care.

"I was taken back to high dependency as I was still very unwell after the delivery and the consultant paediatrician came to see me soon after to say that Luke was ventilated and was doing OK, but he was very 'agitated' and they didn't know why. I was just so happy he was alive at that point! I was desperate to go and see him so they wheeled me up to the unit in my bed and I caught my first glimpse of my beautiful little boy from afar.

"I have such patchy memories of the time in-between and it really distresses me. I have no idea if I was too naive to see the reality of the situation or if I was just blocking out what might happen, but I struggle to remember my thoughts and emotions during the time Luke was in the neo-natal unit up until the fateful night when he was only four days old and the midwife came to waken me to tell me that Luke had taken a turn for the worse and I should go and see him.

"My heart was in my mouth and I sobbed all the way there wondering what sight would meet me. Why was this happening now as they'd told me every day since he was born that he was surpassing their expectations? I still vividly remember seeing his tiny, lifeless body surrounded by hoards of people around his incubator. He was receiving a blood transfusion and I could hear him whimpering in pain. It was awful to hear my baby in so much pain. You could sense the tension in the room as they explained to me that I should prepare myself for the worst and that Phil was on his way.

"I sat and stroked his little body to reassure him but my heart was breaking as I could visibly see by his colouring how ill he was. When Phil arrived they told us that they didn't think he'd last the night and advised us to think about baptising him now if we wanted to.

"The hospital arranged for the priest from the local church to come and baptise him. I'm not at all religious but I did it for Phil. I sobbed uncontrollably all the way through and was numb with pain. I had physical pain and emotional pain and the emotional pain was by far the worse!

"Eventually, a midwife came to check my blood pressure and told me I needed to go back to bed immediately as it was extremely elevated. They gave me a tablet to reduce it and arranged a bed in the family room so we could be close to him. It was tortuous being with him and seeing him so ill, but, even more so, not being with him and wondering how he was. Phil stayed with him until they got him stabilised and they told us they would have to do a brain scan to ascertain the level of damage to his brain.

"The consultant assured us he was comfortable for the time being and that they would let us know of any change in his condition. I just wanted to be with him the whole time but couldn't because I was still so ill. The midwives were amazing as they agreed to run up and down from the ward so I could stay close to him and I'll be forever grateful for that as it meant I could go along when I wanted.

"It was more than 24 hours before they came back to us to say that his brain scan suggested serious brain damage and that he would be severely mentally and physically disabled if he even survived. They suggested switching off his life support and allowing him to die gracefully. They said that they didn't think he would be able to breathe on his own, and that they had no idea how long he would live.

"Luke's consultant was very, very empathetic and understanding throughout the whole decision-making process. He sat and explained everything to us without rushing us. How can anyone make the decision to switch off their child's life support? It was by far the hardest thing I've ever had to do, and I was so grateful for the medical support we received from the neo-natal team. They were amazing. We didn't deliberate for too long as we instinctively knew that he was gone already so we agreed to go ahead and switch the machine off the following day.

"The next 24 hours were awful as we were both in shock and didn't know what to do with ourselves. We both found it so difficult to be with him in the unit, and I'm not sure if anyone can actually understand that until they've been through it themselves.

"It was so hard to hold it together when walking into the unit and you were very aware of the presence of other people – namely, other parents who must have been thinking, 'Thank God that's not us'. Yes, you have a certain degree of privacy with the screens, but that doesn't shield you from the feeling that your emotions are in full view of everyone.

"I wanted to spend every precious last moment with him and Phil was the same, but we just couldn't. We tried and every time we went there we would dissolve into a blubbering mess. We wanted to be there for him and be strong and we failed and both still feel so guilty about that.

"The whole post-mortem issue was a further hurdle to overcome. Again, it's something that just never enters your head. Once again, the team dealt with it with enormous sensitivity. It's very black and white though when it gets down to the detail, and whether or not to have a post-mortem was a huge decision for us when we were still reeling from making the decision to switch off his life support. We had to try and block out the medical aspects of it and think of it as getting answers for Luke. Neither of us could afford to think of what was actually involved and even now, I divert my thinking away from what they did to him.

"The 24 hours leading up to switching off Luke's life support is a total blur. I was still under constant medical supervision and we had lots of friends and family coming in to visit us in the family room. We all made inane conversation and it seemed surreal what was actually happening at the time.

"The doctor came to the family room at 2.30 on the Wednesday afternoon and asked if we were ready. By this point, I just needed to get it over with which sounds so cold when you say it, but the waiting was torturing me. I knew it was inevitable.

"We followed him to the unit where they pulled all the screens around and brought in a two-seater chair for us to sit on and be able to hold him together. I couldn't even tell you if there were other parents present at the time or not. I was in a daze.

"They explained that they had no idea if Luke would pass immediately after switching off the machine or if he would fight death. There was a sense of real tension amongst the medical staff as they desperately tried to get him out of the incubator as quickly as possible so that we had the chance to hold him before he went.

"This was the first time we'd held our baby and he was dying. It just felt so wrong. It seemed to take an eternity for them to unhook him from all the monitors, and I was petrified I wouldn't get to hold him before he passed. We were both sobbing uncontrollably and it just seemed so surreal. When the doctor handed Luke to me it was such a sad moment but also such a happy one too. I was holding my little boy for the first time and it felt so nice, but I would never get to hold him again.

"After about half an hour, the medical staff decided that we should move back into the family room with him for some privacy. He was still hooked up to his morphine drip but other than that, he was free of all cables and monitors. We walked along the corridor to the family room, like any other parents carrying their newborn baby.

It seemed so poignant that we were carrying him to his death, rather than how we'd imagined we would carry him out of the hospital, in his little car seat, to take him home.

"I always remember the midwife saying to me that the last senses to go are smell and sound. She wrapped him inside my nightie as she reassured me that he knew I was there. I treasured every last moment and sometimes I actually forgot that he was dying.

"I still crave his smell and the softness of his skin and his fluffy blond hair. The staff took photos, which I've only been brave enough to look at once, and even that was several years down the line. Phil and I took turns holding him and the staff only came in from time to time to check he was still with us. We were so worried he would pass and we wouldn't even be aware of it. His breathing was so shallow but at times he would let out a gasp and we would think he was gone but he fought it hard for 13 hours and he finally passed in the early hours of Thursday, 31st May 2007, when our lives changed forever.

"My blood pressure soared after they confirmed he was gone, and I was given something to calm me down and to knock me out. I don't remember much about the days following, but I was unable to leave hospital as I was still very ill.

"When I was eventually discharged, I'll never forget that lonely and haunting walk to the car where you inevitably pass couples leaving with their babies and heavily pregnant women arriving to give birth, and it's like a knife in your heart. I still can't hear the buzzer for entry to the neo-natal unit without it sending shivers down my spine and triggering a wash of memories.

"I've gone on to have two healthy little girls. I had a very problematic pregnancy with my eldest and ended up with pre-eclampsia again (albeit not as severe) but this resulted in another emergency pre-term delivery and, again, my baby ended up in intensive care for eight days. It was a very traumatic experience after all we'd been through, and, in hindsight, it affected how I bonded with Keira, as I was so scared of allowing myself to get too attached in case history repeated itself.

"We started a charity called luke4life in memory of our special boy and we have raised over £35,000 which has been distributed between Simpsons, St John's and Forth Park over the years.

"Without the help of SANDS Lothians, I have no idea where I'd be today. I still attend meetings and have made some life-long friends, on whom I can always count for support and understanding.

"I had no idea after losing Luke if I would ever be able to conceive again as I had no reason to believe I would after six years of fertility treatment but I did, relatively quickly. I believe that the treatment I received from the nutritionist I saw in Spain must have 'corrected' something in my body, given the changes I noticed prior to falling pregnant.

"My message here is to all those people out there who have lost hope, like I did, that there is always hope out there and it's not just a cliché. I went to hell and back during my fertility treatment and even more so after losing Luke.

"It was a long road, and I now have my precious little girls and I will NEVER get over losing Luke and my heart aches for him every single day, but I do believe that I am a stronger and more compassionate individual now and his death was not in vain. I want to give something back now, and I have just started a counselling course to hopefully enable me to do that for other people."

Fraser Gary Mcdougall

Arlene had suffered from gynaecological problems for as long as she could remember. When her son Stephen was born in 1980, although it had been an 18-hour labour and she'd had a scare at six months thinking she was going into premature labour, she was over the moon when he was born fit and healthy.

However, her subsequent journey to have another child would be a heartbreaking one. Arlene divorced her first husband when Stephen was three and reared him alone. She met Gary in 1996 and they decided at the beginning of 1999 to try for a baby. In June of that year, they found out she was pregnant with Fraser; however, sadly, they lost him in November 1999. Arlene married Gary Mcdougall in September 2004 when Stephen was 24 and Scott almost 3.

At around 22 weeks, Arlene knew something wasn't right: "My blood pressure was sky high and I told my midwife I was leaking fluid," Arlene recalls. "I was told to go in to hospital and the doctor asked if it was OK if my examination was in front of students as my pregnancy was nineteen years after my first child. Apparently, the students were interested in the background of my pregnancy and why I'd waited so long."

Arlene's blood pressure was controlled better and despite her telling the doctors she was sure she still had fluid coming away, she was discharged from hospital and told just to keep an eye on everything and see her GP if she was worried.

Arlene recalls: "I remember going shopping on the Saturday with my mum and feeling quite ill. I remember buying some Christmas cards and was certain something was wrong. I was wearing a towel but was really wet – but the feeling was coming and going."

Arlene continues: "On the Sunday night, I felt terrible and went to bed. In the middle of the night I woke up. I didn't have any pain, so I'm not sure what woke me," Arlene painfully recalls. "I went to the toilet and I felt my little baby's leg coming out. I pushed it back in. I was numb, I just didn't know what I was doing, I wasn't thinking straight – I think I was just trying to deny what was happening."

Arlene continues: "I got up in the morning and phoned the hospital. The midwife told me to come straight in – they knew me so well as I was in and out all the time. My mum and stepdad took me in as I was too upset to drive. I was sent for a scan and the lady said, 'I don't want you to feel alarmed, but your cervix is open.' I think I screamed at that point. I was told not to worry because they could stitch it. They put me in a wheelchair and took me to the labour ward. All I could think of was – what am I doing in a labour ward?

"I was told the doctor was going to come and examine me, but I told them I didn't want examined as that would make everything worse. They said they had to know how dilated I was. I remember frantically trying to get Gary on the phone at his work but he was on his lunch break. I remember someone saying, 'Calm down, Arlene, calm down'. I was utterly frantic and retorted, 'Just get Gary, just get Gary!'

"The doctors carried out an examination and told me I was nine centimetres dilated. Distraught, I said, 'So that's it, then?' I was told they couldn't stitch me as most of the fluid was away, but that they would try and hold on to my baby for as long as possible. I was told that if we could get to the following Monday, without him having been born, they could attempt to resuscitate him.

"I was put in a bed, upside down. I felt drugged and dazed, it was a horrible time. I didn't want to eat but I remember my mum trying to spoon soup into me but it kept running down my face because I was upside down!

"I really don't remember much from that time but [I] remember people coming and going and praying. I just kept thinking, 'go another day, go another day.' I remember my mum pleading with the paediatrician to please just *try* and save him if he came early.

"By the Thursday, it felt like someone kept moving the goal posts – Monday felt so far away. I just lay there, day after day, with Gary by my side and people coming and going. I remember on the Thursday afternoon starting to experience labour pains.

"I told the nurse and she said, 'Do you think this is time, Arlene?' Heartbroken, I replied 'yes'. Up to this point, I had been scanned each day to check he was alive; we were all worried the trauma would kill him. He had been kicking like mad and I could see it was a boy – I knew I was having a son. Devastated, I listened, as I was told that he probably wouldn't live through the birth as he was so early. They lowered the bed. I was only 22 weeks into my pregnancy with my beautiful Fraser.

"I can't remember much after that, I think I was numb. I remember having pain for a while but it didn't feel that bad. I had my little boy about 7pm that night. All I could say was: 'Is he dead?' I had been told that if he lived he would have a birth certificate and he would then be registered as a birth and then a death, but if he didn't live, he would be classed as a miscarriage.

"I knew in my heart of hearts that if he was born alive, there was no way he'd live for long. Fraser was born alive. I just held him and held him until the nurse said he was gone. He only lived five minutes, but he breathed, he lived.

"Gary was frightened to touch him. Everybody was there and everyone was crying and crying. I don't remember much. I kept looking at all the people around me, crying – it didn't feel like it was happening to me. I was in shock.

"After Fraser was born, I was told that I could put him in a basket, dress him and take some photos. The minister then blessed him in the private room I was in on the ward. After Fraser was taken away, I was taken to the SANDS Lothians' Family Room. When I had to leave the hospital, I remember walking out of the door and more than anything, wanting to stay. I just clung onto the wall – desperately not wanting to leave my baby behind."

Arlene continues: "I agreed to a post-mortem but I had to wait for an agonising two months to get the results in January. I had to endure Christmas, knowing I would have to face this in the New Year. I went to the gynaecologist for the results. I remember feeling such fear sitting in the waiting room. I didn't want anything to be wrong with him. I couldn't hold back the tears. I thought people will think I have cancer as I was not visibly pregnant.

"The counsellor from the hospital was there, I was so upset. They asked if I wanted them to cut to the chase. All I wanted to know was if there was anything wrong with him. If there had been then I wouldn't have considered having more children.

"The post-mortem showed that he was completely perfect. Exactly the right size for gestation. I didn't want anything genetic to be wrong with him but when nothing was wrong, it was almost harder. I had such mixed and confused feelings. I wanted a reason as to why I had lost him, but I was told, sometimes there's no explanation. I was told I could go ahead and try again.

"By the time I got the post-mortem results, I'd read a lot by then about incompetent cervixes and was certain that was what I had – it's when the cervix doesn't stay shut and after a certain length of time, the pregnancy becomes too heavy. Usually they put in a stitch to hold the baby in. And that was the start of my battle to have my third child, Scott.

"I was told that if I became pregnant again and I could get to 14 weeks, they would put a stitch in. Because of my age, they couldn't do it earlier. I knew stitches could cause infections, so I asked if there was a test they could do first, to confirm whether or not I had an incompetent cervix; I was pretty certain they were able to measure the elasticity of the cervix. I had to wait a while for this, so I wasn't happy about trying to get pregnant again at that time.

"I was given an appointment to go in for a test, under anaesthetic. After a long wait, the test eventually showed that I would have lost another baby, and that in fact I wouldn't have even held on to the pregnancy even as long as I did with Fraser. I am so glad I pushed for this – as although they would have put in a stitch anyway, I didn't want to risk it. I was frightened all the time."

Arlene continued: "By the September 2000, the year after I lost Fraser, I fell pregnant. I took a test and then I rang the early pregnancy unit at the hospital and they did another test. I had slight bleeding again, so I had my hormone levels checked and was told to come back again. However, all the time I was bleeding, they thought I was miscarrying. I was. I hadn't expected that... I'd never given that aspect of what could go wrong any thought.

"The doctors said they'd do a D&C, but I said I didn't want them to as I was worried they'd damage my cervix even more. I was given a drug that would bring on the miscarriage properly. I was doubled up in two in the hospital bed as I desperately needed the toilet but was told I couldn't move. I remember phoning my son, Stephen, saying I wasn't being allowed to go to the toilet and the sister had told me I would get my turn. The next thing I was aware of was my son phoning the ward, and I could hear the sister on the phone saying, 'Your mother's been told not once, not twice but three times that we're busy!'

"I was demented. I wanted to leave; I just had to get out of that ward. I phoned the SANDS office and one of the ladies came to meet me outside then advised me to go back in. I was adamant I didn't want to go back in. However, I did but refused to see the sister. Instead I saw a doctor and was told that my miscarriage was complete and I could go home.

"The lady from SANDS came to take me home in a taxi. I remember thinking about an interview Gary had done about Fraser and SANDS that was due to be in the paper that night, and I just wanted to get out of the hospital to get the paper. It all seems so daft now, but I was just at breaking point and felt so angry about everything."

Arlene continues her recollection: "After the miscarriage, I tried and tried to become pregnant again. We'd moved house as I couldn't bear to stay in the same house where I'd endured so much heartache. Both Gary and I were coming up to our 40th birthday and it felt like our lives were on hold. We didn't book any holidays in case I was pregnant. I was constantly buying ovulation kits, yet nothing was happening. By the February, I told Gary, 'If it doesn't happen by the time I'm 40 in March, I'm giving up'.

"I remember Gary saying, 'Right, let's book a holiday for both of our birthdays, we'll go away in April.' We had a good summer, a new house and although I didn't stop caring about becoming pregnant, I stopped being so possessed about it and managed to start thinking about other things.

"I began to relax a little. For two years, I'd done nothing; trying to become pregnant had taken over my life. At one point, while we were working in the new house, I was lifting slabs and I remember saying to my mum, 'I hope I'm not pregnant!'"

Arlene goes on: "Gary and I booked a holiday to Tenerife to celebrate our birthdays. I said to Gary that we should just make up our minds we're not going to have a baby and go away for our 40th birthdays. However, the day before Gary's birthday my period was due but it didn't come. I took a test and held my breath... it was positive. So, there was only one thing I could do – I wrapped it up and gave it to Gary for his 40th birthday.

"We went ahead with our plans to go to Tenerife but we were both scared. I was seven to eight weeks pregnant and completely paranoid. Unfortunately, I got burnt and panicked that I must have done harm to my baby. When I came home, I went for a scan at eight weeks, to check my baby was alive.

"My friend Helen, who was another bereaved parent, came with me and I remember gripping onto her and Gary while I was scanned and was unbelievably relieved when they found the heartbeat! However, very shortly afterwards, my thoughts became fixated on the fear of another miscarriage because the other one had happened at nine weeks. The anxiety and worry just seemed to go on and on. However, I got to 12 weeks, had another scan and everything was on course for a stitch at 14 weeks. I was told to keep an eye on the stitch though, as they could cause infection.

"A short while after getting my stitch, I could smell a horrible smell," Arlene continues "I was hysterical. I showered twice and had a bath, but nothing helped. My neighbour took me into hospital. I was given strong antibiotics and things improved but my nerves were shot the whole time. The worry never seemed to end. I kept having panic attacks and my blood pressure was all over the place. I was scanned nearly every day and I was always on the phone to the girls at SANDS Lothians. I think I should have moved into the SANDS office or the hospital, my anxiety levels were that high!

"Everyone was rooting for me but I was so scared stiff all the time. With every twinge throughout Scott's pregnancy, I thought something was wrong. I kept trying to keep my blood pressure down. I was convinced I was going to lose him.

"At 21 weeks, I went to see the radiologist and was horrified when the first thing she said was – 'I don't want you to be alarmed... but you've funnelled'. Why do people say that? The first emotion you are going to have when

124

someone tells you not to be alarmed is alarm! Funnelled? What on earth was that? It was then explained to me that it meant my cervix had opened at the top and the stitch was holding it together. That little stitch is all that held my baby in from 21 weeks onwards. It was such a difficult time.

Arlene bravely continues: "I was devastated at this latest trauma. I kept having worrying spells with my blood pressure and I was crippled by panic attacks. I was in hospital so much of the time. The doctors kept saying they would have to deliver the baby but wanted to get in touch with my main doctor first.

"Again, by this point, they knew he was boy. I kept pleading with my doctor to deliver him while I knew he was still alive but she was adamant that she wouldn't – she kept saying, "He's not cooked yet, so he's not coming out!"

Arlene remembers: "All the time, I was convinced I was going to lose him. My doctor told me to calm down. She also said, 'I will take the stitch out on the 29th November – not a day before or a day after!' That would make him 37 weeks.

"I ended up being in hospital from the 18th to the 37th week. I used to get a pass to get out on the Saturday for a few hours, to keep me sane, I suppose," said Arlene, and bravely trying to see a funny side as she recalled her experience, said, "I'm not sure why I needed a pass – I wasn't dangerous!"

Arlene explains: "I hadn't taken anything into the hospital; I couldn't bring myself to do so in case anything went wrong. When the time arrived, I was allowed home the night before he came. Stephen took me to the house to pick up everything I needed for the baby, and I took it all to the hospital but even then, I couldn't bring myself to empty the bag. I was told I would be taken up to theatre the next morning to have the stitch out. However, I was told my baby may not even be born that day, and we'd have to see how things went. It could even be another three-four weeks.

"Again, there were students there. The stitch was taken out. I asked to see it. It was like a bit of baby ribbon – that's all that had been holding my baby in. As soon as the stitch came out, I immediately became seven centimetres dilated so the doctor burst my waters. I was then told to go up and down the stairs to get myself into labour! I did this but was still only getting niggles.

"I was then induced, but again not a lot happened. There were machines everywhere with pages and pages of my baby's heartbeat. Eventually, the pain came thick and fast. I asked for an epidural as I was in agony, but I was told there was no time, everything started happening so quickly. My baby's head felt like a football!

"I was over the moon that my beautiful baby boy, Scott, was born safe and well. However, almost immediately, this started leading to a different kind of anxiety. I think when you have already experienced one of the worst things a parent can go through, the death of a child, you know the thing you dread the most *can* happen which I think completely magnifies 'normal' worries that a new parent experiences.

"The panic attacks started again. I was scared stiff something was going to happen to Scott – he was identical to Fraser and to me looked as small, although he obviously was not! I was so scared I'd hurt him. Even the morning after he was born, my anxiety levels were through the roof.

"The first morning I woke up about 4am and went to tend to Scott in the nursery. I was so scared, I called Gary to come in and take over because I had this overwhelming feeling that I couldn't cope. Gary was so confident with him. I had to take Scott off the breast as my medication was making him jittery. He would hardly even feed from the bottle and just slept all the time.

"I remember he never cried in the hospital while all the other babies were screaming but, in short, we never heard Scott crying in the hospital. This of course added to my worry but everyone assured me that nothing was wrong.

"Scott had jaundice too," Arlene recalls. "He was 5lb 7oz when he was born, but dropped to just over 4lb which delayed us coming home in the early days. He was so gorgeous, but tiny. Everyone was frightened to touch him. He was like a tiny doll; I was frightened he might break! Someone then said to me, I bet he's a little strong thing and something just clicked in me – he *is* strong, he's a fighter. However, that didn't stop me having sleepless nights for a year!

"My anxiety levels continued to increase and all my thoughts turned to cot death. I just watched him all the time. He seemed to make a funny noise when he slept. None of the doctors seemed to know what it was but another lady at SANDS helped put my mind at rest and reassured me that her baby had made the same sort of noise and that perhaps premature babies are prone to making this sort of noise.

"So for the first time in years, my fears seemed to ease a little. To most new parents, losing a baby is a distant fear but when one of your babies has already died it becomes a grim and frightening reality. It can happen, it does happen, it's already happened to me – it's no wonder that the unbearable anxiety, panic and fear can become so crippling afterwards."

Arlene reflects: "I probably wouldn't have been here if it hadn't been for the ladies at SANDS Lothians. I remember at one point when I was attending their pregnancy support meetings, it was like they were reading my thoughts.

"I have an anxiety disorder anyway and at times I felt I was going totally ga ga! But their comforting words made me realise I wasn't going off my head. They helped ease my fears and worries about everything I felt could go wrong. They were there for me every time I was worried. They met me at the hospital when I wanted to walk out and their community midwife was wonderful too.

"Two years after Scott was born, I needed a hysterectomy," Arlene continues. "I had fibroids that were causing me a lot of problems and even going in for the operation brought everything back. I remember screaming in the theatre. After you have lost a baby, so many things after that force you to relive all the painful memories. The hospital and my womb were the only place I ever knew Fraser and I was losing that part of me too. The consultant who was to perform my hysterectomy was in actual fact the same one I was under during my pregnancy with Fraser and understood why everything was so difficult for me.

"I would never have got through my ordeal with Fraser and all the worry, anxiety and trauma that came after that without the help of SANDS Lothians. The team there were incredible. They were there for me every step of the way and at every painful milestone. They all went the extra mile for me because they've walked the walk themselves and they care so much."

Zania Mckenzie

"In 1978, I was a young and newly postgraduate specialist nurse, working in a frantically busy unit, hoping to make a career within ophthalmology.

"I got pregnant but threatened to miscarry at 13 weeks. After a week of bed rest followed by a scan, I found my little 'fetus' was still alive, in fact there were two! I was advised to take the rest of my pregnancy calmly and be carefully monitored, so I made a decision to take time out of my career. This meant handing in my notice and living on a tight budget. My husband had not completed his architectural training, but we managed.

"My pregnancy continued well and I was euphoric. However, at 30 weeks, I suddenly went into full scale labour. I was admitted into hospital as an emergency and put on bed rest. I was given an intravenous drug to reduce my uterus contractions in an attempt to stop my premature labour. This was really important at the time, as neonatal intensive care was very risky in those days for babies born prior to 34 weeks gestation. The main reason being that premature lung lubrication treatment wasn't available back then and babies don't reliably make sufficient of their own, prior to 34 weeks. The main risk that comes from this is their little dry sticky lungs rub, causing friction and burst. Air and blood leaks can collect and cause a fatal pressure build-up in the chest and brain area.

"I was helpless and exhausted. After 24 hours of trying, my friends and colleagues could not stop my labour and at 10pm on 6th January 1979, I had two beautiful little babies. A boy weighing 3lbs 1oz and a girl at 2lbs 14ozs, who would sadly drop to 2½ lbs as she became weaker. They were whisked off to intensive care and at midnight I was told that my little boy was fine, but that my little girl may not make it.

"Somehow I fell asleep and the next thing I was aware of was at 8am, when I was asked if I would like to go and see my twins. They were both warm, pink and breathing with assistance. They were beautiful and all the worry and stress had been worth it. My husband came back to the hospital as soon as possible; in those days, they weren't allowed to stay over. We hugged with exhausted, proud delight beside the incubators, admiring our babies.

"After breakfast, a wash and some painkillers, I fell into a deep, relieved and happy sleep. During this time, my husband went to call family and friends to say we had beautiful twins that were doing well.

"I was woken up about 1pm on the 7th January by a staff member who was also my colleague asking me if I would like to have an emergency priest called to christen my babies, and my husband was informed of what was happening, as they had become very sick over the previous hour and weren't responding to the intensive emergency care they had been receiving. My world turned upside down.

"My brain switched to professional autopilot, as my body shook and time stood still. It all just happened around me and there was nothing I could do. Everybody did everything that was needed. My husband came rushing back down to the hospital and we helplessly hugged, numb and shedding many tears.

"At 8pm on the 7th of January, I made the painful decision to have my son's life support disconnected as he had so much leakage into his chest and brain that his long-term quality of life was extremely bleak and it would have been cruel to keep him alive. It's the hardest decision I've ever had to make in my life and it broke mine and my husband's hearts.

"I stroked the silky hair on his little head and held his little hand as he breathed his last breath.

"However, I still had a sick little girl who was hanging on to life by a thread and managing to absorb the blood and air that she was leaking at a steady rate.

"You become something between a shell and a ghost. You aren't quite sure what 'human' is anymore. It's surreal and bizarre and timeless. Then you keep zooming in and out of reality, a bit like playing with Google Earth! It was a helpless no-man's land.

"Then you crash back into your body and brain and your emotions engulf you.

"My little girl needed every ounce of love and positive vibes I could muster over and above all the 24-hour neonatal care she was receiving. After many scary medical emergencies and setbacks during weeks of intensive care, my little girl slowly made it and we got her home at what seemed a massive 4½ lbs on the 5th of March, one week before her actual due date.

"At last she was mine, and I no longer had to share her on a daily basis with the medical intensive care team, although I had appreciated them greatly! I could now give her round the clock professional care and maternal love. Long awaited heaven!

"I brought her up telling her all about her brother in a way that she would understand, depending on her age and we said a prayer for him each day. Sharing things with her meant that we never had to drop a bombshell on her, telling her about our family tragedy later in life. Telling her gradually over the years was also very healing for me.

"In 1981, after more complications during pregnancy and labour with a near fatal haemorrhage and loss of consciousness, I thankfully gave birth to a second lovely and this time, healthy little girl.

"By 1986, I was back to work part time and both my children were at school. I felt I was strong enough to think of some way that I could help others to survive the ordeal of the death of their child, which in no way could be termed deserved or justified in any other way. It just shouldn't happen, but it does.

"I found a very new group called SANDS who met in people's homes. They were establishing themselves as an offshoot of an organisation called SANDS UK and were recognised as a voluntary self-help group working under their umbrella, but it was struggling a little. Together we all shared our stories, drank coffee and tea, hugged and cried and it felt good.

"We met monthly, on Monday evenings. We shared ideas and developed a structure, including providing a helpline to offer support for recently or long-ago bereaved parents. We began to build relationships with maternity and post-natal services throughout the region and started to arrange seminars with staff to help mould and change their views on the care of bereaved parents. We helped teach them that appropriate supportive physical contact and hugs between child and parent were a good thing.

"We got the rules changed to allow cameras to be brought into hospitals. This meant that photos of sick and dead babies could be taken for the parents who will always love their babies, alive or dead, beautiful or ugly. They are a precious miracle never to be forgotten.

"We advertised our group on local TV, radio and in the newspapers and we successfully grew and expanded with the help of sponsorship and the help of volunteers. The work of the organisation that would eventually evolve into what is now SANDS Lothians had begun.

"I needed four years out of my career in order to work out if I could ever go back, regain and maintain my role as an effective compassionate professional clinician. Eventually I returned to work full time. Sometimes it's still very hard, but my experience has given me so much more insight to enable me to relate to, connect with and treat my patients with compassion. There is no doubt, though, that my life and my priorities in life have changed.

"When I was ready to return to work, it was time for me to take a back seat in SANDS, but I would continue to be as supportive as possible when needed. At that stage, one of our other members felt the time was right for her to become more active within the organisation. She and others went on to further develop the society, and I'm very proud and thankful to all the active members and fundraiser's involved in this vital area of work.

"SANDS Lothians is a very worthy charity. It has changed the attitudes towards bereavement from the loss of a baby and has helped professionals realise that parents need a way to remember and recognise their babies and their never-ending love for them.

"Being a bereaved parent never leaves you. You learn to know when, where and with whom to share bereavement so as not to be destructive to your ongoing life and that of your loved ones who are alive. It's a painful work of art, rebuilding a meaningful life with love and happiness.

"The words, 'It takes one to know one' are so true in this field. No one, including professionals, can know what's best for a bereaved parent, unless they have a profound understanding from having suffered a loss themselves."

Kaidyn Cunningham McKeown

28 May 2008

Jamie Kian Cunningham McKeown

20 April 2009

LeeAnn begins: "I am mum to a 9½-year-old son, Corey, but in 2008 I had another son, Kaidyn, who was stillborn at full term. He had been a text-book pregnancy. I had just taken Corey for his first visit to his school, after which I came home, made up the Moses basket and the crib in preparation for the new baby then, a few hours later, all hell broke loose.

"I'd fallen asleep on the sofa and had woken up in horrible pain. Corey had been born by emergency section because the cord was round his neck and the pains I felt now were worryingly similar. So I went up to the hospital to be checked out.

"They initially thought they had picked up the baby's heartbeat, but it was mine. They scanned me again and in the midst of my worry, I couldn't help but feel sorry for the poor doctor. It was obviously the first time he'd had to tell someone such devastating news. I knew myself by that point there was no heartbeat.

"The doctors told me that it would be better if I went through labour rather than have a caesarean section. My labour lasted for around eight hours but, to me, it felt like five minutes. At one point, I remember telling my mum that I really didn't feel well at all and that something wasn't right. I felt so ill at that point and thought that was it, I was going to die. Sadly, by then, I couldn't have cared less, I was so distraught at losing my beautiful son.

"I was catheterised, and it became clear that I had a very severe case of pre-eclampsia, the blood was pouring out of me as quickly as they could get it in. My dad told me later that at one point, the halls were full of medical staff waiting to rush me into theatre. My kidneys had failed and they eventually had to give me an emergency section. My mum, dad, partner David and my brother were all there. My mum had the painful job of having to sign the form consenting to a full hysterectomy if they couldn't stop the bleeding. The next thing I knew I was waking up in intensive care; I was desperately ill and took infection after infection.

"I was in ICU for a few hours, but I was then taken in my bed from ICU to the family room. The doctors and nurses were just fantastic and took such great care of me. The doctor told me that I'd had a placental abruption. I initially gave my permission for them to do a post-mortem, but the process seemed to be taking such a long time that I withdrew my consent and focused on planning my baby's funeral. The funeral directors went to pick up Kaidyn.

Reflecting, LeeAnn says: "I still torture myself over the fact that if I'd had a late scan would things have been different? Although I had been 39 weeks, I didn't actually go into labour. My stomach just went brick hard. It wasn't even like a normal contraction. I hadn't had a natural labour with Corey, so I didn't really know what 'normal' labour should feel like, but I just knew something wasn't right."

LeeAnn goes on: "Kaidyn's funeral was amazing – well, as lovely as something so sad can be. As a family, we all wrote special words and little tributes for Kaidyn. He was buried with my granny and granddad. My mum's sisters are in Australia and America and to open the grave they both had to give their permission, but they did so within seconds of being asked.

"The funeral was just beautiful and so special. There was a lovely choir and everything brought me so much comfort. For something so desperately sad, it couldn't have been better. Through all this tragedy, my little brother was amazing. He did so much to help me and he broke his heart over my pain and the nephew he'd lost. He wrote a piece for Kaidyn's funeral service…

To my gorgeous little nephew, Kaidyn, I met you on Wednesday 28th May, a day that will live with me till I meet you at the gates of Heaven. You had the face of an angel so it is fitting you are now among God's special ones, I will think of you everyday and make sure your big brothers, Corey and Jake, never forget what a special brother they had.

Your mummy and daddy have shown you more love in the past few days than I have seen in my entire life. They are hurting so so much but, with your help, they can become stronger each day. I loved the time I got to spend with you and will take all those memories of a beautiful baby boy with me forever.

You will always be a part of my life, Kaidyn, for all the hurt and sadness I am feeling, the love is so much stronger. I miss you so much, wee man, and I would do anything to make this better. Unfortunately, God wants you with him and He, along with all the family, will look after you now.

You look after Mummy and Daddy from up in Heaven, and I will do my best down here.

Love you loads, Kaidyn
Uncle Chris

LeeAnn says: "I was still quite ill in the days following Kaidyn's funeral and a few days after we laid him to rest, a registrar phoned asking why I hadn't registered my baby. When I took the call I just dropped the phone. My mum took up where I had left off and went to town on them. I know now the girl on the other end of the phone must have felt awful but these things shouldn't happen. It's the last thing you need when you're in the depths of despair.

"It was hard to know what the best thing was for Corey at the time of Kaidyn's funeral as he was only four years old. My partner had a son as well so we decided that both he and Corey could attend the funeral service although we didn't take them to the grave. I knew I would have nightmares about that myself, so I didn't want the boys to go through the same."

My beautiful baby boy

My darling Kaidyn, the minute they told me you had gone to Heaven I felt my heart be ripped from my chest. I had so many plans and wishes for your life, so many things to show and teach you. Tuesday night was the hardest night of my life knowing that when you did eventually arrive I wouldn't hear the glorious sound of you crying or see your amazing smile, though for a short time, I thought I may be joining you.

When I eventually got to hold you in my arms, I felt the love surge through me. You are silent but one of the most gorgeous sights I have ever seen. You seem like you're asleep. I want to scream at you to open your eyes, to cry, to breathe, but I know this is impossible.

As the tears rolled down my face, I knew you were special and obviously someone needed you in Heaven more than I did here, though it doesn't make it any easier.

I'd give anything to have you here in my arms but I know you are watching over me and Daddy and your brothers. We will always miss you, Kaidy, and not a day will pass I won't think about you. Every time I close my eyes I see you looking back at me. I'm sorry I couldn't keep you safe, Kaidyn, but I promise I'll look after you again one day.

Goodbye, Kaidyn, I love you with all my heart and soul and will think of you and miss you every day.

Take care, my Angel
Love Mummy xxx

LeeAnn continues: "I fell pregnant again the following year with my third son, Jamie. I had spotted a bit early on but was reassured it was nothing to worry about, but I couldn't help but panic after Kaidyn. Then one day, I was at my work on my break and felt an almighty pain. I sat on a chair curled up in agony. We phoned the hospital and they told me to take paracetamol. Nothing helped. I couldn't move.

"One of my colleagues wanted to take me straight home, but my brother came in to pick me up. When I got home, I had a shower but again, had a gut-wrenching feeling that something wasn't right so I went straight to the hospital. I was admitted straight away, I was only 18 weeks.

"I was put on the doppler and reassured that my baby was fine, his little heart was beating away like mad! I was told to go and get a urine sample so I did and all of a sudden, blood started pouring from me. I was put back on the doppler and again my baby's little heart was beating away strongly. They told me I may have an infection of some sort. The medical team were so brilliant. I was put on the bed on the ward and was told if there were any problems I was just to press the buzzer and however busy they were, they would come to me. This went on for days. I was so carefully monitored, and they did everything they could to reassure me.

"Everything settled down as we progressed through Sunday and that afternoon and I thought, fantastic, I'll get out tomorrow. Then, heartbreakingly, that night all hell broke loose once again. I was in agony. I was put on morphine but nothing helped. I had to be lifted off the bed just to go to the toilet and I couldn't stop shaking. I was wheeled along to the scan room. I always remember one doctor saying, 'Why is she not walking, why is she in a chair?' That was so hard to hear. I was scanned again and at that point I was told it was a boy.

"My mum and dad had come to the hospital, and I told them once again that I didn't feel well. I was moved down to the labour ward but not told that I was in labour. It never occurred to me. I was monitored on gas and air. Then at 5.15pm I told my partner to go and get the nurse and later I delivered my baby. When he was examined closely, we saw he had a little mark on his head – like a little clot – but no one could be sure when that had happened.

"When Kaidyn had been born, almost three-quarters of the placenta had come away and with Jamie, they could see marking on the placenta again, so they thought perhaps the same was happening with Jamie, but they couldn't be certain.

"At the hospital, the priest who came to bless Jamie said he had never seen such a tiny baby. I remember he said he could understand why some people's faith was tested at times like these. He was leaving for Rome the next day and told us we would be at the top of his prayers. He's still our priest to this day.

"Jamie's funeral wasn't as big as Kaidyn's as it was private with family only. At Kaidyn's funeral, the priest said he'd never seen anything like it! He'd never had to do a child's funeral before and with Kaidyn's, despite it being a big chapel, you couldn't move. Then when everyone arrived at the cemetery they were lining up outside.

"I decided not to have a post-mortem for Jamie, but I remember asking for his footprints and his length measurements – the same mementos I'd received with Kaidyn, but I was told I couldn't have them because he was classed as a miscarriage. I always find it so hard to accept that it's still classed as a miscarriage at that early gestation, despite the fact that you have to go through a delivery.

"The midwife, and one of the auxiliaries that had come to see me went away and managed to get me Jamie's little footprints. I was so grateful to them for that as I know they could have got into trouble, but they did it for me anyway. Everyone was so kind to me and they couldn't have done more. I do have photos of Jamie but keep them private as he was so little.

LeeAnn painfully recalls: "After I'd given birth to Jamie, I buzzed the nurse and asked if someone could come and take him away. I didn't want to remember him going a different colour. When the nurse came back, they just put a cover right over Jamie's face and walked out. I was so upset by this. He was still my precious little baby, and I wanted him treated with care. However, most of the staff were wonderful and cared for me so well and I can never thank them enough for everything they did for me.

"The first day I was up on my feet I felt so strongly that something good must come out of losing two of my sons. When my mum had cancer, we fundraised for Macmillan nurses and, when my friend's grandson died of cot death, we fundraise for SIDS. There was a little leaflet in my memory box about SANDS; that's how I got to know about them. I went on to fundraise for them.

"In the months and years since losing the boys we have had a number of fundraiser's. We had one in our local bowling club. Our family and friends were amazing; 100 tickets were sold in minutes! Companies were so generous, Slaters, jewellers – the prizes were wonderful. Another of our fundraisers involved a sponsored walk around Arthur's Seat in tutus and leggings! We have some great pictures of the men dressed up like that; it was so funny.

"Then on another occasion we had a band playing in our bowling club and all the tickets were sold out before they even went up for sale. We had so many raffle prizes donated that the band hardly got a chance to play. It helps me so much to do fundraising events in memory of the boys and it helps give me focus. As others started to learn about my losses, so many people started to tell me about their experiences and this helped me greatly in my grieving process."

Mummy's little angels
Written by LeeAnn

My heart was happily jumping,
The days I got the news,
The plans, the thoughts, the dreams for you,
I already began to plot.
I never dreamt they wouldn't be
I'd hoped for such a lot.

My heart was torn apart those days,
Those days I won't forget.
My precious boys
I lost you both
But never will regret.

I have you both in my heart
Both truly precious gifts,
Gone too soon
And loved so much
I'll always just say why?

I'm told so much
You were too good
To struggle here on earth
You went to heaven to be safe
And watch us from above.

I love you both and always will
Until we meet again,
In Mummy's arms you will be
We all will smile again.

Mummy's little angels
I know you have your wings
I love you my small angels
I do now and always will.

"I split up from my partner, Kaidyn and Jamie's dad, in the August after Jamie died. I'm sure it was all down to the stress or it at least played a part. I haven't had any more children since, but I have my lovely, precious son, Corey. I honestly feel if I hadn't had Corey, I don't think I would have been here today.

"Both Kaidyn and Jamie have beautiful headstones at their grave. My boss, my partner, parents and Nancy, a close family friend, all helped me with the cost of paying for these at the time. Jamie is in the same place as his big brother.

"We encountered a little problem trying to ensure they could stay together as the plot was full, but the funeral director was amazing and went above and beyond the call of duty to make sure that it could be reopened. It was so important to me not to split the boys up and they are now both laid to rest together on the same level.

"My brother and his wife have just had a baby, and he is amazing. If I'm honest, there were times that I found this quite upsetting and I feel so bad about that. I felt my brother couldn't enjoy his baby because of me and I felt terrible. Right up to the end of the pregnancy, no one could relax because they were terrified something would go wrong. I feel awful that I've made everyone feel that way. I got in touch with SANDS Lothians again during this time, and I know they are always there for me when I need them. It's hard feeling my experiences have put everyone else on edge.

"Kaidyn and Jamie will always be a huge part of our family. Even Corey will always say he had two brothers if anyone asks. When I lost the boys, I tried to explain it to Corey by telling him my tummy was broken. It had been so hard on him as he'd seen me in the hospital with an oxygen mask on and drips in my neck, but, despite all that, he often talks about both his brothers."

LeeAnn continues: "SANDS Lothians helped me to find a way forward. I couldn't stop what happened to my babies, it's just life and these things happen. However, I wouldn't wish my experience on my worst enemy! It's so sad that when losses like this happen it's often still seen as such a taboo at times and that in itself makes you feel you've done something wrong and it's your fault.

"You often blame yourself anyway, so it really doesn't help to feel like you can't talk about it. SANDS Lothians helps you get rid of all those feelings and helps you deal with all the difficult emotions. God knows where I'd be if it hadn't been for SANDS Lothians.

"My parents have been so great too, both when I lost my boys and now. They are also focused on helping SANDS Lothians help others, and they continue to help me through everything, allowing me to talk whenever I need to and my dad drives me everywhere I need to go – the cemetery, the SANDS Lothians' office and the SANDS Lothians' memorial service. I don't know what I'd do without them. Without my mum, dad and brothers, I couldn't have got through this. It was they who urged me to use the services of SANDS Lothians then and now, whenever I still need to. As a family, SANDS Lothians is now a very important part of all our lives.

"I would always say to anybody who has suffered this sort of loss to talk to others and share your experience. I can't praise my SANDS Lothians' befriender enough. She was such a great help to me and she is like a member of our family now."

Samantha Elizabeth Pennycook

"Samantha was my first pregnancy. I had a small bleed early on but all was progressing well. The summer was very hot towards the end of my pregnancy, but still, everything was fine.

"At 36 weeks, I had a midwife appointment, during which she told me that my baby had moved and was lying transverse (across my tummy) and she was worried that the baby was too big now to move back. She made me an appointment with the hospital for a week later. During this appointment, I was told the baby had moved back, and I overheard the doctor saying I was 'a paranoid first-time mother'. Naturally, I wasn't happy hearing that, but at least the baby was back in the position she should have been.

"My pregnancy continued and I was seen again at 40 weeks, at which time, I had another scan. At this point, they told me I would be seen again in one week's time if I had not gone into labour, since my blood pressure was rising, though it was still in a range that was acceptable.

"At 41 weeks, I was told my blood pressure was getting higher and I was booked in to be induced on the Saturday.

"On the Friday night, I went out to a Speedway match. I had a little pain but didn't put it down to labour starting. I went home but couldn't settle. I was in and out of a bath until my contractions went into full swing. I phoned the hospital, told them I was seven minutes apart, and was told to start thinking of coming in.

"I went in at around 3am and was admitted at 3.30am. I had a monitor put on. My blood pressure was stable and the baby's heartbeat was good. The midwife told me I was in text book labour and went to get her notes. As she left the room, the alarm went off on the baby's heart monitor. The midwife came back in and checked that everything was attached properly. I was then put in a wheelchair and rushed up to the delivery ward.

"There was a doctor in the room and also a midwife… they both confirmed that my baby had died. I would deliver a stillborn baby. We were totally devastated. My contractions stopped as my body was in total shock. Surely they were wrong, or I was having a nightmare.

"I assumed that I would be rushed to theatre and the baby would be born by caesarean section, but how wrong I was. They said there was no point putting me through a major operation. The midwife and doctor left the room and we were left completely devastated.

"When the midwife and doctor came back in, they inserted an analgesic pump and a drip for restarting my contractions. I was exhausted and devastated and couldn't believe this continuing nightmare.

"My husband (at that time) phoned our mums about 6am to tell them I was in labour, but the baby would be stillborn. They were distraught. This would have been the first grandchild on both sides.

"I had a midwife with me all the time and every time I dropped off to sleep, she increased the contraction drug to keep me going. Around 8am, the doctor was made aware that my blood pressure became very high and my analgesia was changed. My blood pressure settled down a few hours later.

"At 12.25, my daughter was born normally, as she should have been. I had been praying to myself all through, that they were wrong and when she was born she would cry, but it didn't happen. I had torn, so I needed stitches, which were done. I was given a very painful anti-D injection as I was an O-negative blood group.

"I was asked to give consent for a post-mortem as there were no signs of what had gone wrong and no evidence of cord compression.

"Once all the blood tests were done, I was kept in overnight. My husband stayed with me, and we had Samantha with us overnight. I still couldn't believe what a nightmare I was in.

"Our parents came in to meet and say goodbye to their granddaughter.

"We tried to get a hold of our minister, as did the hospital chaplain as he knew him, but to no avail. Samantha was christened by the hospital chaplain.

"We left the next morning without our beautiful daughter, who we had named Samantha Elizabeth. I can remember thinking, that antenatal clinics never told me that there was a possibility I could leave without my baby. The worst-case scenario, they told me, was that my baby may need the special care baby unit for help. I remember feeling great anger about this.

"I was told my GP would visit me later that day and my consultant would see me in six weeks as an outpatient. However, it would not be in a post-natal clinic, but would be in his other clinic in gynaecology.

"I went to SANDS Lothians, who supported me through the very dark days after losing Samantha.

"About two weeks later, Samantha was buried in the Rose Garden at Mortonhall. I couldn't believe the amount of people who turned up, there were so many. I buried Samantha in a lovely little dress with matching hat. It was an outfit I had seen during my pregnancy and loved. I knew if I had a baby girl I would buy it, I just didn't expect it would be to bury her in it. I also had an Ermintrude toy that I had bought. I wish, when I had gone to see her in the funeral directors, I had asked to hold her again. I was in a very dark place at that point and was being forced to eat and drink, as I thought there was no point, all I wanted was my baby.

"I went to my six-week appointment and was told they were still waiting for all the final post-mortem results. I remember staring at the U bend on the sink as the consultant said the best thing for me was to have another baby. This just caused me more devastation and the thought that this could happen again filled me with fear. There was nothing that had come back so far from the post-mortem to confirm what had gone wrong.

"I didn't go back on the pill and I had two miscarriages very early.

"I was referred to the miscarriage clinic eventually after seeing my professor again. He felt sure I could have a successful pregnancy.

"I was four weeks pregnant at my appointment, and I was given an internal scan. All looked fine, and I was booked in to have all my ante-natal care at the hospital.

"I have gone on to have two boys, both delivered by caesarean section as I couldn't go through another labour. Unfortunately, my professor wasn't very happy that I insisted on a section. I ended up having to write to him, stating that if he could not authorise a section, I would move hospitals and consultants, and I would make sure the hospital would be made aware of why. I got a letter back apologising, and saying that it was my body and my baby and he would give me a section if that was my choice and he would give me his backing.

"I went to a SANDS UK AGM that incorporated all SANDS branches, as it was hosted in Edinburgh for the first time.

"The professor speaking at the AGM delivered a talk on the post-mortem side of things. It was then that the penny dropped: Samantha's brain was not with her. I went into a blind panic. As soon as I could, I got in touch with my professor's secretary, saying that I needed to speak to him urgently. He was away doing a lecture overseas, but would be back in a few days. She said she would make him aware of the fact that I needed to speak to him urgently.

"He called me a few days later and after we talked, he then realised that no one had ever told me. In fact, he admitted that he would not tell other doctors in any lectures about baby post-mortems and of the fact that the brain would not be with the baby afterwards. He offered his apologies and then arranged to get the head of pathology to meet with us both and explain what had happened to her brain and what they had kept pictures of.

"The meeting was arranged, but was cancelled when the professor suffered a family bereavement. I sent him a sympathy card and he sent me a note back in which he admitted he had not realised the pain and heartbreak I went through since Samantha was born. He apologised for the fact that this was a side of having children he had not really got involved in, but I had drawn him into it and that had made him more aware.

"We had the meeting with the head of pathology, who explained my daughter's brain had been incinerated after all the tests were complete and she was sorry that this had not been explained to me. She said, in hindsight, I should have been given a choice as to what happened to it and perhaps this was something they could learn from. She also admitted it would help if more student doctors attended post-mortems of babies, so that they were more aware of what happened. My professor assured me that more of his junior doctors would be made aware of procedures, and he would expect them to attend more post-mortems. I was told that there was a picture in Samantha's files, but that these would be marked as not to be used.

"The help and support I got from SANDS Lothians stopped me from having a complete mental breakdown. I felt utterly devastated and completely alone in my experience. When I walked into their meeting, I was amazed at how many people were there and they had all lost a baby too and understood how I was feeling. The time and support that everyone offered me gave me a huge amount of comfort when I needed it most.

"When I lost Samantha, it was an uphill struggle – even doing the simplest, everyday things. I couldn't even go to my local supermarket, and I had no motivation to even eat or drink. SANDS Lothians gave me the help I needed to allow me to begin to try and move forward. They also supported me through my next pregnancy with my son, Andrew, which was priceless. Even all these years down the line, I know I can still pop in or pick up the phone and chat about my beautiful daughter.

"Samantha would have turned 18 in July 2012, which is totally unbelievable. It still seems like yesterday, even though my boys are 12 and 16. The 23rd of July is not a day I look forward to in any year, but her birthday in 2012, would have been a special age for her.

"I make sure she is not forgotten at Christmas and birthdays, and my sons are both aware they have a sister that they will never know.

"I will never forget my daughter or what I went through. Silly things trigger me shedding a tear even after 18 years, and I suspect they will, for the rest of my life."

Caitlin Poppy Ryce

19 May 2005

"My husband and I have been together for fifteen years," Natasha begins. "We're both from Edinburgh, where we lived for a while. We got married 12 years ago and wanted to start a family, so we moved down to the Borders, mainly because it was cheaper – we couldn't have afforded a tent in Edinburgh!

"I'm diabetic so we had to go for a lot of pre-pregnancy tests and counselling. If your sugars are out of control that can cause problems with the pregnancy and malformations of the baby, and it can be too big. I spent two years seeing my obstetrician about six or seven times a year working on my health, and we got the go-ahead to start trying in the middle of December. So we thought we would have Christmas first and if we wanted to have a drink we could, and then we'd start trying properly in the New Year.

"By the second week of January 2005, I was pregnant – one cycle and I was pregnant. I was initially a bit freaked out by how quickly it happened, even though we'd been working towards it for two years. When it happened within three and a half weeks, I got a bit jittery. I have very little confidence anyway and I just started panicking. Was I going to be a good mum? Would we be OK for money? I was six stone heavier back then, and I was worried about how I would cope physically having to run around after a little one, but we were delighted.

"I had extra scans, one at six weeks and one at 12 weeks, when we saw her for the first time. I also had one at 16 weeks but my husband Dave hadn't been able to come to that one as he couldn't get time off work for every single scan. I remember at the 16-week scan she was lying on her back and she sort of waved. In fact, the sonographer said, 'She's waving at you!'

149

"Later, I would go over that scan in my mind, again and again. I kept thinking, did she know? Was she waving goodbye? It's always made me so sad that Dave didn't make that scan, but of course, at that time, we had no idea what the outcome would be. We didn't know she was a girl until after I'd had her, but I was convinced I was having a boy. We'd chosen a name if it was a boy – Oscar. There was no rationale behind my belief that I was having a boy, I was just convinced."

Natasha continues: "When I was about 19 weeks, on the Friday, I didn't feel very well. I felt dizzy and really sick. I phoned up the hospital and they told me to go down and they'd check me out. My mum came down from Edinburgh with Dave and by the time we got to the hospital it was about 6pm. They couldn't do an ultrasound as the one sonographer had gone home for the night. They listened and could hear the baby's heartbeat, so I was reassured that everything was fine. They did some additional tests, told me not to worry, and to go home.

"The next week I was due for my 20-week scan, and Dave and I literally skipped along the corridor as we were so excited that we were finally going to find out the sex of our baby. They turned the lights off in the room and put the gel on my tummy. They started checking my tummy.

"Shortly afterwards, my obstetrician was brought in, and by this point Dave and I were getting a little edgy, wondering why he was being called. The sonographer then said the words I'll never forget, 'I'm so sorry, Natasha, the baby's got no heartbeat'. My reply was a heartbroken and disbelieving, 'Are you joking?' Naturally, she replied that she'd never joke about anything like that.

"The obstetrician then came in and confirmed the terrible news. They showed us the flat line on the screen. Time then felt like it started to stand still. I'd spent a long time on pregnancy websites, so I knew I would have to give birth and that a caesarean section wasn't an option. They took us away to a special room that was funded by SANDS UK where we could discuss what would happen next, and we could ring our families.

"I phoned my mum at work – I've always felt so guilty about that. I just phoned her and blurted out: 'The baby's dead'. I should have phrased it better, more gently, but I just wasn't thinking straight at the time. Mum was so understanding."

Natasha says: "They gave me tablets to take, and I was told to go back two days later on the Thursday to be induced. On the Wednesday night, Dave and I went to bed. Dave just pulled the duvet over his head and started sobbing. The whole bed was shaking with his sobs. Initially, I felt so freaked out that there was a dead baby inside me but by the next day, reality set in and I knew that in 24 hours my baby would no longer be inside me, and I didn't want that to happen either.

"On the Wednesday, I started getting pains around 9pm, and so I phoned the hospital to ask if this was normal and was there any chance I could be going into labour? The midwife on duty said there was a possibility it could be and said I could go in if I wanted to. We live about 20 miles from the hospital and neither of us drives.

"I didn't want to be at home if there was any possibility I was going into labour. We phoned a taxi and waited downstairs on the street. It was so strange as we actually felt the excitement you would feel if you were going in to have your baby under normal circumstances. Regardless of what we were going through, we felt a real sense of anticipation and glee at the thought of meeting our baby.

"Dave sat in the front of the taxi and I was in the back. I was in a lot of pain but was trying to stifle it as I didn't want to have to try and explain to the driver what was happening. We arrived at A&E and at the reception desk, told them we were here to have our baby. The receptionist exclaimed, 'Oh, how lovely!'

"When I explained we would deliver in the special SANDS room, the receptionist obviously knew what that meant and the smile left her face. They put me in a wheelchair and took me to the room. They kept saying that I couldn't be in labour as it was too soon. They said it would be my body experiencing a bit of stress but since I was due to come in the morning anyway, they were going to keep me in.

"They gave me some paracetemol and encouraged us both to get some sleep. The painkillers didn't work. An hour later, the pain was getting worse and worse, so, around three hours later, I was given pethidine. Dave realised, straight away that it was labour because the pain I was experiencing was coming in waves that were getting closer each time.

"The whole way through, the doctors were saying it wasn't labour, it was my IBS. In hindsight, this made everything worse for me. I was so frightened. If they'd acknowledged it was labour it would have made it easier; at least I would have understood why I was in so much pain. They were very busy that night. The normal labour suite was just across the corridor and at one point I heard a baby being born and the crying. I asked if the baby was ok. In the morning, Dave had gone for a coffee and the new dad was on the phone, excitedly calling all his relatives about the new arrival. Poor Dave had to cope with the new father's understandable elation and then come back into the room to deal with our devastating reality.

"Because of my diabetes, they put me on a drip. They put it into my arm but forgot to put the cap on properly so there was blood all over the floor. I had to get up while they changed the bed, despite my being in so much pain. They continued to tell me I wasn't in labour, and that we should both try and get some sleep.

"Eventually, they gave me morphine and brought in gas and air. Poor Dave kept putting the gas and air tube in my mouth because it was keeping me quiet, and he must have thought it was helping take the pain away, but it wasn't. It was just making me feel jellied and out of it, but it was hard to express myself as I was in complete agony.

"Actually, none of the pain medication helped until after I'd had her. Literally, the second I gave birth, all the pain completely stopped. The drugs suddenly took hold and I fell asleep for about three hours. Again I felt terribly guilty about that as we both fell asleep in the hours after having Caitlin.

"Later, the nurses brought her in. There was a brief moment where both of us were really nervous about seeing her, and, if one of us had said to the other that we couldn't do it, we wouldn't have seen her. However, we are both so glad that we did see her or we would have regretted it forever."

Natasha says: "They brought her in to the room in a little Moses basket. We were sitting on the bed a little scared about what she was going to look like. She was so beautiful. She was tiny, only 16 centimetres, but she was a little baby. She looked like Dave when he sleeps, the way her arms and legs were. I could see the little wrinkles on her fingers; you could even see her little nostrils. There was so much detail even that early. She was a perfect baby, our tiny little perfect baby. Now they thought when I'd gone in on the Friday that the heartbeat they'd heard was mine and not hers, as they thought she'd been dead for about a week."

Natasha continues to reflect: "Her little head was a bit misshapen because it softens. We had a post-mortem done and initially it showed nothing. However, as I had spent a lot of time on pregnancy forums, I'd asked them if they would test me for Hughes syndrome, which is a disorder of the immune system that causes an increased risk of blood clots and miscarriages.

"I'd spoken to a woman on the forum who'd had 11 losses around 20 weeks, and all had shown the baby was totally healthy, but when they tested her they found she had Hughes syndrome. Apparently, it's the leading cause of late to mid-term stillbirths and recurrent early miscarriages."

Natasha continues: "We spent about three hours with our beautiful daughter, Caitlin. It was amazing. So peaceful. The sun was streaming through the window. I clutched her close to my breast and we read her a story called 'Guess how much I love you?' The words 'love you to the moon and back' were part of this book and we put them on her gravestone.

"We showed her pictures of our cat, and since it was our wedding anniversary the next day, we showed her pictures of her mummy and daddy's wedding. It was such a precious, peaceful time and the sad thing is, I haven't felt that peace since then. We promised Caitlin we'd give her a brother or sister one day and we would keep going."

"My mum had come down. I was meant to be induced at 9am but I'd already had her by 7.30am. The nurses weren't in the room when I gave birth to Caitlin. I told them I needed the toilet and, because I was still attached to all the drips, they put me on a commode. Dave then heard a splash and immediately thought I'd passed the baby. He called the nurses back in, and they confirmed that I'd had my baby.

"I've always felt dreadful about the way she was born. Afterwards, my midwife told me that there are lots of women that have live babies on the toilet and that made it a little bit easier but at the time, I felt horrendous. However, right up until the point I gave birth to Caitlin, I was told I wasn't in labour.

"My mum also had reservations about seeing her granddaughter. Again, she didn't know what to expect but eventually, she did. She is the only person, other than Dave and I, who saw her and she always says she's never ever regretted it.

"Shortly after having Caitlin, they asked me if I wanted a bath," Natasha goes on. "I know it sounds disgusting, but I didn't bathe for about four days. I'd held my baby on my chest. If I had a bath, I'd feel like I was washing her away and I couldn't bear that. The precious time we'd had together as a family of three was so short, and I wanted to save and cherish every moment and everything associated with it.

"When the time came to leave her, I felt terrible. I had all these awful images in my head of her and what would happen next as I knew she was going to have a post-mortem. Everything felt wrong. As a mum, you're not supposed to leave your baby in the hospital and go home with empty arms and get on with your life. How do you ever begin to move on from something like that?

"I remember such strange things from that time. We were waiting for the lift and the hospital porter went by whistling 'My secret love' by Doris Day. There's a line in that song that goes 'Once I had a secret love that lived within the heart of me'. Now I can't hear that song without thinking of Caitlin.

"I didn't want to go home. I wanted them to bury me with her. It's seven years ago now, but I still remember when I first met the SANDS Lothians' team and they talked about how the grief never goes away, but it changes. I remember thinking that must be impossible, as I couldn't believe that I would ever feel anything but devastated.

"Dave had two weeks off work and then went back to his job. He needed that, he needed to get back into a routine, but I think for me that's when I started losing it. I had no routine in my life anyway, so I felt completely lost. I didn't want to phone Dave up at work crying, so I started to fill my time by going on the internet and talking on forums. I was talking to complete strangers, which in a way was easier than talking to my husband. There was such a lot I didn't know – the hospital didn't tell me that my milk would come in. I found that out through a forum so then understood what was happening when it happened."

Natasha recalls: "It was so scary how quickly everything had changed during what should have been such a happy time. The Monday of the week before we found out Caitlin had died, we'd booked the village hall for a 'Welcome to the world' party for when she was born. Mum and I had been designing a cake to have specially made and then by the Friday, we were organising her funeral.

"At the funeral it was just Dave and I, my mum and dad, Dave's parents and his sister. We didn't know Melrose very well and, initially, we went to the wrong cemetery! We knew it began with a W, but there were two with a W.

"Dave carried Caitlin in her little coffin from the hearse. I'm so proud that he did that, but no dad should ever have to do that. It was a tiny little white coffin with white ropes and a silver plaque.

"The weather was dreadful, it was pouring. The minister read a poem and I read a poem. Dave had his arm around my back to help steady me, but I could feel him shaking too. The poem was called 'What makes a mother?' It was so beautiful and so apt and I would later go on to read it at the SANDS Lothian's memorial service years later.

"Some people ask if you can be a mother when your baby has died as a result of stillbirth? This poem asks that question and makes it very clear that every woman who has loved and lost a baby to stillbirth is, without doubt, a grieving mother."

What makes a mother?

I thought of you and closed my eyes
And prayed to God today,
I asked, "What makes a mother?"
And I know I heard him say:
A mother has a baby,
This we know is true
But, God, can you be a mother
When your baby's not with you?

Yes, you can, he replied
With confidence in his voice,
I give many women babies,
When they leave it is not their choice.
Some I send for a lifetime,
And others for the day,

And some I send to feel your womb,
But there's no need to stay.

I just don't understand this God,
I want my baby here.

He took a breath,
and cleared his throat,
And then I saw a tear.
I wish I could show you,
What your child is doing here...

If you could see your child smile
With other children and say,
"We go to earth to learn our lessons
of love and life and fear,
but my mommy loved me so much
I got to come straight here!"
I feel so lucky to have a mom who had so much love for me,
I learned my lessons very quickly,
My mommy set me free.
I miss my mommy oh so much
But I visit her each day.
When she goes to sleep,
On her pillow is where I lay.
I stroke her hair and kiss her cheek,
And whisper in her ear,
"Mommy, please don't be sad today,
I'm your baby and I am here"

So you see my dear sweet one,
Your children are okay.
Your babies are here in my home,
And this is where they'll stay.
They'll wait for you with me,
Until your lessons there are through,
And on the day that you come home,

they'll be at the gates waiting for you

So now you see
What makes a mother,
It's the feeling in your heart,
It's the love you had so much of
Right from the very start.

Author unknown

"The SANDS Lothians' memorial services are amazing and they help me so much," Natasha says. "They somehow help me mark my progress. I can see such a difference in how I feel from the most recent service compared to the first one I attended. At the last one we were at, there were newly bereaved parents attending and we could see the same look in their eyes that we'd had at the beginning. The look that says – I don't want to be here and this isn't how it should be.

"When you lose your baby you become a member of a club that you don't want to be part of, but if you do have to be part of a club you're glad it's there.

"We've tried so hard to have more children. We've had four miscarriages. The year we lost Caitlin, we got pregnant another twice, then miscarried twice and in the November of that year, my cat of 13 years died. She went from completely fine to dead in ten days. It was almost like losing another baby. By that point, I was completely distraught; all the losses were just far too much to bear.

"For three years, Dave and I started to drift apart without realising it. We've always been able to communicate a lot but we just stopped talking. The grief weighed so heavily and I was eaten up with guilt. I was convinced that everyone thought I'd killed her and I was sure Dave and his parents thought the same thing. I was so convinced everyone blamed me.

"I used to say to Dave, 'I know you don't say it but I know you must think it – just say it, just get it out'. He hated hearing me say that, it was so upsetting for him. I didn't want to hurt him anymore, so I stopped saying it, but I didn't stop feeling it. I started to internalise everything and the guilt was so corrosive.

"I had a very traumatic childhood and grew up with very low self-esteem and no confidence. I used to self-harm and even now, I never feel worthy of Dave. I still don't know to this day what he's doing with me! Every month when I get my period, I tell him he should go and be married to a proper woman who can give him babies. I do believe that he loves me, but sometimes I don't know why.

"My weight got worse and worse going up to 20 stone and my diabetes was deteriorating because I wasn't looking after myself. I was supposed to have six insulin injections a day and I had about two. I just didn't care about anything. It was an effort to simply get out of bed in the morning without the extra stress of having to deal with pills, injections and inhalers.

"I ended up embarking on a slimming programme and I lost a lot of weight. Dave and I then went on a holiday and it was the first one we'd been on where I was slimmer and fitter. I could go for long walks and we could do more together and slowly but surely, Dave and I fell back in love with each other.

"When we got home, I found a bag of letters and cards we'd written to each other over the years, and it was as if we'd forgotten who we were as a couple before we lost Caitlin. The last seven years, with all the grieving and all the problems getting pregnant, were the only reality we'd known for so long. We'd forgotten the happier times. Our friends used to call us Romeo and Juliet and ask how we could still be like honeymooners after so many years together! We'd lost that, and we'd forgotten how to be happy.

"I kept working on my fitness and we started trying again. About two and a half years ago, I got pregnant again and had another miscarriage and since then, nineteen months later, I've never been able to get pregnant again. It's never taken us that long, five months is the longest it's taken before. We've had tests – mine are fine, but Dave's still waiting for his results. The Hughes syndrome means that tiny clots formed in the umbilical cord, but that shouldn't stop me being able to have a baby again although I would be a high-risk pregnancy and would be monitored closely. I suppose we just have to be patient, but nine and a half years is a long time to be patient.

"It seemed so ironic, but having taken me so long to get my diabetes under control, I was then diagnosed with this blood disorder that I'd never heard of before. It was weird when we found out. Being told losing Caitlin was 'just one of those things' was never a good enough answer, so at least we had an answer of sorts. This helped Dave a little, but I just felt worse thinking even more that it's my fault. It's me, it's my body, and I've failed her."

Natasha bravely goes on: "One thing that really upset me in the days before Caitlin was born was feeling movements: I remember lying in bed one night and when I put my hand down on my side I felt what I can only describe as a little bubble. I was so excited as I felt it must have been my baby moving. Then one of the midwives said that, since she'd probably been dead for a week, it probably wasn't her moving, it was just her corpse bumping about in my womb. Those were her words, and I was devastated. It was one of the few things I had to hang on to and with a few careless words someone took away one of my most precious memories, haunting me ever since.

"When your baby dies, your memories are all you have because you don't have a future. For years, I couldn't get to sleep as I couldn't bear to have my hand on my side as it reminded me of that."

Moving on, Natasha recalls: "I first heard about SANDS as the special room in the hospital is sponsored by SANDS UK, and they gave me a number for a branch local to me which has sadly since folded. However, they gave me the number of someone else who could help. It was only about two weeks on and I wasn't really ready. The lady whose number I was given had had a son who was stillborn at full term and I felt it would be wrong for me to talk about my earlier loss which I know, now, isn't the case. A loss is a loss.

"My best friend in the whole world got pregnant after a holiday romance and she was terrified about telling me because she knows anytime anyone announces a pregnancy it's really hard for me. She said to me she would understand if it was too hard for me and too difficult to see me through the pregnancy. It was at this point I thought – no – she's been my best friend since we were seventeen. She was my maid of honour. If it had come to this, it was time for me to talk to someone."

Natasha continues: "Dave and I came to one of the SANDS Lothians' meetings in Edinburgh. It was amazing. There were all these people that understood how we felt and knew what we were talking about. They even understood our frustration at the bizarre, thoughtless comments that people make when they think they're being helpful.

"One of the most ridiculous ones we got was when someone said, 'Well, babies die every day in Africa.' I've no idea how on earth the person who said that ever thought it would be of any comfort to us! People often say things like, 'Oh, you can try again', as if that's a replacement. Another child helps but it never makes the loss go away."

Looking back, Natasha reflects: "I remember feeling that maybe the doctor had got it wrong and the baby would be fine when she was born. They had been wrong about hearing her heartbeat on the Friday; maybe they would be wrong too about the outcome they expected?

"I don't think you ever get over something like this and it affects so many people. Often I'm asked how I am, but people forget to ask how Dave is. Just because the father hasn't carried the baby, doesn't mean they have less of a connection. From the moment we found out we were pregnant, Dave used to talk to my tummy. He was just as bonded with our daughter as I was.

"We have both felt unbearable grief but we have dealt with it differently. He's very stoic in general and just got on with things, while I turned it all inside and completely fell apart. But I've never ever thought that he doesn't grieve for Caitlin or that the loss is any less for him.

"We both came to about three meetings," Natasha says, "and then three or four of the Christmas memorial services. Then in March of 2012, we took part in the Mother's Day sponsored walk, which included the balloon release. We released a balloon with Caitlin's name on it and that was just the most brilliant feeling. It was the most perfect day – not too hot, brilliant blue sky and glorious sunshine.

"Going for a walk with other bereaved mothers and releasing a balloon on Mother's Day is, of course, not what I really want to do on Mother's Day, but if I can't be with my baby, it was the next best thing. It's that club again! Being part of that special day meant I was acknowledging my baby and recognising what a huge part of my life she was.

Natasha says: "Dave and I remember reading a quote that said something like 'when an adult dies, you lose your history with them, but when a baby dies, you lose your future with them'. I think that's why the little mementos on babies' graves mean so much, the little windmills, snowstorms and toys. Sometimes, people say that's morbid but it's all we have of our baby so we hold on to those things as they are so precious to us. We like to make her grave look pretty and celebrate her anniversary each year. We wrote 'Love you to the moon and back' on her little gravestone – they were the words from the story we'd read to her in the hospital.

"It helps me so much just to know SANDS Lothians is here for me if I need it and that brings me huge comfort, even if I don't attend meetings regularly. Sometimes I find it hard to ask for support and often I don't, but I've found SANDS Lothians Facebook page and the people on it a huge help. I'm not great at talking to people on the phone, so I'd never ring up for a chat, but it is great to be able to interact with others on Facebook and share my feelings.

"I remember in the early days when I first came to SANDS I felt quite uncomfortable as I didn't feel that I belonged in a group for people who'd had a stillbirth as she was an early loss but equally, I didn't feel I belonged in a group for miscarriages because she wasn't a miscarriage either, as most people understand them. I know in medical terms she would be classed as such, but if you go through labour and hold your child that has ten little fingers and ten little toes, how can it be a miscarriage?"

Again reflecting, Natasha says: "Dave and I lost hope for a while. Hope in general, hope for having another child and hope for our marriage. We were so devastated and our life had changed so much. However, there is always a way through SANDS for getting help, one way or another. If one group doesn't work for you, try another. If you can't phone, look at their website or the Facebook page, but there are so many sources of help. Reach out – you're not on your own."

Asked what advice she can pass on to others, Natasha says: "Your baby is your baby. It doesn't matter whether it's a full-term baby or an early loss. It's still your baby. There is more to having a baby than just the physical bit.

"For me, from the moment I found out I was pregnant, I started dreaming and planning for the future. It's not just about you anymore.

"One of the things we both felt when we met Caitlin for the first time was our love for each other made her, made this beautiful perfect little girl. Whatever else has happened between us or whether or not we are ever able to have more children, we fell in love with each other and we made a beautiful little girl."

Natasha concludes: "Sometimes, people say you're not a proper mum because your child is not alive, that you're not really parents, you were pregnant but you're not any more. They may say, when you're pregnant again, then you'll be parents. But by coming to SANDS, I've learnt that we *are* parents and I *am* a mum. I am glad I went through labour, it was all part of me being a mum. I wasn't able to grow her to full term but Dave and our love for each other made her. My body housed her for as long as it was able to. I was, and still am, a mother."

Joseph McCormick Safdar

"I experienced a miscarriage at 13 weeks in April 2005 and was left reeling at the emotional pain it caused. I fell pregnant the next month, but it felt like the innocence and delight of pregnancy had gone and, instead, I was left with a wariness knowing how easily things could change. I had an early scan to reassure me and then my usual scan at 12 weeks. Things progressed how they should and, gradually, I began to look forward to the future and visualised life with our new baby.

"Around 33 weeks, I began to have a pain at the top of one side of my back. I put it down to a strain and just carried on. The pain did not go away after a few days and was starting to wake me from my sleep, so I went to my doctor who told me to go straight to the hospital.

"My bloods were taken and I was put into a room to wait. I could hear women coming into the hospital in labour, and I mentioned to one of the midwives that I was a bit conscious that I was taking up a room, as I was not in labour and just had a back pain. They told me that it was fine and not to worry.

"A few hours later a senior doctor came in to explain that my blood tests had found something and showed I was suffering from a condition called HELLP syndrome (this stands for 'H' Hemolysis, 'EL' elevated liver enzymes & 'LP' low platelet count). It was explained to me that my red blood cells were rupturing. The platelets that make blood clot were disappearing, so bleeding could be fatal and that the pain in my back was my liver starting to break down. They explained that the only way to treat me was to deliver my baby by an emergency section and that this would take place that day, as soon as they could arrange it.

"I called my partner, Nicky, to break the news but tried to reassure him that the midwives had told me that babies born at 33 weeks generally did well.

"Nicky arrived in time, but because I was to be given a general anaesthetic, due to the fact that I needed a blood transfusion afterwards, he was told to wait in a separate room from the operating theatre. Nicky was told that he would be advised as soon as there was any news.

"He remembers waiting for some time until he was eventually told that we had a son born at 20:43, but because of the long wait, he already had his suspicions that all had not gone well. Our baby was transferred into the neo-natal unit due to breathing difficulties and the next 12 hours for me were a blur. I was in the high dependency unit and seemed to drift in and out of consciousness, I assume due to the morphine I had been given. At some stage, I had been given a Polaroid picture of our baby – I was distressed to see him attached to tubes and wires but grateful for the photo, nonetheless.

"Finally, the next day, on the 21st of December, I was allowed to be taken down to see our baby. I had been convinced it was a girl so had not yet decided upon any boys' names, but I knew I wanted his middle name to be Joseph, the same as my father's middle name. Nicky took me down in a wheelchair, and I instantly broke down as we entered the neo-natal unit.

"The sight of so many small, poorly babies, the beeping of the equipment and the shock I was still in, all seemed to take their toll on me. Our baby looked big and healthy as he weighed 4lbs, quite different to many of the other tiny babies in the unit. He was beautiful with a shock of thick dark hair.

"We met the neo-natal nurse, who explained what the equipment was for and what the beeps all meant. It was lovely to spend time with Joseph and some of our family visited too. We were advised that they were doing some checks on his heart and lungs to see what the matter was. I went back to the maternity ward.

"Thankfully, I had been given my own room, although I could still hear the other babies crying in the wards close by. As I had wanted to breast feed, I was woken up in the middle of the night to collect some colostrum that would be stored and given to the baby when he was well enough and to help establish my milk flow. The midwife who sat with me that night was a great shoulder to cry on, as she listened to all my fears.

"On the morning of the 22nd I went down myself to the neonatal unit as Nicky had not yet arrived. I spent time with my baby but noticed that the neo-natal professor asked me a few times during my visit if Nicky had arrived yet and told me that we should both go to see him when Nicky got there. When Nicky reached the hospital, we went to see the professor, who took us into a separate room.

"He explained that the test results had come back and that our baby had been diagnosed with a chromosome disorder called Patau syndrome or Trisomy 13. Nicky and I were stunned and asked him what this meant for our baby and how disabled was he going to be? We were advised that the diagnosis was 'incompatible with life' and that it was highly likely our baby would slip away from us very soon.

"I just remember myself and Nicky in tears of disbelief as we clung to each other, trying to make sense of this news.

"We decided the best thing to do was for us to spend as much time as possible with our baby, who I now decided would have his first name as Joseph as it felt more important for him to have a family name, rather than his own individual one.

"I discharged myself from the maternity ward some several floors up from the neo-natal unit so that Nicky and I could stay in the family room, close to the neo-natal ward. We spent all day with Joseph and the neo-natal nurse made sure we got to hold and cuddle him out of the incubator and took some pictures for us. Nicky even got to change a nappy, which was so important to him, as he needed to feel that he had helped care for his son.

"The night-time neonatal nurse started her shift and, again, we worked closely with her, sharing the care of Joseph, bathing his skin gently with cotton wool, stroking his fingers and hair. We were with Joseph all day and late into the night and were exhausted. The nurse suggested we go for a sleep in the family room. She promised to let us know if there was any change.

"A few hours later, she came along to alert us that things had gone downhill and that time was fading away. We ran to the ward and all the tubes and wires were removed from Joseph. He was wrapped in a blanket and placed in my arms, whilst Nicky cuddled us both. We comforted Joseph tenderly and quietly as he slipped away from us so gently as we held him. He died at 3.10 in the morning of the 23rd December.

"The nurse asked if we wanted to help her dress him and we agreed. We went back to the family room with Joseph tucked up in a Moses basket. The three of us bathed him, put him in a clean nappy and dressed him. We were asked if we wanted to have his hand and feet prints taken and a lock of hair and we agreed to all this. The hand and footprints, a certificate of Joseph's life, a clipping from his hair, his blanket and little hat were all placed in a beautiful box. The nurse left us with Joseph, wrapped in his blanket. We cuddled him and for a few hours, we fell asleep soundly and peacefully for the first time in many days as a family.

"Again, the next few days went past in a blur. Joseph's grandparents arrived the next morning as this was the first flight they were able to get from Belfast, due to the time of year. I had one final night in hospital, spending time with Joseph before coming home on Christmas Eve.

"As we were leaving and getting a death certificate from the professor, he explained that he would document Patau syndrome as the cause of death – to confuse the registrar. We felt this was a strange and insensitive 'joke' to make at the time, but did not comment – we were still numb with shock and grief. There was no celebration on Christmas Day, and my thoughts were now centred on arranging a funeral.

"A few days later, at the funeral directors, we met a lady, who was kind and thoughtful and took us through all the arrangements. We decided we wanted a humanist ceremony and met with a man we could discuss this with. He was so kind and we worked out a suitable ceremony together. I remember the man we were talking to started crying and I was surprised at how upset he was. I believe I was still numb from everything, and I was simply being carried forward on autopilot. It was like being an outsider looking in. I chose not to see Joseph in the funeral parlour but picked his clothes carefully. I know that his grandparents visited him and, as well as a letter and a teddy, they put a bar of chocolate in with him in his little coffin. We decided to lay Joseph to rest at Mortonhall Rose Garden, where there were other babies. It meant everything to me, to know that Joseph would not be alone.

"On the day of the funeral, we were picked up in the hearse. Joseph had a beautiful tiny white coffin and was in the front seat beside the driver, who told us that he had sung him nursery rhymes on the journey. We then held him ourselves on the remainder of the journey and Nicky carried him in to the service.

"The funeral was beautiful. We picked three songs: 'The first time ever I saw your face' by Roberta Flack, which reminded us of all the first moments we had with Joseph; then we chose 'Thank you for the days' by Kirsty MacColl, which summed everything up perfectly; and finally, we chose the theme from the film 'The Deer Hunter' which was a beautiful, melancholic piece of music. Strangely, I did not cry on the day. I think I felt I had to hold my grief in so I would not alarm others.

"Looking back, I honestly do not know how I did this, but again I can only assume I was still in shock. The image I have of the day, which brings me to tears even now, was of me walking beside Nicky and him carrying Joseph out at the end of the ceremony, past our family and friends, to take him to the grave. Later, we had a heart headstone engraved with a rainbow as a sign that we would never forget.

"The days afterwards were the hardest. The tears came. I couldn't stop thinking about how unfair it was to lose my baby. That's when I thought of SANDS Lothians. I contacted them and Nicky and I attended some meetings. It gave us immense comfort to be with parents who knew exactly what we were going through. Unless you have experienced this type of bereavement, it is simply impossible to imagine the feelings of grief you have to endure following the loss of a child and your future with them.

"Three months later, and I was pregnant again. Whether it was a twist of fate or a sign of comfort, our baby was to be born around the same time as Joseph had been born. Again, I attended the SANDS Lothians' groups but this time the pregnancy support groups and these meetings were invaluable to me. I found that I was able to really speak about my fears openly here, as I felt awkward around friends and colleagues who were also pregnant and I didn't want to spoil their joy about pregnancy with my own worries.

"I received lots more tests, checks and care this time and was advised that our baby boy would not have any such health problems. Joseph's little brother, Leon David Safdar, was born on the 28th December 2006 by elective caesarean section and looked very similar to Joseph. He has been our blessing and, although he is his own person, it is as if we get a peek to see what Joseph may have been like, too, which is a great comfort.

"Leon has been brought up knowing about his brother – it simply felt too big a story not to share with him and his photo is beside Joseph's in my bedroom. Leon will be six this Christmas, Joseph would have been seven and, although time is a great healer, I have no doubt that I will always feel like there is a missing gap in my life.

"I have learned the lesson of gratitude that comes with having Leon and I am also thankful every day for the little boy I had the privilege of knowing for those few days. He shaped my life and being for evermore. Thank you for sharing our story."

Elijah Smyth

Cathie Smyth adored her two little boys, four-year-old Oliver and three-year-old Rory, and was over the moon when she fell pregnant for a third time. She found out the good news in September 2011 and was told her due date would be May 19th, poignantly, a date that had just passed at the time of telling her story.

On a Wednesday at the beginning of December 2011, Cathie started bleeding a little, not much, so she wasn't overly concerned. However, she'd also had a little bit of pain across her tummy. So because of the combination of things and a few other little niggles, she phoned the hospital just to make sure. She spoke to a midwife who, fairly matter-of-factly, told her that even if it was a threatened miscarriage, they couldn't do a lot about it and Cathie was just told to go to bed with a hot water bottle.

Cathie recalls: "The Thursday wasn't too bad, but then on the Friday, I had a couple of small clots. I had a shower before bedtime but was still worried."

Cathie continued: "I had another clot on the Saturday morning and remember thinking, 'this really isn't right', but I went about my day. We had a family photography session in the morning and in the afternoon, I dropped my eldest boy off for a party. Then I decided to phone the hospital because I just knew something wasn't right. This time I spoke to a lovely midwife, who told me to come in, even if it was just for a little reassurance. When I went in, the midwife listened for the heartbeat, but she couldn't find one.

"At about 4 in the afternoon, the doctor came in with a portable scan machine, but couldn't find the heartbeat either. I was 17 weeks pretty much exactly to the day. I was on my own at that point as I had said to my husband, Ronan, that Oliver needed picked up in the afternoon. I said I'd just let him know if there were any problems. I had just carried on as normal that day with no idea what lay ahead. I couldn't drive myself home, I was devastated, and so Ronan came to pick me up. I phoned my mum, too, and we went home. It was hard to take it all in. I always thought if I were to suffer a miscarriage, it would be before the 12 weeks, but, technically, any loss before 24 weeks is classed as a miscarriage. My 12-week scan had gone really well, so to be 'miscarrying' at 17 weeks hit me like a ton of bricks."

Cathie recalls: "I wasn't given much information but the hospital told me I'd have to come back in on the Monday morning. I was told to phone first thing to find out when my appointment was. I was told this, but not much else."

Cathie continued: "I went in on the Monday morning and was given a full scan to confirm for certain that my baby was no longer alive. I was then taken into a side room and given some information about what would happen next. I was going to have to take a tablet to soften everything up and get things started. I took that on the Monday and was told to come back on the Wednesday to be induced. However, I was actually told it could happen at any point.

"At this stage, I was glad I'd had babies before now. I wasn't equipped emotionally for anything that was happening during this awful time, but at least I knew what to expect with an induction, having gone through it previously, with both my boys.

"All sorts of things were going through my mind...having never gone into labour naturally, I was panicking that something might happen before the Wednesday and I'd give birth to this 'thing' at home that I didn't know what to do with. It was a very frightening and anxious time from the Saturday to the Wednesday – it was all very surreal.

"Mum came down on the Sunday evening and we all went in on the Wednesday. We were put in the family room, and then it was just a case of waiting. When it all started, it was just like normal labour. However, I remember turning to Ronan and saying that it was far more painful than my labours had ever been, but in my heart of hearts I was aware that it was probably because I knew how dreadful the outcome was going to be.

"My emotions and feelings were all over the place because, despite everything, I still felt excitement about meeting my baby for the first time. He was a little person, he was still my son."

Cathie goes on: "I started getting contractions about 1.30pm and my little Elijah was born at about 3.30pm. It was such a weird feeling giving birth to him, because under normal labour you get this urge to push since the baby is so big, but because Elijah was so small I didn't get this urge as fully as before. Initially, I wasn't sure if I wanted to see him as I thought I would just see all kinds of mush. My fears were unfounded because when he was born he was a perfect but tiny, tiny baby.

"The midwife cleaned him up and brought him back in a little blanket. I didn't know if it was a boy or a girl before I went into labour, and I had been told they might not be able to tell so I may have to wait for blood tests – but he had everything so it was quite obvious! I was really glad about that as it meant I could name him straight away.

"I spent about six hours with him, leaving the hospital around 9.30pm. The time with him was so precious and gave us a chance to take photographs. It was so hard though – he was so tiny, I couldn't give him a proper cuddle. I had a little blanket for him, but I couldn't really wrap it round him, but at least it was there, providing a little comfort.

"I wanted to do all the normal things you'd do with a newborn but was unable to; it was so hard. It was so difficult to understand how he was classed as a miscarriage, when I'd had to go through labour and he was a tiny baby. Legally, he wasn't classed as a 'person' but he was to me and I wanted to recognise this. I phoned my minister and he came to christen Elijah before we left. That was lovely and meant so much to us.

"It was such a difficult time," Cathie recalls. "Ronan had felt awful about not being there when we'd first found out there was no heartbeat, and he became very upset when Elijah was first brought through to us. In fact, understandably, we all burst into tears.

"When the time came that Ronan and I had to discuss plans about what to do next, things became a little fraught – hardly surprising when you are faced with decisions you hope you'll never have to make. My husband didn't want a big funeral and I would have been happy with a cremation but was told that because Elijah was so small, I'd get nothing back. I couldn't bear the thought of this. I wanted to bury him.

"The midwife that had been with us throughout was amazing. She phoned the funeral director and made an appointment for us to go and see him to help us make a decision. It helped us both to know we could have a small, private ceremony.

"My dad, who had always been very practical, had, some years ago, bought us all plots in a cemetery in Aberdeen. We decided to put Elijah in a little wooden casket, in my plot. On December 29th, we picked Elijah up from the funeral director and I found comfort in holding him on my knee in the car for part of the journey up to Aberdeen.

"We were all there, including my mum, dad, sister and brother and the minister from our local church held a lovely little special service for us. We'd picked a beautiful poem called 'Snowdrops' (see page 70) which the minister read and we had put it in Elijah's little coffin, along with his blanket of love that we'd been given in a little memory box at the hospital.

"Whenever we visit mum and dad in Aberdeen, we visit him. He's in a lovely sheltered sunny corner. Our eldest boy, Oliver, now knows about his little brother and one time when he came with us he called Elijah's little grave his 'Angel house'. It was so sweet."

Cathie bravely took a breath and recalled: "I was 17 weeks when I found out Elijah died and 17½ weeks when I lost him. Doing this interview, I'm exactly 17 weeks with my current pregnancy, and I've just been to hospital for my scan. I'd had a tiny bit of bleeding last night so you can imagine my relief when all went well. The dates and milestones of this pregnancy almost mirror to the day those of Elijah's."

Cathie continues: "I had a full post-mortem done on Elijah but no reason was found as to why he died. They said there were some closed blood cells on the placenta, but that could have happened at any time. In a way, I was glad not to have a reason as I knew that would make me worry that it could happen again with any future pregnancies. I almost felt relieved that is was 'just one of those things'."

Cathie reflects: "Although Elijah was an early loss, the impact and feelings of loss are still the same. Sometimes when you tell people the loss was at 17 weeks, they just think 'miscarriage' and they don't think beyond that and the fact that you actually have to go through labour. Even though, in medical terms, it's classed as a miscarriage up to 24 weeks, it must be incredibly difficult to lose a baby at 23 weeks as it is still not classed as a person in the eyes of the law but you are only one week away from legally having to register the birth.

"I had a lot of mixed feelings when I lost Elijah. I felt I shouldn't grieve as much as people who had suffered late stillbirths, but then I felt guilty for Elijah as I felt I was then not giving him the recognition he deserved. It was like a circle of guilt, I felt I didn't deserve as much sympathy as others but then I carried so much guilt for Elijah as he deserved to be remembered.

"Coming to SANDS Lothians meant so much to me. It meant shared understanding and I have made so many friends with whom I can talk openly. We don't talk about our losses all the time, but there is an underlying connection and understanding between us all. We can share thoughts and feelings with each other that we may not be able to express to our families."

When asked what advice she could offer others in a similar position, Cathie says: "Do what feels right for you at the time. It was good for me to see Elijah as a person and give him a name and recognise that he had been part of my life. Acknowledge that you had a baby, keep mementos and treasure memories. Talk about them with your family and keep their memory alive."

Cathie continues: "My minister was so lovely, and I'll always remember his saying that he'd christened a lot of babies but would always remember Elijah. I also often recall something someone else said to me which has stayed with me to this day and that was 'grief lasts longer than sympathy'. I know I will carry my grief for the loss of Elijah for a lot longer than people will remember it, but with the love and support of my friends, family and everyone at SANDS Lothians, I am so happy to able to keep his memory alive."

Chloe Catherine Sommerville

2 July 2009

Hope Margaret Sommerville

8 January 2011

Jennifer begins: "My husband Grant and I had our first daughter, Louise, in 2002, a healthy baby after a textbook pregnancy, with no concerns. She was and still is an absolute delight and we adore her.

"When we tried for another baby in 2009, I fell pregnant fairly quickly. I wasn't troubled much with morning sickness, so I was able to work a bit more than I had with my first. I got past the 17-18 week mark and everything was progressing well.

"We decided to announce our good news on my 30th birthday and the weeks passed by. I was working part time as a teacher and one night I was attending the Primary 7 end-of-year dance. It was a hot June evening. I remember not feeling quite right. I felt very hot and just wanted to be on my own.

"When I got home, I still didn't feel one hundred percent. I'd had a little discharge but wasn't overly concerned. Next day didn't bring any improvement so I persuaded Grant to take the day off work. He got the fan out and helped keep me cool.

"I remember going to the toilet and having a strange sensation that felt like something was going to pop out of me. I couldn't figure out what it was so I phoned the midwife and then went to see her. She said it was probably just a prolapse, examined me and said there was nothing to worry about. She said it may sort itself out or I may simply have to put up with it. I was 19 weeks and two days.

"I went home but I was still convinced something was wrong; it was really worrying me. I phoned to get an emergency appointment that evening with my doctor. I also got in touch with the hospital during the day and they told me to keep my appointment with the doctor and if he wasn't happy he'd send me in.

"I remember so vividly at one point during the day I was standing at the dining room table and had an almighty sneeze. Again, I was convinced that something was going to pop out and, by this time, I had started bleeding. I went to get my husband and told him that we had to go straight to the doctor. By the time we saw the doctor, I was bleeding quite heavily so he sent me straight to hospital."

Jennifer continues: "We sat in the hospital waiting room for about 20 minutes and the bleeding was getting worse. I was then taken into a little room and after being examined, the news was broken to me that I was already ten centimetres dilated and there was nothing they could do to stop the labour. The delivery was imminent and there was a ninety percent chance that my baby wouldn't survive at 19 weeks.

"I was then transferred to the family room. The midwives who were looking after me were so kind. The next few hours were a blur while I lay on the bed. My husband called our parents to give them our news. There were no contractions: I just had to wait to deliver. I remember being quite excited at the thought of finding out if my baby was a boy or a girl. I don't think the reality had quite hit me yet.

"When the time came to deliver my baby, I remember saying, 'I can't look' and the midwife just told me to do what felt right for me. She'd tried so hard to prepare me. She told me that my baby may try to breathe and not to be alarmed or frightened. She prepared me as best she could.

"After my baby was born, I had trouble delivering the placenta. The same thing had happened when giving birth to Louise, and I ended up having to go to theatre. Before I was taken, they brought my daughter through. I'd had another little girl. We named her Chloe Catherine. We'd always loved the name Chloe and Catherine was after my husband's grandmother. I remember thinking how beautiful she was, just like her big sister. I couldn't get over how perfect she was for being so tiny. She had beautiful long fingers and she looked like she had a little smile on her face.

"After going to theatre, I spent the night in hospital. My husband went home to care for Louise, and my parents slept either side of me in the room. I woke in the morning wondering if I had dreamt everything and as reality sank in – I relived, it again and again.

"That afternoon, I left the hospital. It was so hard to leave my baby behind. It was gut-wrenching. The next few days became a blur and all rolled into one. I can still remember sitting in the garden with Mum as Louise played happily, and Mum and I sat in utter bewilderment as to the events of the last 24 hours.

"At first I said no to a post-mortem," Jennifer says, "but after being told that they were very respectful to the babies and that it might help work out what went wrong, I agreed.

"About a month later, we held Chloe's funeral. All our close family and friends were there. The minister who married Grant and I conducted our daughter's funeral service. It all seemed so surreal. However, it was a wonderful service and exactly what we wanted, with special poems and songs. We'd made little candles and, on them, we put the relationship everyone was to Chloe and handed them out at the funeral. Never in a million years did I ever think I'd have to lay eyes on my daughter's tiny little coffin.

"I remember such a special moment when I got back home. I was in the sunroom and it was so hot that I had to open a window. Then all of a sudden a tiny little white butterfly came in and stayed, fluttering around for a good five minutes before flying away again. I took it as a sign from my daughter and it was made all the more poignant due to the fact that there was a little butterfly on all the candles we gave to people at her funeral."

Jennifer goes on: "The weeks and months that followed were so difficult. I tried to go back to work but my head teacher chased me away as I clearly wasn't ready. I took some more time off and just sank lower and lower. I felt no one was looking after my girl. I felt that I shouldn't be here, she should be here or I should be with her. During one of my darkest spells, my mum told me that Chloe had died on the same day her dad had died and that she wasn't alone and was being looked after by her granddad. That was the first time my mum had shared that with me and it brought me great comfort.

"After Louise was born and before we lost Chloe, I had spent a long time putting footage of Louise on our computer, and I realised for months I'd done nothing. It started to dawn on me that I'd missed a huge chunk of her life. It was the kick start I needed to begin to move forward. All the hopes and dreams I had for Chloe, I had to give them back to Louise.

"Life began to carry on. I went back to work and I had good days and bad days. Then my husband and I started to discuss whether or not we should try for another baby. It was a hard decision to make. I didn't want to do it to replace my baby, but I had this deep desire to have another baby. Chloe's post-mortem results had shown that she was a perfectly healthy baby, so there was no genetic reason not to have another baby; my body had just decided to deliver early.

"I had also got the results back from some of the blood tests that I'd had after Chloe was born. They showed that I had a condition that meant my blood was twice as likely to clot, so I began to take aspirin every day. This was not thought to be the cause of Chloe coming early, so we felt there was at least no medical reason why we couldn't try again.

"It took me about a year to fall pregnant for the third time. We cautiously told our parents our news. The morning sickness came back tenfold, so I got straight back in touch with my doctor and consultant and they told me they would keep a close eye on me and I would get regular scans.

"We tentatively took the step forward of telling the rest of our family and friends, saying we were delighted but understandably scared. It was the year of the very bad winter and the snow kept me at home, but I happily did nothing and wrapped myself up in cotton wool!

"My 20-week scan was due to fall around Christmas time so in my mind I felt Christmas Day was my milestone. That would mean I was past the 19-20 week stage and I could relax a bit. Christmas came and went and everything was okay. Hogmanay arrived and we had a safari supper planned with our neighbours.

"I remember standing at the cooker, thinking - I don't feel right, I need to lie down. I phoned the hospital explaining that again I'd had a tiny bit of discharge. I then phoned my parents to ask if they could look after Louise, as, just to be on the safe side, I was going to go into hospital to get checked.

"When I arrived at the hospital, I again sat in the same waiting area and then they took me into the same room, then the same doctor came in. There was an awful sense of déjà vu. The doctor checked my baby's heartbeat, which was good and strong, but for the second time she then had to break the news to me that I was about 3 centimetres dilated. I completely broke down. I was so gutted. This couldn't possibly be happening again. Grant was with me and simply looked me in the eye and said, 'If this happens, it happens. We won't go through this again, we will concentrate on Louise.' The doctor told us to go home and that there was still an outside chance that my labour would stop as I hadn't had any actual contractions.

"I was told to lie flat on my back and not move. I have the most amazing family. They have this uncanny knack that if anything goes wrong, they all appear and rally round. So we all sat together, on Hogmanay, in a rather sombre mood. Every time I moved, I had a contraction. I phoned the hospital to let them know my concerns.

"I had to go back in and again was taken back into the same little room, where I was examined again. I'd dilated a little bit more, but not much. However, I was told I should stay in. The shift changed and then in came the midwife who had delivered Chloe and it was like everything that had happened before was happening all over again. I was reliving a nightmare.

"A doctor then came in and wanted to prop up the bed so that my feet were raised for as long as possible. My contractions were so few and far between, with no pattern to them. The doctor felt that we had a chance, an outside chance but it was still a chance. We were cautiously optimistic and simply had a waiting game ahead of us. I was 21½ weeks.

"I stayed in hospital and every time my thoughts drifted back to Chloe the tears would come. My parents basically moved into the room to be with me. Grant stayed as long as he could while juggling caring for Louise. I stayed in for about a week. My baby's heartbeat was checked regularly, which was a great comfort to me. I needed that; it was my hope and I clung to it. The midwives were amazing and, incredibly, found a way to lighten the mood when it was needed.

"The days became a blur and we were into the new year. My lowest day was the anniversary of the day my grandmother had died. I woke up in floods of tears. I just didn't want to deliver on that day. It was a bizarre week. They were trying to get me to 26 weeks. I was so worried that the inevitable would happen that I wanted them to speed everything up. My consultant then explained to me that if we did that, we would effectively be terminating my pregnancy. I know he didn't mean it quite so matter-of-factly, but his words hit home and led to another turning point for me. I was going to fight for my baby whatever it took.

"Sadly, my contractions became more and more regular and, by this point, the baby was feet down. Eventually, I got to the point where I was in so much pain, they thought my baby must be turning. I remember waking up suddenly and feeling something between my legs. I told my dad to hit the help button. I had, in fact, delivered a massive clot, but it brought a relief in the pressure I'd been experiencing. I thought by that point, I must be fully dilated but everything stopped. It was a relief to be pain free for a while and be able to stand up.

"Unfortunately, by this point, they wanted me to deliver because the contractions had been coming thick and fast and delivery was now inevitable.

"I was taken down to the labour ward and given the drugs that move things along. I was examined again and prepared once more for the inevitable. At this point, my baby was still alive and I could feel her moving around inside me. I was then told to give one big push. My baby was born alive. I had another beautiful daughter. In amongst all of this sadness, I briefly remembered having a laugh earlier on when we had been talking about names. I'd said if it was a boy I wanted to call him David and I always liked the middle name Cameron. However, someone then pointed out – did I really want to call the baby David Cameron!

"We decided to call our third child, Hope. On her difficult path in getting here, not one person had ever given up hope for her. She would be called Hope Margaret, Margaret after my granny.

"When Hope was delivered, she let out the tiniest of cries. I was only 22½ weeks and the midwife said she'd never heard a baby that small give a cry. Hope was gasping for breath, as we thought she would, but her movements got slower and slower. I remember asking my dad if he wanted to hold her. At first he said no, but then I said, 'That's your granddaughter, dad' and he cradled her in his arms.

"When I held her, I lavished her with kisses and cuddles as I had done with both her sisters before her. She was so like Louise and Chloe. They were all so similar and all so beautiful.

"Hope survived for an hour. She was such a fighter, I often wonder if she would have made it if given treatment, but I knew they wouldn't intervene with such a premature baby as it was seen as unethical. Watching her take her last breath was so hard. I understand that there has to be a cut-off point, but it's incredibly hard to simply watch your baby slip away when they are born alive.

"The consultant said that medical professionals had to make a decision that wasn't based on emotion, but it's hard to understand how emotion can't play a part. I suppose it must be hard for everyone when things go wrong. I don't suppose every story can be a happy one.

"Hope was taken away for a little wash, dressed in tiny little clothes and put in the most beautiful little cot. The midwife was so lovely and gave me such a big cuddle. She shared with me that she'd had a little cry too and offered me words of comfort and reassurance that I would get through this.

"I was wheeled from the delivery room, back up to the family room in the bed, carrying Hope over my shoulder. I suddenly realised that, as they smiled at me, other people thought I was carrying a healthy baby. We then chose a quieter route to save me any unnecessary pain.

"I wanted to leave the hospital. I wanted to go home and give Louise a cuddle. My three brothers had all arrived and I gave them the choice of seeing their niece if they wanted to. They agreed that they would like to meet her, but it was so hard to watch everyone else's grief too.

"We finally decided that the time had come to leave the hospital. For the second time, I walked out of that building, without my baby. My brother tried to shield me from another family that were leaving with their baby, completely elated. It was so hard to drive away yet again. I left with another memory box. As special as they are to my life, I didn't want a second one. I had to leave Hope alone in the room. The hospital was understaffed that night and there hadn't been anyone available to take her before we left. Leaving her on her own was complete agony.

"We always thought Hope may be our lottery win, our miracle and everything might work out, but it wasn't to be.

"We phoned the minister again to ask him to do another service. Again, we chose special music and poems. This time, there were three times as many people in attendance.

"Once more, my life became another blur, with days rolling into each other. I had more time off work to try and come to terms with everything. I received some counselling through the hospital with the bereavement midwife, but at that time I couldn't bring myself to go to a SANDS meeting."

Jennifer continues: "I gradually moved on a little and began to do some meaningful things. I got a group of 29 people together to do a sponsored walk and run, and we raised over £1500. It was something positive for me to focus on in memory of my girls. As things gradually became a little easier, I remember having a joke with Grant, asking how he would have coped with three girls and me?!"

Looking to the future, Jennifer says: "My husband is pretty certain that we shouldn't try again and we should spare ourselves from any more pain. However, realistically, we are at the point where we need to make a decision as to whether or not to try again, but I'm just not sure if I could go through that pain again, should things not work out. I had the strength of my cervix tested and was told it was borderline. My first pregnancy with Louise held tightly but, for some reason, weakened my cervix. If I had another pregnancy, they would have to put in a stitch. I feel that, unless this would be 99.9 per cent safe and work for certain, I'm not sure if I could go through it.

"Louise is older now and more inquisitive so if things were to go wrong again, she would require a bit more explanation of things. She does already know that she has two sisters. Sometimes in her sweet innocent childlike way she says to me, 'Mummy, you have to go and get another baby. Daddy needs someone in the van with him - you've got me at home so he needs someone with him.' Such simple logic to a six year old.

"It helps so much to share stories and hear about other people's experiences. The death of a baby can be such a taboo subject. Some people don't know what to say, so say nothing and sometimes that's even worse. Even if they just said they were sorry, that would be enough.

"I heard about SANDS Lothians through a cousin who lost a child and had used their services. They were like a safety net for me. I knew I could phone them if I needed to. They would be my first port of call during a difficult spell. The advice they give comes first hand and they have a wonderful support network. I would like to do another fundraiser soon to help raise money for SANDS.

"When you get so far down the grief road, you can look back at where you've been. I remember in the depths of my grief one of my coping mechanisms was housework. My house had never been so clean, it was spotless!

"I think I am now almost at a point where I could help others by sharing my story and give a little advice and comfort. I find it very therapeutic. To let someone else know that in their darkest hours and darkest times there *will* be light at the end of the tunnel is very rewarding.

"Sharing stories is vital. Bereaved parents telling of their experiences will help give midwives and medical professionals first-hand accounts and help them to be better practitioners."

Offering advice to others, Jennifer says: "You'll never forget your child. Don't be afraid to talk about him or her the good and the bad. I always made a promise to myself that if anyone asked about my children, I would be honest. I would say, 'I've had three children, but I only have one of them at home.'

"Never be afraid to tell people you've had a child and lost a child. Acknowledge them and remember your children. It's true what they say – what doesn't kill you, makes you stronger. Never let what's happened defeat you; if you do, you're not honouring your baby's memory. As hard as it may be, you will come out the other end."

Isla Thomson

"In January 2011, during my 20-week scan, Francis and I discovered that our baby girl Isla was suffering from growth restriction. At that point, she was four weeks behind in her growth. Following this, her growth was monitored via fortnightly scans. Sadly, instead of catching up on her development, like we desperately hoped she would, her growth rate fell further and further behind. She hung on for about two months but lost her fight for life in the first week of March 2011. I was 26 weeks pregnant at the time. Her birth was medically induced and she was delivered on March the 12th. Francis and I held a lovely but very sad funeral and cremation ceremony for her.

"The following months were a time of severe grief for Francis and I, although the way it affected us was different. For the first month or so I was tired, numb and felt like I was floating around. I became very withdrawn from the world. I couldn't bear to look at pregnant women or babies. I felt intense anger at anyone whom I perceived not to be sensitive to what Francis and I were going through. Two months later I went back, one day a week, to my job as an arts therapist in Glasgow. On a few occasions I suffered panic attacks in the underground. Francis continued to suffer panic attacks for quite a while longer.

"It was in April that I was contacted by a senior befriender at SANDS Lothians. She told us how sorry she was, how she was a parent who had experienced the stillbirth of her twins and that SANDS Lothians could support us.

"The first time I went to a befriender at SANDS Lothians, I felt instantly comfortable with her. I felt that here was a person who really understood, on a very deep level, what Francis and I had been through. One thing that really struck me was her ability to be completely present, attentive and attuned to whatever I needed to share with her. It felt like she had all the time in the world for me.

"This type of support has continued and was instrumental in helping me work through my grief. She had also recently completed her counselling training at Edinburgh University and so has in fact helped me in numerous different ways. She has helped me work through other deep-seated issues, and the result is I am a much stronger person for it.

"For almost a year I was visiting SANDS Lothians weekly which was like a lifeline. Around the one-year anniversary of Isla's death I became very upset and another befriender was there at the end of the phone supporting me.

"SANDS Lothians run a monthly meeting on the first Monday evening of each month, offering an opportunity for bereaved parents to meet, share stories and support each other.

"The team also offers pregnancy-after-loss support. Recently I fell pregnant again and although I knew it would be an anxious time for Francis and I – we were reassured knowing that SANDS Lothians would be there when we needed them.

"Sadly, this pregnancy ended in miscarriage on Monday the 14th May. Francis and I are once again very sad but find things so much easier to bear this time round, because we know that the team from SANDS Lothians will be there to get us through this again. Our future is brighter knowing their unwavering support will be there.

"The team at SANDS Lothians are angels. There is always at least one or two of them available when you need them. This is no mean feat when they are a tiny charity in terms of numbers of staff, who, apart from having to support a huge amount of bereaved parents, also need to find time to raise vital funds. The pressure on them is immense but they stand by bereaved parents in and around Edinburgh like a rock.

"A classic example of this was recently when I started miscarrying. They contacted me three times to see how I was going, and to remind me that someone would be there for me although my befriender was on holiday at the time.

"SANDS Lothians very recently won the 1st prize award in the *Daily Record* 'Our Community Hero' category, and I know that other bereaved parents would join me in saying that it couldn't have been given to a lovelier team of people."

Molly Traynor
14 April 2011

Grace Traynor
4 May 2012

"We found out we were pregnant with Molly in mid-December 2010, five months after our wedding. We were delighted, but couldn't help worry as we had miscarried at six weeks just two months earlier. At a scan on the 6th of January we saw Molly for the first time. A little bean, with a flickering heartbeat. We were in love! We were delighted and let our parents in on the news early on.

"Things were going well, despite being sick constantly. We decided to let our brothers and sisters in on the exciting news too. They were all over the moon. We started to relax and counted the days until our 12-week scan so that we could properly announce our happy news. Valentine's Day arrived and with it, my 12-week milestone. Our scan wasn't until the following week. My husband Paul's mum came with us and we were amazed to see our little jellybean waving away at us. All was well and the sonographer said things were progressing nicely.

"We announced our happy news to friends and family. No-one was more excited than my 5-year-old niece. She was so excited about being a big cousin that she started having regular conversations with my growing bump. The 'morning' sickness continued morning, noon and night.

"At 16 weeks I had a small bleed. A trip to the maternity unit showed I had cervical erosion which we were told was nothing to worry about at all. We also had the chance to hear Molly's heartbeat through the doppler. It was one of the most amazing sounds I have ever heard. In the next few weeks, I started feeling movement. Every time I sat down, I had flutters in my tummy.

"At 19 weeks, I had another bleed. Again, a trip to the hospital confirmed the erosion was the cause of the bleeding and we had another opportunity to hear the heartbeat. Perfect! We were looking forward to our 20-week scan the following week.

"On the 12th of April, at just over 20 weeks, we headed to the hospital for our scan. I hadn't felt any flutters for a couple of days but was waiting patiently for the real kicks to start. We were looking forward to seeing how our jellybean was coming on. We were shown into the usual room, but this time the sonographer did not turn the screen round.

"All was quiet and I knew something was wrong. She took my hand and said, 'I'm sorry but there is no heartbeat'. I will never forget that moment. She went to get someone to come and confirm that our baby was gone.

"We were shown to a tiny room and told a doctor would come and speak to us. We were in shock. The next couple of days are a blur. I was given tablets to take and told to come back in two days to be induced.

"We arrived back at the hospital a couple of days later and were given a side room in the labour ward. All around us we could hear the cries of healthy newborns. It pulled at my broken heart. At 10am, I was given the first pessary to induce labour and the contractions started soon after. That whole day is a blur to me.

"Molly was born at 21 weeks on 14th April 2011 at 9:04pm. I didn't look straight away. The midwife took her away and brought her back to us all clean and wrapped up. I was scared to hold her, scared to touch her. But she was perfection in miniature and so beautiful. Our little girl. Her hands were perfect, complete with long fingers and tiny fingernails. She would have played the piano, I knew that.

"We held her and spoke to her. I was scared to unwrap her and look at her. I was scared to keep her with me. We spent a few hours with her, then the midwife took her away.

"I was in complete shock. I don't think I would have survived had it not been for my husband. He was there every moment with me; he kept me going. Leaving the hospital the next day, without Molly, was one of the hardest and most horrendous things I have ever done. Walking away that day was the worst part of the whole experience. I don't know how my legs carried me. We buried our beautiful girl two weeks later on a warm, sunny morning.

"I have regrets …that I didn't look at her feet, that I didn't hold her for long enough …I just didn't know what we were allowed to do, and I didn't have the presence of mind to ask. I look at her footprints and I wish I had looked at her tiny, perfect feet.

"July brought results of the tests carried out on my placenta. Molly had been perfect, my body let her down. Placental results showed that she had died due to a very rare condition called Massive Perivillous Fibrinoid Deposition (MPFD). This basically meant that fibroids and clots had formed on the placenta, gradually taking over until it was no longer fit for purpose and unable to support a growing baby.

"Consultants put in place a plan for the future: daily aspirin tablets and daily self-administered heparin injections. It was hoped that this combination would stop clots forming and keep the blood moving through the cord. Time would tell.

"We went on to have another early miscarriage at the end of July 2011, and then a pregnancy test on New Year's Eve confirmed that we were pregnant for the fourth time. With a treatment plan in place, we were hoping that finally this pregnancy would give us our take-home baby. What a fantastic start to 2012! Our rainbow baby was on its way!

"We were booked in with the midwife straight away as we needed a quick referral to our consultant and an early scan before we started on the medication. Six weeks brought us to our first scan.

"With a little bean appearing along with a heartbeat, we began the medication. At night, I was taking my aspirin, folic acid and vitamin D. Also, I began injecting the Clexane. This was a bit strange at first but I got used to it quickly, and a vast array of bruises began to decorate my tummy. I was not bothered, I would have injected myself a hundred times a day to keep my baby safe.

"Eight weeks showed us our little bean was coming on well and things continued to progress including my 24-hour morning sickness. I was losing weight and couldn't keep a thing down. Evenings were particularly bad but I didn't care. It was reassuring.

"After a small bleed, we were scanned at 10 weeks for reassurance and our little teddy bear made a spectacular appearance. Possible future gymnast, perhaps? She was twirling and turning the whole time.

"Things quietened down and we waited patiently for our 12-week scan. It came around quickly and we were relieved to see our baby waving at us and measuring perfectly for dates.

"Things were going well and baby was coming on a treat. We were delighted but still very apprehensive. Molly had also been measuring perfectly at this stage, so we knew we had a long way to go. Our next scan was booked in for 15 weeks.

"Fifteen weeks arrived (it was a Wednesday). Baby was measuring slightly behind but the sonographer wasn't worried and said it was normal to be out by a few days. The worry was in the back of my mind, though. We went round to see the consultant to make sure all was going well with the medication. He offered extra scans for reassurance at a community clinic every Friday which we gratefully accepted.

"We went two days later for the first of those scans and a registrar scanned us on a very old machine. She was concerned about the fluid level but, after looking at our scan photos from the big machine from the Wednesday, she said they were the same and not to worry about it if the hospital hadn't mentioned it. So we tried to put it out of our minds and hubby happily went off on his future brother-in-law's stag.

"On the Sunday I had a major bleed. My husband was still away so my mum took me to the hospital. A Doppler let us hear a nice strong heartbeat and put my mind at rest a bit. A scan was also arranged for the coming Wednesday when I would be 16 weeks. This was when our world started to crumble all over again.

"The scan on Wednesday showed that there was no amniotic fluid and the blood flow through the cord (EDF) was absent. We were devastated and could not believe that it was happening all over again. The doctors advised us that our baby would die within days and that they would scan us weekly until the inevitable happened.

"We met with our consultant the following day. He thought it was the same thing again and told us that this was the first time the hospital had dealt with anyone with Massive Perivillous Fibrinoid Deposition (MPFD). In fact, they hadn't heard of it before and the treatment we were on had been their best guess.

"The 17-week scan showed the baby still had a strong heartbeat although growth had majorly slowed down. However, some small pockets of fluid had appeared and EDF was present. This gave us a tiny sliver of hope and the doctors doubled the amount of Clexane I was taking. I also began taking steroids to see if it would help halt the damage to the placenta, which was assumed to be the cause rather than loss of waters. It looked like the condition which had taken Molly from us had returned with a vengeance.

"By this time, I was in contact with a fellow silent mum (a mummy with no living children) who had also experienced multiple losses in practically identical circumstances. We realised we had the same condition! This wonderful person had already done so much research and gave us hope that whilst it might be too late for this little one, we still had a future. There were treatments available – we provided our doctors with all the research.

"18 weeks: my bump was popping out and growing well. I was still being sick. The scan showed our little star was continuing to fight hard. There had been some growth but the small pockets of amniotic fluid were gone, although the EDF was still present.

"19 weeks: our little fighter continued to baffle the doctors and the heartbeat was still going strong. The growth was minimal and EDF still present, but the bump was still growing and the baby was kicking regularly.

"20 weeks: our little one still not giving up without a fight. The EDF was still present but no growth. We spent the weekend on the coast, remembering Molly on her first birthday and anniversary. We still couldn't believe we were going to lose our rainbow baby, and we had such a horrendous sense of *déjà vu* as it was all happening at the same time of year again.

"21 weeks: the heartbeat was still there, but the EDF was now absent again. I was advised to stop all the medication.

"I woke up a few days later on the 2nd of May and knew our little one was gone. I had movement the night before, but I knew when I woke up that something was wrong. A scan later that morning confirmed our little one had finally lost their battle. I was booked in for induction two days later.

"4th May 2012, 22 weeks pregnant: after six hours of labour, Grace came silently into the world at 3:15pm, in the same room where her big sister was born. She weighed exactly the same as Molly, perfection in miniature. She looked so serious and deep in thought in her forever sleep. She would have been our little thinker. I wasn't so scared this time. I held her. I looked at every part of her, including her tiny feet. I didn't want the same regrets as I had the last time. We had little clothes for her and teddies and blankets. We cuddled her for hours.

"We kept Grace with us all night, and her grandparents came to meet her. A bright, lone star also appeared in the sky outside the window. I think Molly had come for her sister.

"The next day, we said our goodbyes. It took us a long time to walk away. Once again, I found this the hardest thing to do. There is nothing worse than walking away and leaving your child behind. It is the most horrendous thing I have ever experienced. I don't know how I did it either time. I don't know how my legs carried me out. I know that each time I did it, I left a piece of my heart behind. I'll never get those pieces back.

"Tests on the placenta have confirmed that, like Molly, the placenta was again attacked due to the condition massive perivillous fibrinoid deposition (MPFD). They are still not 100 per cent certain of what causes the MPFD to happen, possibly an immune response, possibly an as-yet undiagnosed Thrombophilia issue. They are not committing to either school of thought. What they have said is that the condition is aggressive and recurrent, and they are struggling to find anyone else with as severe a condition. We are a unique oddity.

"So they have agreed to the treatment plan that we have researched, as long as we go into this with eyes open and accept that we are now sailing in uncharted waters with no guarantees. This treatment will include aspirin, high dose folic acid, heparin, steroids and Intralipids. So we move forward with a quiet optimism and a realistic pessimism.

"In the October, after losing Molly, I became aware of the SANDS Lothians' West Lothian support group, run by a colleague of my mum. I began attending the monthly support meetings and it has been a huge source of support for me. The girls in the group were also a fantastic support through our journey with Grace.

"The group has been a lifeline for me and I have made many new friends. I have been very lucky to have this and also to have a supportive family network behind us. You have to take every positive you can, though some days these little positives are the only thing that keep me going."

Theo James Welsh

Nicola begins her story: "I had my first son, Lucas, in 2007. He was born early but everything was fine. My husband Gary and I really wanted to expand our family and not have too big a gap between each child. We were very fortunate that it worked that way, as there were two years between each son.

"When I became pregnant with my second son, I went to the midwife for a ten-week check-up. I remember saying I just wanted to be sure everything was OK. I had a bit of a gut feeling that I had never had before that something wasn't right, and I felt that it was important to check the baby. Perhaps it was some sort of mother's intuition, but it was important to me. It wasn't really like me to be this anxious but I was desperate to know, so in the end, we paid for a private scan to ease my mind.

"On the face of it, everything seemed fine, but later on when we went into the reception area the midwife said there was a little bump on the baby's tummy and that sometimes things like that happen at this stage. There can be a placental hernia, where the tummy is the last part to close up and it could look like this at this stage.

"Looking back, I think the midwife knew something wasn't right and that triggered great worry for me. I couldn't relax and trawled the internet for research as to what it might be. I phoned the midwife back and told her I was concerned now. I had learned that there were two conditions: it could be gastroschisis or exomphalos. With gastroschisis, the baby's bowel protrudes from a hole in its abdomen and with exomphalos the tummy doesn't close properly and the protruding organs develop within the umbilical cord and can include the intestines, stomach and liver. It is the more serious of the two conditions.

"I wanted to know if this was what the hospital were thinking too. I was told that it wouldn't be gastroschisis and, if anything, it would be exomphalos, but it was so early it was impossible to tell. I was left hanging. I asked if I could get an early scan, but I would have to have it at 13 weeks as that would be the best time to see properly."

Nicola continues: "I tried so hard to remain positive and convince myself that everything would be fine. When I finally had the scan, I asked if they could specifically check the baby's tummy or I still wouldn't be able to relax. It took a while and the room fell very quiet. I then remember the lady saying, 'I've seen the baby's tummy and it's not what I'd like to see'.

"I can remember everything so vividly, even the colour of the walls and I remember lying there thinking, 'Oh my God, that's it'. From that moment on, I knew my baby was going to be sick and from then on, we had such a long journey through the pregnancy.

"Theo's tummy looked mostly flat and then it looked like he had a big balloon, almost the size of his head, on his tummy. When I went in the next day, I saw a specialist who confirmed the diagnosis and said they would do a CVS where cells would be extracted from the actual placenta to see if there were any other conditions linked to the original diagnosis that Theo was suffering from.

"Babies with exomphalos can also have a host of other birth defects, like chromosomal anomalies, and heart and neural-tube deformities, and they can also have respiratory problems.

"The CVS carried risks of its own but we decided it was still best to go ahead with it. That was a very difficult time. We had to wait for the results and it landed over a weekend so the wait felt endless. It was horrendous for us as, realistically, the results would mean we either keep or terminate the baby but already in our minds, we were keeping that baby, it was ours and while he still had a heartbeat, we would do anything for him.

"They phoned with the results on the Monday and they were fine – well, fine to the extent that the baby wasn't suffering from any further difficulties and he just had this one condition, which we would manage. We would look after our baby and give him everything he needed. We tried so hard to turn the negatives into positives. If anyone could cope, we could."

Nicola continues: "I was constantly on the internet and talking to other people who had had babies with this condition and interestingly, there were never any stories of the baby not surviving. When I was about 28 weeks, we went to meet at the hospital one of the surgeons, who advised us that they would treat Theo's condition conservatively, i.e., paint the external with dressings and let the baby's skin heal up over it so the baby has a large hernia. When the skin and muscles are strong enough they would operate to close the hernia.

"I didn't really like the surgeon; he wasn't really a people person. We were still trying so hard to stay positive and he became the first to bring up the issue of mortality and mention that Theo's condition could be fatal. I know perhaps he was trying to prepare us for the worst, but I still didn't want to hear it. It was the first time the seed of that outcome as a possibility had been planted in our minds. It was the first time we had had to think along those lines and it was like being hit by a train. After we left, we just sat in the car outside, weeping and unable to speak to each other.

"We went home and I felt numb, still unable to talk. It was one of these times when the impact of terrible news affects you physically. It was like I shut down and I was oblivious to everything happening around me. I was in complete shock.

"After a few days, I got a bit stronger and asked to speak to another surgeon. I wanted a second opinion. I wasn't just going to accept that my baby would die. We then spoke to a wonderful surgeon who was very experienced and who actually ended up as Theo's surgeon.

"He was of a totally different opinion with regard to the outcome for Theo. He was far more positive and said he had treated hundreds of exomphalos babies who had been fine. Comfortingly, he said, 'We'll deal with it when the baby comes out. Just look after yourself at the moment and the baby inside you and everything will be fine.' By this time, I was around 30 weeks."

Nicola recalls: "I went into early labour at 31 weeks. When I went into hospital, again, fate seemed to be playing its part. The consultant who had seen us throughout was there that night and delivered Theo. His birth was wonderful. It was a natural delivery which is unusual for exomphalos babies but the consultant was a firm believer in a natural delivery as it was less traumatic.

"My midwife was so lovely too. I always remember her saying afterwards that Theo came out with his hands clasped as if he was praying. Maybe he knew he'd need a little extra help. Theo was so beautiful. He was very, very blond with little waves and tufts of hair. I saw him so briefly when he was born, then he had urgently to go to the Sick Kids Hospital in Edinburgh. I was in labour for around 30 hours, but I was so proud that I managed the birth. Now, when other people talk about the birth of their babies, I can include stories about Theo's birth and share pleasant memories.

"Almost as soon as Theo was born, he went to the Sick Kids and Gary went with him. The end of my labour wasn't straightforward as my placenta didn't come away. The very bit that should have gone well, didn't! I ended up having to go to theatre at the same time as Theo was taken into theatre for the first time. This must have been such a difficult time for Gary. Both his wife and baby were in theatre. I had to have an epidural to get rid of the placenta but I'd never needed one for any of my labours!

"Gary had very quickly taken photos of Theo in the minutes after he was born and as I was being dealt with in theatre, I was being shown pictures of my baby, but it was so comforting for me. However, I still didn't know what was happening. It turned out that Theo had a tiny tear in his exomphalos so that's why he had to go straight into theatre.

"Poor Gary, how on earth did he drive?" Nicola reflects. "I don't know how he coped, he must have been on autopilot. The first time he ever spoke about that time was when we had to return to the Sick Kids when our third son, Oscar had to go into hospital for an operation.

"He recalled meeting the surgeons and even where he'd sat waiting that night. Gary had had to wait to check Theo was all right for around three hours and even after that he drove back to check how I was. By that time, it was around one in the morning."

Nicola recalls: "I felt physically really well after coming out of theatre after Theo's birth. I was up and dressed as nothing about me mattered by now. It was all about Theo. It was so difficult to see him the first time at the Sick Kids. It would later transpire that the nurse who looked after him on his first day would be the nurse who cared for him the day he died, and that was so special for us.

"I was home the next day and so began three weeks of visiting him in hospital. We kept a blog, partly to keep everyone informed and partly as it was therapeutic for us. I couldn't hold him. The exomphalos was just so huge and he was so tiny. He responded well after the surgery and for about three days everyone was really positive and optimistic. Then the surgeon wanted to have another little look at him under anaesthetic and he called us in to talk to us.

"At that point, we knew there must be something else wrong. He was going to have to operate again on our baby boy as soon as possible. Theo's organs were outside of his little body and his tummy was trying to close and heal itself. This was then restricting the flow of blood to the organs which of course, was very serious. Sadly, in the end that's what killed him.

"Looking back, they had actually thought he would be a stillborn if I had gone full term as the space would have been more restricted. If I had been full term, I would never have met him. I just feel so blessed that I got the chance to meet him and that's why he came early. I remember reading his star sign for the time around his birth and it said something like 'I think you know the tide is turning and you need to make moves now because you know what the other option is'."

Nicola continues: "They cut his tiny tummy to give him as much space as possible, put a silo over it, then attached that to something that basically looked like a washing line as he lay in his little incubator. The line would hold the exomphalos up and they would hope gravity would in time, make it go back into his body. They would gradually squeeze it down a little bit each day."

Nicola reflects: "Looking back, Theo really struggled during this time. I had been expressing milk since he'd been born – I was determined to do this. It was about all I could do for my baby, but he wasn't tolerating feeds. I couldn't hold him, I could only touch him."

Nicola painfully recalls: "The first time I cuddled him was when he was going to die. I'd really struggled to produce milk and then, cruelly, the first time I held him as he was dying, my milk came in. Mother Nature's timing really wasn't great.

"During the three weeks, we were at the hospital every day. We couldn't stay overnight but there were nurses there 24/7. The nurses never leave your baby's side for a second, they are truly amazing. I always phoned through the night. Ten days after Theo's second operation, he was stable-ish. We still thought he'd be fine and at that time 'normal' life was mainly about juggling stress, hospital visits and a two year old. We were lucky, though, we had a lot of family help.

"On Lucas' second birthday, they decided to take the silo off, then everything got a bit wobbly again. They didn't know where to go from this point. They had to phone hospitals around the UK and ask other doctors' opinions, since what they were having to deal with was so rare. They took the dressing off and had an emergency team ready to take some skin to a laboratory so they could grow skin to cover the exomphalos and try to treat it conservatively again.

"They tried so hard for Theo, spending thousands of pounds trying to save him. It was amazing. That was the most positive and optimistic time. His exomphalos was so much smaller and we still had hope.

"We were told it would take about 14 days to grow the skin then they would graft it on. Everyone was so optimistic and Theo looked so well. Then one evening, he had a bit of leakage. When I phoned in the middle of the night, I could hear in the nurse's voice that something wasn't right. I was told that the surgeons were going to have another look at him in the morning. I didn't think anything of it, and I stayed at home with Lucas.

"Gary decided to go through. I was strangely calm but drove through later. Gary was edgy and upset. We went up to ICU and the best way I can describe what I saw was Theo looked really done [in], he looked so ill, like he'd just had enough. I remember saying, no more pain, I had a strong sense that we just couldn't do anymore to him.

"The surgeon took us into a room and told us there was nothing else they could do and that his intestines were dying. Gary somehow found the strength to thank everyone and somehow we both remained composed. We were both certain that our son should not endure any more pain.

"We were then moved into a room on our own to come to terms with everything. We weren't sure if his passing would take hours or days, but we were told that we could turn his machine off and, reading between the lines, I think that's what we were being advised. We slowly came round to the realisation that's what we, as his parents, must do for our son.

"We were able to phone people and let them know what was happening. I phoned our minister and he asked if I wanted him to christen Theo. Again, fate played its part here. The minister had been on his way out and had just that second returned to the house as he'd forgotten something. I wouldn't have been able to get a hold of him otherwise. He came to the hospital and Mum, Dad, Gary and I were all there as he christened Theo. He gave us a lovely christening certificate which we treasure. It was recognition of Theo's little life.

"We put him back in his incubator right beside us but we couldn't sleep and barely dozed. Those hours were total agony. The grief was so unbearable. It was like being eaten from the inside out, as if someone was constantly clawing at me, reminding me – your baby's going to die. Family members came to say goodbye. I felt so sorry for everyone else, but I felt so numb. We brought Lucas in to meet his brother and we have some lovely photos of that.

"I remember we went down to the Sanctuary for about half an hour and there was a little card there to provide comfort to parents whose baby is dying. There was only one card and on subsequent visits to the Sanctuary, I have never seen those cards there again. I remember so clearly. The words on the card said, 'You can hand your baby over, not to feel guilty and God will look after him.' I remember then saying to Gary with renewed strength, 'We can do it now, he's not dying; we're just handing him over'. Theo would always be with me in my heart, throughout my life.

"We were quite certain now about what we had to do. It was about 4pm. It was the first time I got to hold my baby without all the tubes and apparatus. He was so beautiful. The doctors would keep checking him and he stayed with us for a long time. We just kept holding him as his breathing became shallow. Theo told us when the time was right, he squeezed my hand so tightly before he died and we knew. I kept telling him it was ok for him to leave, he could go now. I knew when he'd finally gone, it was like a passing of him, and it felt like energy passed from him into me. It was like a total impact into my chest. Maybe it was just my heart breaking."

Nicola says: "Theo looked so peaceful, so lovely, beautiful and angelic. I could never see him properly before. He was a perfect little baby. In a way, we were lucky. We had him alive for three weeks. We saw the colour of his eyes. He got the greatest care, and all the right people were there for him at the right time throughout his life.

"I found it hard to let go of him and lay him down. I couldn't decide how best to leave him. We decided to put him in a little Moses basket and I handed him over to the midwife.

"After we came home, we had a week to prepare for the funeral. I don't know where we got the strength from. I asked them to play one of my favourite pieces of classical music which we played during Theo's birth. We played the same piece when people came into the church. It was later that I found out that the piece had been written for a mother grieving for her son she had had to bury and for the loss she felt.

"We also played 'Hallelujah' by Jeff Buckley and 'Somewhere over the Rainbow' by Eva Cassidy. I remember the sunlight was beaming into the church through the window, and I could feel its warmth on my face when I shut my eyes. We wanted Theo's funeral to be all about love, not sadness, and about remembering his little life."

Nicola continues: "True to form throughout this experience, when our son Oscar went into the Sick Kids for his operation, we went to the café where we had often gone when Theo was in and suddenly, over the speakers, the song 'Hallelujah' started to play and immediately after that, 'Somewhere over the Rainbow.'

"There are many versions of this song but it was the exact same recordings as we'd played at Theo's funeral. What were the chances of that? One after the other. As if that wasn't enough, Theo's surgeon then walked in. It was as if Theo knew what we would need at that time. I know most people would say it was coincidence, but it brought me great comfort.

"Theo's funeral was at Grangemouth and he was buried at Kingscavil. We chose not to see him in his coffin and I think that was the right thing to do. We knew him as a live baby and wanted to keep it that way. The burial was horrendous watching his tiny white coffin going into the ground.

"That night, the grief engulfed me like a tsunami. I felt like I'd been hit by a freight train and the next day I just didn't want to be here. If I could have done something easily, I would have. I remember thinking it all through – Lucas would have Gary but Theo needed me. I was so grief-stricken, nothing else mattered but being with Theo."

Nicola continues: "After the funeral, I got through the weeks and months with great difficulty. I'm a realist and a positive person but I had no idea what to do or how to cope. I really pushed myself and I did crazy things, like still going to my friend's child's birthday party weeks later, in an attempt to keep some normality for Lucas.

"Some of my friends were still pregnant and I remember saying to people - don't treat me any differently. I spent time around newborn babies and I always felt it was Theo sending me a baby to cuddle! It was so strange. Perhaps it was my coping mechanism. Maybe I pushed myself too much but I'll never know.

"Six months later, I had a miscarriage, then fell pregnant again immediately after that. Then at eight weeks I had to have a D & C because that baby hadn't formed properly and it was just an empty sack. Looking back, I am sure I was just too sad to carry a baby. That was such a dark period for me.

"I wanted to be pregnant again so much as I was desperate to have a baby, but it just didn't happen. It took up until the end of June but by that time, I'd allowed myself to grieve for Theo and was probably in a healthier place for my next pregnancy. I tried to stay so positive throughout that pregnancy, and Oscar is such a happy, contented baby so hopefully, it worked!"

Nicola poignantly says: "You can try and go round grief but really, I think the only way is to go through it. Give into it and work through it. It's harder to go back and grieve, so let yourself give into it when it's raw. If you need to stay under the duvet, if you just can't face the day, then do it and don't force yourself to do anything you don't feel up to.

"When Theo died, I was so lost and I didn't know where to turn. The hospitals didn't point me in SANDS' direction and my GP didn't refer me for any help. I'd had support from a wonderful bereavement counsellor who helped me when I was pregnant with Theo and then again, after he was born and died. She left to go back into the labour suite and then she just happened to be the one who delivered Oscar! She was retiring shortly after and said to me that she'd been there for my darkest and brightest times and said delivering my healthy baby was the best ending to her career.

"After I had Oscar, I felt so much better. I had dealt with my grief and I was ready for him. I spoke to the bereavement midwife about doing a support group in my area if there wasn't already one running.

"While I was researching on the internet and looking at various websites to see what was out there, I found SANDS Lothians' website. I contacted SANDS to see if I could go along and see what their Edinburgh group was like, with a view to setting one up in my area. I was then told that there was already a SANDS group in West Lothian and perhaps I may like to consider taking it on as they were looking for it to be run by someone more recently bereaved.

"I now run the SANDS group in West Lothian and liaise with staff at St John's Hospital, and by doing this I am able to help support others and I find it very therapeutic. It's a way forward that works for me. Theo's short life must hold meaning and more good still needs to be done in recognition of his being with us, even if it was for a short time. My work with SANDS Lothians is a tribute to him. I've done my befriending training now and, as well as running the West Lothian group, I get great pleasure from helping with SANDS work in general.

"It's so good to be able to pass thoughts and ideas onto parents in meetings and help them find ways of turning sad days into positive days and find ways to celebrate their baby's life rather than be overwhelmed by grief. People look for comfort in different ways and we try and make the groups as uplifting as possible. I try and get the parents to think how their baby would want to see them – would they want to see them devastated or doing something positive and happy?

"I am a great one for looking for signs and finding meaning in them. Some people may think it's daft or coincidence but who's to say what's right or wrong, and if it brings you comfort in your grief, then that has to be a great thing.

"Recently we all went to Findhorn in Scotland. I love rainbows, I always have, but especially because we played 'Somewhere over the Rainbow' at Theo's funeral. While we were driving up to Findhorn, the most beautiful rainbow appeared and our eldest son Lucas exclaimed, 'Look, Mummy, Theo's come on holiday with us!'

"On Theo's first birthday, I said to Gary that I just wanted a little time on my own and I wanted to listen to 'Somewhere over the Rainbow'. It was a cold winter's day and we'd had the first heavy snowfall of that year. I was looking out of the window, listening to the music. Suddenly, out of nowhere, there was a little white feather floating down from the sky, incredibly slowly, like a pendulum as if it were saying, 'Look at me, look at me.'

"I feel Theo sends us signs all the time. It's so wonderful and so comforting. Some people may be cynical about that sort of thing but I think believe what you want to believe. If it helps turn a difficult day into comforting positive day, where you are able to acknowledge your baby and it helps you through – do it."

"On 28th November last year, I had a phone call no one wants to receive, my 25-year-old daughter was on holiday in Ireland, [and] she said: 'I'm in hospital, I've had the baby and it's dead'.

"She had left us deliriously happy, three days earlier from our home in Spain. She was with good friends but I couldn't go to her till the next day. She was 22 weeks pregnant, she was in the hospital in Dublin where she couldn't have had better care.

"When I got there, we spent time with our beautiful girl and named her Elissa. I was broken hearted for myself, my daughter and my granddaughter. Also, my husband was left in Spain, unable to comfort us and relying on phone calls and texts.

"We have our darling baby's ashes, photos, etc here and her mum has since moved to England – I'm going over to spend our baby's birthday with her. We had so much love to give her [and we] feel cheated and so sad [but] will never forget our beautiful girl x."

Karyn Bates Grandmother

Rosalind Edith Christina Westendarp

"I fell pregnant when I was 29 years old. It was planned – we were three years into a happy, loving marriage. When the reality sank in, I remember feeling a little panicked and wondering if I was ready for motherhood, but my excitement soon outweighed any fears I might have.

"The first 25 weeks were completely problem-free. Unlike many women who are aware early on that something is wrong, I had no inkling of the heartache that lay ahead. My scans showed that our baby was developing well and, other than the odd cold, I was in good health – such good health, in fact, that I was still going for regular jogs in the park.

"Then one weekend, out of the blue, I started getting cramps. I remember thinking it was probably nothing. They were so mild that I still did my weekend jog as usual. My husband Luke was away down south with his work on the Tuesday night after this, and as the cramps were a little worse by then, I thought I would get an early night.

"The next day, Wednesday the 9th of February, I was due to go to Glasgow for a work meeting. I walked quite briskly to the station to make the train on time and, about half way there, I suddenly realised I was soaking wet down below. As it was my first pregnancy and I was only 25 and a half weeks in, I had no idea what it felt like when one's waters break and no expectation of it happening at that stage. I thought maybe I'd had a 'little accident' and was so embarrassed, especially when I had to attend this important meeting.

"I bought some sanitary pads and went into the toilets on the train to try to sort myself out, but by the time the train arrived in Glasgow I was all wet again. I decided to call the hospital in Edinburgh for advice and was told to go straight to hospital to get my symptoms checked out.

"I remember saying, 'No problem – I'll just take the train back to Edinburgh and get a taxi to the hospital'. However, the lady on the phone gave me a shock as she replied, quite firmly, 'No, I want you to go to the hospital in Glasgow right now – you haven't got time to come all the way back to Edinburgh'.

"At that point, I started to realise the situation might be more serious than I had thought. I ran out of the station feeling shaken and tearful, and took a taxi to the hospital. When I arrived there and found my way through the maze of corridors to the right place, I walked into a waiting room full of couples. I remember thinking, 'I can't do this – I'm on my own, miles from home, and all I can see are happy couples with perfect bumps'.

"I went up to reception in tears and explained that the hospital in Edinburgh had said I needed to be seen urgently. To my relief, the staff immediately sprang into action. They showed me to a bed for an examination and quickly realised that I was already dilated. I had a scan as well, which showed that my baby's heartbeat was strong and she was still moving. They weren't sure exactly what was going on, but it was clear that I had lost a lot of fluid.

"Then everything began to happen very quickly and, before I knew it, I was being whisked into a delivery room. Despite contractions coming on fast, I managed to phone my husband's office and told them I had to get in touch with him urgently, that I needed him to be with me as soon as possible.

"It was then that the harsh reality dawned – Luke was at least three hours away and I was all on my own in Glasgow giving birth to our baby, 15 weeks too early.

"Now as it happens, although both our families live in England, we are lucky enough to have a very supportive church community. Luke decided to ring a few friends from church as well as the church office itself. Without hesitation, the support worker at the church leapt on a train to come to be with me in Glasgow.

"It also turned out that a girl called Jess – the flatmate of another friend – was already in Glasgow studying at a bible college. This amazing girl – whom I had never even met – just dropped everything to come by my side. The kindness of people motivated by their faith is amazing. Judith and Jess had never been at a birth before, but they just walked into the delivery room, rolled up their sleeves and got stuck in. They were an incredible support – offering soothing words, massaging me and praying with me.

"I've often asked myself since then – if I got a phone call in the middle of my working day saying, 'There's a girl in Glasgow whom you've never met, but can you go and help her?' would I have? It's a challenging question for us all to ask ourselves.

"One of the worst moments of the whole ordeal was before Jess and Jude came, when the midwife asked me if there was anyone at all who could be with me. I remember feeling so crushed by that and so alone in a city where

I had no friends or family. The selflessness of Jess and Jude when I needed them most was amazing and my husband and I will be forever grateful.

"Everything happened very quickly in that delivery room and my labour was over in around three or four hours. I was on gas and air and morphine and was a bit spaced out, so I probably experienced an unreal sense of peace. I was aware that my baby was coming, but I don't think I had really processed what was happening, emotionally.

"I remember trying to focus on praying and on visualising a beach in Northumberland that is very dear to me. By pure coincidence, both my husband and I both know this stretch of coastline from holidays we had there as children, and it is somewhere that we still love to go to and where we had always imagined our children playing.

"When Rose was born, she was breathing but very limp. I didn't get to see her as she had to be taken quickly to a resuscitation table in the corner of the room. There must have been seven medics or more around that table trying to help her. I remember asking the doctor, 'Why can't I hear her cry?' They told me she had a tube in her mouth.

"I'd known that our baby was a girl since the 20-week scan. I'd always wanted a daughter and we had already named her before she was born. We had a very exciting five weeks buying baby girl clothes and I had been finishing off a patchwork baby quilt that I'd started long before Rose was even conceived. Now our baby girl was fighting for her life.

"They tried to resuscitate her for about 25 minutes, but she just wasn't responding at all. Then came the worst moment of my life – the doctor came over to tell me they were going to stop trying. There was nothing else they could do to save her.

"Poor Judith had the terrible job of phoning Luke to tell him his daughter had just died. I don't know how she made that phone call. At that point, he was in the taxi just arriving at the hospital, so he missed Rose coming into this world by a mere five minutes.

"As soon as he arrived, everyone left us alone together, which was exactly the right thing to do. I just clung to him for strength; I was so pleased to see him. It must have been such a dreadful room for him to walk into and I can only imagine the sense of frustration that he must have felt needing to be somewhere and not able to get there.

"Looking back, I think the midwives and the doctors handled everything very well – everyone was so kind and sensitive. One of the doctors knew that we were Christians and suggested that my husband and I look at Psalm 91, which talks about finding refuge under God's wings. It brought us great comfort then, and still does now.

"I didn't actually want to hold Rose; I found it too traumatic. There was a time when they tried to put her in my arms but I just couldn't bear it. It wasn't how I'd imagined holding my first child, I just couldn't do it. However, I remember at one point after she had died they tried to take her out of the room and I just cried out, 'Where are you taking her?' I didn't want to be parted from her.

"They handled that situation well, saying they would put her in a cot in my room and when I felt ready I could go and look at her. Again, that was exactly the right thing to do. Luke looked at her first and I remember his telling me she was so sweet. That helped me pluck up the courage to look at her, and I stroked her lovely little face and gave her a kiss.

"They let us both stay in the hospital that night. They suggested I have a shower while they took Rose away for a little wash and so they could take photos of her and copies of her footprints to give us as mementos. The midwife said she wanted us to know that all she was doing that night was looking after our daughter. That was just what we needed to hear.

"Sometimes, even now, I feel my attitude to her photos change day by day. There are days I can't believe she was actually inside me, this little person with perfect little hands and feet and a perfect little nose, a mind and soul and a heart. She was a perfect mixture of my husband and me. There are times I am in awe of the miracle of life. She was alive inside me for five precious months.

"Other times, I look at her picture and feel shock and sadness. This wasn't something I thought would ever happen in my life – you never think it's going to happen to you. I'd done everything right to get in optimum shape for having Rose, which made it harder to understand what had happened. I think that was a lesson in humility learned for both of us – the loss of a child can happen to anyone.

"The post-mortem showed that Rose was, as we thought, developing beautifully. However, I had got a urinary infection and the liquids in my womb had become infected as a result. Poor little Rose had been breathing that liquid in, which had caused her to develop pneumonia. It was the infection that caused me to go into labour early and tragically, because she was so small and because of the pneumonia, resuscitating her was just too difficult.

"We wanted Rose to be buried in Northumberland. It seemed the perfect place – it meant so much to both of us and to our families too. The funeral director agreed to bring her body down to Northumberland from Glasgow and arranged everything else. There is a peaceful little graveyard just near the coast where we were allowed to bury Rose.

"By weird coincidence, long before sad events took place, we'd actually booked a family holiday home in Northumberland on a date that turned out to be just two weeks after her death, so organising for family to be at the funeral was very straightforward, which was lucky, as neither Luke nor I had any fight left in us at that point.

"Planning the funeral service was actually very healing for Luke and I – choosing the readings, prayers and music gave us both something to focus on in those bleak, sorrowful days after her death. It also allowed us to express our love for our daughter.

"In fact, ever since losing Rose, I've found making and doing things for her very healing. I've done pottery for several years and so I made her a tile decorated with the words from one of the songs we had at her funeral. I have also made her a patchwork bag to keep her cards in and am planning to frame her footprints next. Any way I can show my daughter love is a help – especially since I can't hold her and kiss her as other mothers can their daughters.

"My husband and I also find it very peaceful to pray at her grave and plant flowers there – we have snowdrops there that bloom around the time she was born.

"Luke and I had long had a deep faith, but it was strengthened during this dark time. We really felt that God was looking after us. We are sure he played a hand in all the things that happened that helped bring us comfort and smooth an otherwise agonising path. Jude and Jess coming to help me when I was all alone and needed them the most, the funeral being so easy to organise and the fact that we had the holiday planned just in the right place at the time we needed it.

"Day by day, praying got us through the darkness. Even now, anytime I feel really upset I ask God to hold my daughter extra close and love her. I take comfort from knowing that Rose has peace, joy and light and is completely free from all the trials of this life. Sometimes on the days when my pain has been at its worst, I have found consolation in knowing that my daughter will never have to feel this.

"In terms of what friends and family can do to help bereaved parents, it's important that they don't think they shouldn't mention the child you lost 'in case it upsets you'. What they need to realise is that you think about that child every day, and not talking about her or acknowledging her makes things worse. It doesn't have to be a long conversation, just a simple 'I'm so sorry' is enough.

"I know people often feel awkward around grief – it's the elephant in the room. I understand it's hard, but even just sending a text or a card, or making a clumsy attempt at saying sorry is better than nothing. Rose is our beloved first born – part of our family – and we love to hear that people remember and love her too.

"The other advice I'd give is to just spend quiet time with the parents – be there to listen, but don't try to distract them by talking about other things. When you are so raw inside, it's hard to focus on other things and it can really wear you down trying to engage in conversations that just don't seem to matter. You feel like an absent party in those conversations and it can be very draining.

"Perhaps people's intentions are to remind you that life goes on, but a grief that is raw and that deep is all consuming and the cracks can't simply be papered over. Rose was such a blessing to us, she taught us so many things. I used to always panic that if someone told me about some terrible circumstance they were going through, I would have to say something clever to ease their suffering. Rose taught me that of course you can't fix things for them; you can just listen and be there when people need you.

"Going for counselling was incredibly helpful. I first heard about SANDS Lothians from my Edinburgh midwife when she came to visit me at home in the fortnight after Rose died. She too, was so moved by everything that had happened and she just listened when I needed to talk. I think one of her colleagues had done some work experience with SANDS and she recommended that I go and see them, so I did soon afterwards.

"I had 'one to one' sessions at SANDS Lothians as I found the group atmosphere wasn't quite right for me. I remember feeling as if I was made of eggshells – I was so fragile – talking with the counsellor at SANDS Lothians was exactly what I needed.

"I saw a counsellor at my church as well, and together with SANDS Lothians, I drew such strength from these two sources of help – both after losing Rose and then again when I was pregnant with my second child, Rufus and terrified of losing him too.

"I found seeing other people with their babies very tough for a long time after Rose died. Five of our friends gave birth that year, and it was incredibly hard to read their texts and emails announcing the births, and looking at the happy pictures of them with their newborns was just too much to bear.

"It was really difficult to send them a card with my love and best wishes, but I remember thinking that as much as showing love was painful, not showing love would be even more damaging. It took all my strength to send the cards though, to write that I was happy for them, even though I was yearning for my own child so desperately.

"I feel I endured two types of grief when I lost Rose. The first grief was because she was my first child and I was left with the terrible feeling that I would never hold a healthy child in my arms. I can't even begin to explain the pain of that grief. Every time I saw a mother pushing a pram, it hurt. Every time I saw a mother with a baby in her arms, it hurt.

"Then there was the grief of losing a particular child, who is completely unique and irreplaceable. Even if I go on to have another fifty daughters, none of them will ever replace Rose. It is really important that people understand that – even if you have other children, you still always grieve for the one you lost.

"When I found out that my second child, Rufus, was a boy, I had a brief moment of wishing he were a girl. However, I quickly realised it was much better to have a boy – he was his own wonderful little person and perhaps that would help people understand that one child doesn't replace another, a son doesn't replace a daughter.

"I know SANDS are there for me if I need them in the future. I have this niggling hunch that we won't have another girl. I would of course absolutely love another son to be a brother to Rufus too. I find it easy to contemplate that and to think of boys' names, but I can't even bring myself to think of girls' names – I just can't let myself go there.

"One comfort I take is that even if I don't have another daughter of my own, perhaps one day Rufus will marry a lovely girl and I will have a daughter-in-law. Or maybe someone may make me godmother to a beautiful girl or one day I may even have a granddaughter."

When asked what advice Amy would give to other bereaved parents, she says: "The thing that kept me going was my faith, but I think my advice could be interpreted in a non-faith based way too. I would start each day praying to God and asking Him to show how I could learn a bit more that day, how I could love more. I asked Him to put someone in my path each day whom I could love, so that I could feel there was a point to going on.

"So my advice is to take things day by day, and try to do something small, like send someone a card, or buy a gift or make a phone call, something that takes you out of yourself and helps you think of others.

"Doing something for charity can really help you feel like life has a point too. I found my work for the Kenya Street kid's charity that I am trustee for very, very helpful in my recovery. Doing things like this help you feel there is meaning to each day and a reason to go on, and, gradually, you begin to find your way through the darkness.

"Also, I would advise you to talk as much as you can to good listeners with sympathetic ears. Check in with your partner at the end of every day and talk about anything that has upset or hurt you that day. I would say that the most difficult thing of all is to forgive people who hurt you by saying or doing the wrong thing, but that as hard as forgiving may be, carrying anger and resentment is far harder.

"Above all, try to trust that one day. The deeply painful grief you feel will be replaced with feelings of overwhelming love towards the child you have lost. Try to trust that your child is in God's loving hands, and that they have all the peace and joy that you could wish for them."

Grace Wilkinson

Lesley begins: "Grace was my first baby and my pregnancy was perfectly healthy all the way through and I always only had a very neat little bump. Everyone said one morning I'd wake up and suddenly have this huge bump! At around 30 weeks, I went to a midwife appointment, where I was measured. Then at the appointment after that, at 34 weeks, I was asked if I felt I was getting any bigger. I said no, not really, but they reassured me that everything was ok.

"I was told that since the last measurements, I hadn't grown but that my baby was fine and the heartbeat strong. To be on the safe side, the midwife arranged to send me to the hospital for a check up. I couldn't get an appointment for a growth scan for over 2½ weeks. It was frustrating as it seemed a very long time to wait if the growth of my baby was a concern, but I'd been reassured everything was fine, so I tried not to worry.

"The day of my scan eventually arrived and I asked my husband, Gordon, to come along. I think I may have had a gut feeling that something wasn't right. I was scanned thoroughly, the heartbeat was strong but the scan continued for some time. I was then sent up to the ward and put on a machine to do the baby's heart trace. The sonographer said she wanted a doctor to look at the scan results, and that she would get him to come and speak to us.

"I then became aware of a doctor and nurse standing talking at the door to the ward, and I just knew something was wrong. They came over and began to ask me a lot of questions – had I been a smoker or a drinker, but they still didn't tell me what was wrong. It was horrible and I had to ask outright what was going on. They said the baby was really small for its gestation. I asked them how small, 6lb? Less? Then came the shock reply – 3lbs.

"They explained that they couldn't see anything obviously wrong, but the baby wasn't growing, so the best thing was for it to come out. I was booked in for an elective caesarean section on the Monday morning but had to go in every day until then to be kept an eye on.

"I went in for my section and had a beautiful baby girl. They showed her to us quickly. She wasn't crying, just whimpering quietly, and then they took her away. My husband went with her and came back shortly afterwards, saying she was fine.

"Back on the ward, a young doctor came to speak to me. I'll always remember the gentle and kind way he spoke to me. He knelt down so that he was at my level rather than standing over me and talking down. He touched my hand, comfortingly. He told me my baby, whom we'd named Grace, was in the neonatal unit. He said her condition was grave. She was breathing on her own but they thought there was something wrong but they weren't sure what."

Lesley continues: "They moved me into a side room which instantly increased my anxiety levels. I felt I was being separated from everyone else. All the other women on the ward had lovely healthy babies and I didn't. I was heartbroken.

"Mum and Dad and Gordon's mum were due in that afternoon. The midwives had come down with a few Polaroids of Grace and shortly after that, Gordon came into the room and walked over to the window. He was white as a sheet. I asked him what was wrong and he told me that a doctor was coming to see us.

"Soon after that, the doctor came in. We were told that they thought our daughter had Spina Bifida. Apparently, she could dislocate her thumb and when she was born, she had a bit of skin on the back of her head about the size of a 10p piece, that hadn't knitted together properly. The spacing between her eyes wasn't as it should be either. She was in perfect proportion and normally newborns' heads are bigger than their bodies. These were all indications that something was wrong.

"The doctor then dropped a bombshell on us and, brutally to the point, said that, if Grace did have Spina Bifida she would be disabled and have severe learning difficulties. She'd never walk and she'd probably have epilepsy. A long list of terrible possibilities was reeled off, but still they couldn't say for certain what was wrong with our baby. I remember thinking, I must be dreaming, this wasn't happening.

"As the doctor turned and walked out, my mum and dad appeared and I had to tell them the terrible news. We were all left to digest this dreadful turn of events, but nothing else was explained to us further.

"My husband took my parents up to see their granddaughter and then we all had a good cry. Later, the doctors came back in and confirmed that there was definitely something wrong with Grace and they had to send her to a specialist children's hospital for further investigations and tests. They had taken blood to do chromosome testing, but the results of those tests would take a few weeks to come back."

Lesley recalls: "All the time we'd been in the hospital the midwives had been amazing. They made up a makeshift bed so that Gordon could sleep on the floor so that he didn't have to leave me.

"The following morning they put me in a wheelchair to take me up to see Grace. She was breathing on her own but was having her pulse monitored. They gave me a cushion so that I was able to hold her before they transferred her. It was so lovely to cuddle my baby and to see her up close at last. Later in the afternoon they brought my daughter into my room in her incubator so I could have some more time with her. Then I had to be parted from her as she was transferred to the children's hospital and I had to stay where I was. Her daddy went with her so she wasn't alone. He wanted to stay with me, but I made him go.

"While Gordon was away with Grace, they let my mum come in out with normal visiting hours as normally it's only the father who can do that. Gordon travelled between the two hospitals to check on his wife and daughter. This was what he was determined to do but, clearly, he was exhausted.

"He would go and see Grace in the morning then come straight back to tell me how she was, then he would return to see Grace in the afternoon, and then come back to me again in the evening. Some days, he would go back to see Grace yet again, later at night before going home.

"On the Thursday morning, I just woke up and decided I was leaving the hospital. They wanted to keep me in until the Friday to give me more time to recover but I was adamant. I had to be with my baby. They agreed to let me go on the understanding that I wouldn't walk far and that I took it as easy as possible.

"A few days later, the doctor wanted to see us. He and a nurse took us into a little room. He told us that Grace's brain scan had shown a few pockets of air on her brain but nothing substantial. They knew there was something wrong with her eyes. They had done a heart scan and an MRI scan which were fine, so they thought the problem was congenital. By the time doctors at the children's hospital had done their tests, they were no longer saying it was Spina Bifida, but they still said they didn't know what it was and were finding it hard to narrow the possibilities down.

"I remember wishing it had been something obvious as nobody seemed to know anything for certain. They then said she was well enough to go back to the hospital where she was originally born, so that night she was transferred back in her incubator and we were right back where we started, no further forward.

"Gordon and I spent the night with our beautiful daughter and she seemed to be doing OK. The next morning she was in a little Moses basket as she was managing to retain her body heat. She only had a feeding tube in by this time and she looked like a normal tiny little baby. Before Grace was born, my sister had had a premature baby who was only an ounce heavier than Grace, so I was still optimistic that everything would be fine.

"We were encouraged to look after her like a normal baby and were allowed to change her clothes and bathe her. Still we had no firm diagnosis and no long-term prognosis for our daughter. We continued like this for about two weeks then we were called in for a meeting with the genetic counsellor.

"The blood tests had shown that part of one of Grace's chromosomes was missing. It was quite a large deletion and they say the larger the deletion, the more pronounced the problem. They now knew which chromosome it was and at last we had a diagnosis. Our baby had Wolf-Hirschhorn syndrome, a very rare condition that only affects 1 in every 50,000 births.

"We were given leaflets for a support group to help us get more information and help. We were told that this condition would be quite debilitating but there were records of sufferers living until their late thirties. Apparently, the syndrome could come in varying degrees but affected everything down the centre of the body and usually there were also problems with their heart, kidneys, eyes and their skin not forming properly. It would also come with quite profound learning difficulties and epilepsy.

"It felt like we'd been on a rollercoaster ride of emotions. It was so hard going from thinking I had a healthy pregnancy, then a perfect but tiny baby, then to try and come to terms with the fact that she wasn't well, then to be given a little hope after being discharged from the children's hospital, only to come crashing down again and be hit with just how ill she was and how uncertain her future was.

"This was made all the more difficult by the doctors' telling us that they were still only 85-95 per cent sure this was what they were dealing with. Neither Gordon nor I were carriers of the faulty gene; it was just one of those things."

Lesley continues: "We were allowed to take her out of the cot for cuddles. As Gordon and I came to terms with the news we had received about our daughter, we quickly decided – stop, no more tears. This was our baby, she is what she is and we love her dearly. I would send anyone away who came in and cried. We had to be strong, find a way to cope and move on for our daughter. We found inner strength from somewhere and quickly agreed that there was nothing to be gained by dwelling on what might have been.

"It had also been discovered that when Grace was born, she had a heart valve that didn't close properly and we had always been aware that she may need to have some keyhole surgery. I would go into the hospital to be with her all day and wouldn't leave until about 9 o'clock at night. There was nowhere else I wanted to be.

"I was able to feed her and bathe her. Then one day I went in and Grace was a terrible colour and immediately, I just knew that something was wrong. However, the midwives told me not to worry, they thought it was just a little infection and they had taken urine samples to find out more. I held and cuddled my baby and told Gordon to come to the hospital because I just knew something wasn't right at all, and I was getting really agitated.

"Her breathing was very strange but I was told it was just because she was sleeping on and off. Again, I had a gut instinct it was something more and asked one of the midwives to take another look at her. We were then given the terrible news that her heartbeat had become erratic and her heart was failing. They told us they thought the end was near, and we were moved to the family room.

"We were then just left with Grace, holding her waiting for her to slip away. Our hearts were breaking. We had stayed so strong and positive for our daughter and now we were losing her. I held her close. The doctor came in and checked her, then they asked again what we wanted them to do.

"They could still try and operate on her but her chances of coming through were slim because she was so small. We came to the decision that she'd had enough, and we didn't want to put her through any more. I just remember looking at her eyes and I knew she was tired and weary. I didn't want people to think we were giving in. I just knew it was the right thing to do.

"We sat with her and our little Grace continued to cling to life. There were a number of times I thought she'd gone but then she'd move again. The midwives were wonderful and they encouraged us to make the most of this precious time. We talked to her and took lots of photos and got pictures of her foot and handprints. Then a doctor came in and said there was still a possibility that it was just an infection and there was still a chance. No one seemed to know anything for certain; it was utter agony for us, like a slow torture. The doctor just kept asking us if we were sure, which just made everything so much more difficult.

"So, in desperation, I just said, 'If you think you can save her – just take her.'

"The doctor took Grace away and was only away about ten minutes or so when the midwife came running back into the room and said, 'You need to come with me, quickly'. We followed her to our baby and were told that her heart was finally failing. We were just in time to hold her once more then she passed away in my arms. It was the 8th of August. Grace had fought for her life for nearly three weeks."

Lesley bravely goes on: "It was desperately hard to leave her, but we eventually went home. The day after, we had to go back in for a meeting. We had to walk through the ward to reach the doctor's office and that was so difficult. Then while we were sitting in his room waiting, I saw a clear plastic bag sitting on the shelf and suddenly realised all my baby's things were in the bag.

"The doctor explained that they wanted to take samples from Grace to examine. Because she had had a chromosome disorder, they wanted to take samples of her brain tissue. That was so hard to hear. On one hand, I wanted to know more but on the other hand, because we had a good idea already what was wrong, I just didn't want them to touch her. However, they encouraged us to have a post-mortem so they could learn more about the disorder and more about what had happened to Grace. I then agreed, as long as they didn't touch her brain or her heart. I just couldn't bear that. They explained fully about everything that would be done during the post-mortem and that they wouldn't and couldn't do anything without our consent.

"We then believed that Grace was taken somewhere in town for the post-mortem but we didn't know where. We kept phoning the hospital to ask what was happening and they just kept telling us she wasn't back yet. We felt stuck in limbo; it felt like everything was taking an eternity. This frustrated my husband so much that he got the Yellow Pages out to try and find out where she could be. He looked for the phone numbers of any of the places she could possibly be and rang them one by one.

"We eventually found where she was and soon after got a call from the funeral director to say they had released her body, and we were finally able to have her funeral.

"The funeral was very comforting. She was in a little white coffin and they let us hold her in the front seat of the funeral car. We buried our beautiful little Grace in our local cemetery. We bought a family plot so that we could all be together again one day."

Recalling how they gradually moved on, Lesley says: "I fell pregnant again the following summer. We'd been on holiday in Turkey and, afterwards, my husband always said he had felt all the way through the holiday that I'd been pregnant. There was no firm reason why he thought that, it was just a feeling. Then one day, while on holiday, we had been looking for a watch for him and my husband had been busy trying on various styles. Then, bizarrely, out of the blue, the shopkeeper then turned to my husband and said, 'You get discount because your wife is having a baby'- we were both gobsmacked!

"It was all so strange. I hadn't even suspected I was pregnant at the time. The day I came back from holiday I did a pregnancy test and guess what – I was pregnant! So my husband and a Turkish stranger knew I was pregnant before I did!

"Because of my history, I was monitored carefully and given regular scans. My first scan was when I was only around 7-8 weeks pregnant. They had warned me not to get upset if there was no heartbeat as it was so early, but the scan showed there was a heartbeat already. I then had scans almost every month. They then sent us to a genetic counsellor to discuss all the testing that they could do. I opted for nothing, no tests, not one. People close to me thought I was absolutely crazy.

However, after Grace had died, I had asked if I'd been tested during her pregnancy, would anything have shown up? I was told, probably not as it was such a rare disorder. I then thought, what would I have done with the information even if I had it?

"Gordon and I decided the new baby would be our baby, and we would love her with all our hearts, whatever happened – just as we had done with Grace.

"My pregnancy progressed well and, in January 2007, we had another little girl whom we called Georgia."

Asked when she first heard about SANDS Lothians, Lesley reflects: "We'd been given leaflets at the hospital but in the beginning, I didn't feel comfortable about going to meetings. After Grace's funeral, I went into lock down and isolated myself from everybody. The only person I would see would be my husband and my parents. I would only offload to my husband when he got home from work.

"Months after that time, I remember thinking, my poor husband, he must have wondered what would be waiting for him every time he turned the key in the door!

"During that bleak spell, if I had to go to the shops, I would go at night-time for fear of bumping into anyone who didn't know what had happened and I'd have to explain things to them. Sometimes, I would see people who did know what had happened and they'd cross the road – that was worse! I felt I didn't get much support from my GP and almost felt left just to get on with things. I wasn't referred to a counsellor or anywhere else for extra help.

"I gradually became more and more depressed and my mum started to come round every morning to make sure I was ok. One day, around three to four weeks after Grace died, there was a knock at the door. It was the health visitor. I originally thought she'd come to check how I was healing after the caesarean section but in fact, she said she was here to do Grace's six-week health check. I just sat there in shock. My mum was furious and in anger, retorted, 'Grace died two weeks ago and they've just buried her!' The health visitor simply said, 'Don't worry, dear, these things happen, you'll get over it', and left.

Lesley continues: "You wonder how there can be these catastrophic errors in communication and record keeping and it wasn't the only one. When I had gone for my post-natal check up I'd had to tell them again that Grace had died, then when I fell pregnant with Georgia, the doctor said, 'That's good – your babies will be nice and close together' and again, I had to tell them my first baby had died."

Lesley says: "I know that SANDS Lothians produce little 'Teardrop Stickers' that can be put on your medical records to show that you've lost a baby to stop these very painful blunders. It is such a shame because the charity is working so hard to try and stop you being asked awkward questions and still these things happen.

"Luckily, when Georgia was born, the midwife told me that everyone in the delivery room knew my situation so there was no chance that anyone would ask anything that would cause me distress. That helped me so much. I wanted that time to be about the joy of the new baby arriving and not be spoilt by there being a difficult atmosphere. To save me unnecessary anxiety, I was induced with Georgia and she was born three weeks early. Despite this, she weighed in at 7lb 13oz, double the size of Grace.

"It was after Georgia was born that I went to the SANDS Lothians' meetings in my area. Initially, it was more to see if they needed any help. By helping others, it helped me. I used to feel my life was over after losing Grace and it was good to be able to reassure others in the position that I once was, that life goes on.

Asked what advice Lesley can give to others in a similar situation to hers, she says: "Don't look too far forward, don't give up hope and take each day as it comes. Just because it happened once doesn't mean it will happen again. With a genetic disorder comes a lot of guilt but try not to blame yourself. You can be bombarded with information and it can get quite overwhelming but pick out the pieces that matter and process everything a bit at a time. Try not to over analyse things or read too much between the lines. Take things at face value and most of all, do what's right for you."

And concluding, she says: "Come to the group meetings. You can say anything and you will never be judged. We're not the old-fashioned style of support group where everyone sits in a circle thoroughly miserable. We sit having cups of tea and cake and although we have a shared grief our meetings are light hearted and fun and very often we end up having a really good giggle!"

Erin Wright

For Lisa Wright, the stillbirth of her daughter Erin was not the end. It was the beginning of the most tortuous phase of her life, and closure still eludes her.

Lisa met Erin's dad in 2006 and they were only together a short while before Lisa fell pregnant with Erin, a much wanted and planned pregnancy. Lisa had suffered an early miscarriage shortly before falling pregnant with Erin so, to put her mind at rest, she had extra hospital checks and paid to have some additional scans privately to ensure all was well. She was reassured that the pregnancy progressed smoothly. She had wanted children all her life and was determined to keep her unborn baby safe and well.

Erin was due on July 1st and Lisa went into labour on July 3rd. The labour was long and very painful and would change Lisa's life forever. Sadly, not in a good way.

"We didn't know it at the time, but Erin had been facing occipito-posterior (back to back) and this was perhaps a contributory factor to the level of pain," Lisa recalls.

"Since Erin's birth, I am an avid watcher of *One Born Every Minute* and I'm pretty certain that the way Erin was lying should have been picked up through an internal examination or, at the very least, I felt that I should have been checked and monitored more.

"My labour continued to be very painful and I was convinced something was stuck in my ribs – perhaps it was a foot, I don't know. I had started with gas and air for pain relief, then had pethidine injections before moving onto an epidural which didn't work properly and I could still feel severe pain down one side."

Lisa continues: "I was on a lot of drugs, but I was aware that something wasn't right. Both present at the birth, Erin's dad and my mum, who has four children, became increasingly agitated that things were not progressing as they should. Even the midwife in attendance seemed to become concerned and called In the consultant.

"Unfortunately, the presence of the consultant didn't improve the situation one bit, and real fear began to take over. The consultant spoke in broken English, and he was hard to understand. There seemed to be a great deal of confusion, and there appeared to be a breakdown of communication between the consultant and the anaesthetist. I was very, very scared, but it was my first child. I didn't know any better. I trusted them."

Lisa goes on, tearfully: "Everyone tried to reassure me, telling me my baby was fine. However, I'd been pushing a long time and nothing was happening and that's when the doctor first mentioned he would use forceps to deliver my baby. As my contractions had stopped, the doctor said he didn't want to use the forceps without the aid of a contraction so I was given something to restart my contractions. Again, this had no effect, so the doctor decided to go ahead with the forceps delivery anyway.

"When Erin was finally delivered, she was purple and floppy. I remember my mum saying, 'Should she be that colour?' Erin was rushed away, and, again, I was reassured everything was fine and she would just need a little help with breathing. By this time, I was bleeding heavily."

Lisa continues: "My mum sent Erin's dad out of the room to find out what was going on as they had been gone a while. Shortly afterwards, he returned with the paediatrician to tell me, that Erin had been born with no sign of life.

"No sign of life. How could that be? How? She was strong and active throughout the pregnancy. She had been monitored closely. Her heartbeat had been strong throughout labour. She was a good weight – 6lb 15oz. They *must* be wrong.

"The following hours and days were a complete blur. After the birth, I was put in what I now know was the family room – a room specifically for parents that had lost babies. I was lying on the bed there with Erin in between me and her dad – she just looked like she was sleeping. There was nothing wrong with her. I just couldn't understand what was happening.

"The next day they asked if I wanted a post-mortem carried out – I said no. I went to pieces. I *knew* there was nothing wrong with her; she'd been alive up to the last minute. I didn't want her subjected to anymore trauma. The irony of the request for a post-mortem was magnified when the doctors told me there was a 99 per cent chance they wouldn't find anything.

"The nightmare continued. On the day of Erin's funeral, I had to be taken to the doctors as I'd been stitched so badly after the birth that I was in agony. At the service, everyone tried to offer words of comfort, but all I wanted was my baby. My mum thought she saw the midwife who had been in attendance at the birth, at the funeral, but we couldn't be sure. However, someone sent me a lovely bay tree shortly after the funeral and to this day I have no idea who it was from.

"In the days after Erin's death, we involved a solicitor and made a complaint against the hospital. Horrifyingly, it came to light that the same doctor had been involved in another traumatic birth that had resulted in the death of a baby the year before.

"After Erin's delivery, the consultant involved in my case was put on supervised duties, then his contract was not renewed. I also heard shortly after that the midwife involved had gone on sick leave. Later, when I would go on to have my next two daughters, I was treated like royalty, from start to finish. Yes, there's every possibility all these events happening together were all coincidences, but if it were you, what would that tell you?

"The complaint we made against the hospital went to an independent authority. The notes had been written up after the event, but there were bits missing. When the query was raised about Erin's heartbeat being strong throughout, I was told it must have been my heartbeat they were picking up. How? The baby had its own heart monitor and isn't the baby's heartbeat usually much faster than the mother's? It was unbearably hard.

"I felt we weren't being listened to because we weren't medically minded. Nothing in the notes seemed to reflect the chaos in the room, the confusion and the lack of communication. It wasn't an accurate portrayal of what happened. Surely, the fact that the staff had had to resort to writing up their notes on paper towels speaks volumes. Unbelievably, the outcome of the complaint was *'nothing untoward'*. My baby should never have died. I'd been subjected to the most traumatic experience of my life involving a doctor already implicated in another baby's death and yet the conclusion was 'nothing untoward' happened. How?"

Lisa continues: "To add insult to injury, I had to go back to the hospital around a month after Erin's birth for the results of the hospital's internal investigation."

She then painfully recalls how the senior obstetrician rolled out the graph showing her baby's heart trace during the birth. Incredulously, she relays the doctor's words as he pointed to various stages on the graph, 'This is when Erin's fine, this is when she's distressed, this is when I would have delivered her,' and then moving considerably further up the graph, he continues, 'and this is when she was delivered'."

His words, combined with the graphic illustration, were like a knife through Lisa's heart, which was twisted further still when the doctor concluded, 'I'm really sorry. This should never have happened.'

Nothing untoward? Lisa had to live with the fact that because there was no proof, nothing in writing and nothing to substantiate negligence, no action could be taken.

Lisa's life fell apart. The year that followed was a complete blur. She says: "Erin's dad and I had stretched ourselves financially to get the best house we could for our baby and to live in as a family but I couldn't go back to work. I ended up on antidepressants. I went from being a strong independent woman to a shell of the person I had once been.

"Erin died in the July, her dad proposed to me at Christmas, perhaps his way of trying to paper over the cracks, and then he left me for another woman in the March.

"Looking back, I'm sure he was trying to deal with his grief too, but I was so angry with him. He told me I was no longer the same person. How could I be?! I still feel anger towards him – he left me at the worst time of my life."

Lisa continues: "I eventually tried to go back to work, but it was too much. My boss had restructured everything, which made it incredibly hard for me to integrate back in. I felt like I was on autopilot. I was having panic attacks and I just couldn't function. I lost my job, then my house, then came the inevitable debt that piles up from having no income, yet just trying to live and get by. I struggled desperately to come to terms with my loss. I felt like my baby had been murdered and, despite everything, no one had been held accountable."

The torture of living with 'why' stays with Lisa daily, but the agony of imagining the 'what ifs' is just as hard.

"I have two more beautiful daughters now and they are my world. They are amazing – they do something different and magical every day. They bring me such joy and are a great strength to me. However, having other children doesn't change my pain. You can never replace a lost baby. I've wanted children my whole life but after I lost Erin, going on to have my girls, Laila and Rosie, just amplified my loss and the devastating circumstances under which it happened.

"I almost feel really guilty saying this, but I even began to envy parents who knew why their child had died and could find some solace in their grief."

Lisa continues: "I never get closure – I thought it would get easier having more children, but it just gets harder. I adore my girls, but there's still one missing. I can't help but make comparisons when my other girls reach milestones like birthdays and going to nursery and school. My feelings of loss and anger over what happened to Erin are getting stronger, they're not subsiding. I always find myself thinking 'What if Erin had lived, what would she have looked like? What would her first day of school been like?' The ache of losing her never leaves me.

"My experience even tainted my pregnancies with Laila and Rosie. Rosie's pregnancy mirrored Erin's so my anxiety levels went through the roof and, with Laila, I almost cut myself off from my pregnancy. I almost didn't register I was pregnant. Perhaps it was denial, perhaps self-preservation. I needed counselling throughout my pregnancy as I was so nervous about the birth, and I was adamant that I wanted to know who was going to deliver my baby. I was petrified of giving birth. I elected to have a caesarean section. I couldn't bring myself to go through a normal delivery – I even felt I'd been robbed of that experience. I don't think I will ever be able to give birth naturally again.

"The circumstances under which I lost my beautiful first-born daughter have caused me irreparable damage. It is a bereavement I know I will never get over; I just have to find a way to live with it.

"I feel I've had everything. I had a miscarriage before Erin, then the trauma of losing Erin, then the anxiety around Laila's birth, then after Laila, I tried for two years to get pregnant, but I then had an ectopic pregnancy and had to have an emergency operation to have a fallopian tube removed. Luckily, I then fell pregnant with Rosie a couple of months after losing the fallopian tube.

"I hope nature will take its course and one day I'll have more children, but it's not been an easy journey. Erin died the day before my birthday. I have never celebrated my birthday since. I have to wait until afterwards – it's too much of a jump in emotions – it's too hard going from being devastated one day to celebrating the next.

"I've told the girls about Erin. They know they have a big sister and she's very much part of the family. I have her picture and a photo of her little footprints at home. We go to visit her at the cemetery two or three times a year.

"I married my husband David, Laila and Rosie's daddy, in 2010. We have been friends all of our lives, so he knows my history and what I have been through. He looks on Erin as part of his life, and he instinctively knows when to give me space when I have off days.

"I often try to think how best to describe the mixture of grief and happiness that I have to live with, and the best thing that comes to mind is that it is a never-ending race. Most days, I am in front but, on some occasions, grief overtakes me briefly, until my happiness kicks in again – mostly, thanks to my girls and my husband – and then I am in front again, pushing the grief behind me a bit more.

"I was in touch with SANDS Lothians from the day Erin passed and received some counselling. When I became pregnant with Rosie, I came to the pregnancy support meeting. This was such a massive help to me and I quickly realised that here I could say anything and no one would tell me I was being daft or neurotic! Although all our circumstances were different, our feelings were the same.

"I will definitely come back to SANDS Lothians for more counselling. I know it won't bring Erin back. She was taken from me and there is nothing more I can do about it, but I know the team at SANDS Lothians are there for me at every stage of my grief and they will help bring me a little relief from my heartbreak and hopefully, one day, some peace.

"I wish I could say my grief goes away, but it doesn't. It never goes away, but I am gradually learning to live with it every day, and it is a great comfort to know that SANDS Lothians are here for the days that I can't."

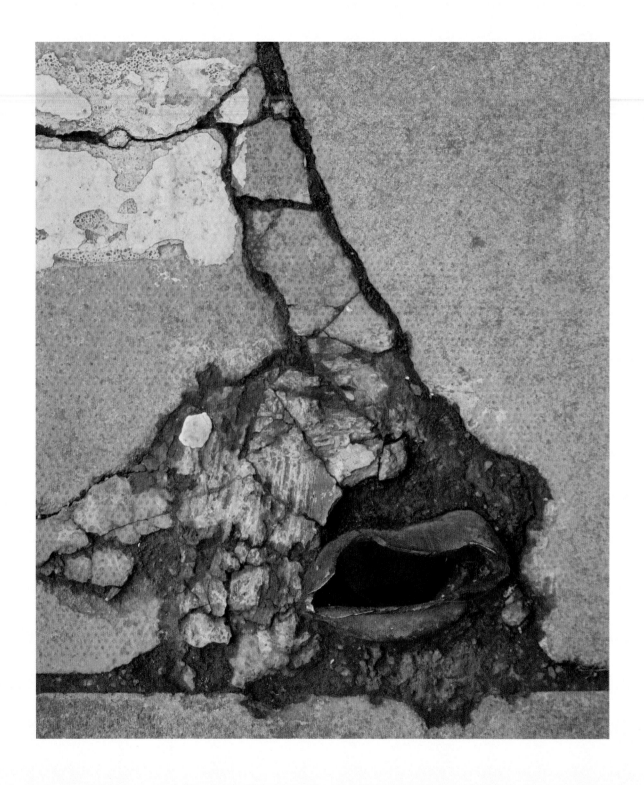

FATHERS' STORIES

"There is a sacredness in tears ...They are not the mark of weakness but of power.
They are messengers of overwhelming grief ...and of unspeakable love."

Washington Irving 1783-1859

Graham James Dickson

9 October 1998

Terry begins: "Graham was born on the 9th October 1998, and about 16 hours later on the 10th he died. He was born at 28 weeks, 12 weeks too early.

"All the way through the pregnancy, my ex-wife Sharon had various scares and some bleeding. At 23 weeks, 6 days, and a few hours into the pregnancy, she started having contractions, but they put these down to being Braxton Hicks. We went into hospital but because she was below 24 weeks they seemed to give her fairly basic monitoring. Then as the hours continued to pass and she passed the 24-week milestone, the attitude of the health professionals completely changed. The next four weeks she spent the majority of the time in hospital.

"Then, on Friday the 9th of October, she started to have contractions again. This time they seemed more worried and moved her from the downstairs ward to the labour suite upstairs. That had happened a few times throughout that four-week period, but this time everything seemed more imminent.

"My son Graham was delivered at 7.40pm on the Friday night. Sharon had pressed the buzzer to say the baby was coming, but we were told she was mistaken. She continued to insist he was definitely coming and everyone then leapt into action."

Terry reflects: "Shortly after my son was born and they had cut the umbilical cord, I remember seeing a doctor in blue scrubs come running along the corridor. He took Graham away and took him straight up to the neo-natal unit. For the next two and a half hours, we weren't told anything or given any information as to what was happening. It was about 11pm before we were able to go up to see Graham.

"I was aware of the fact that the same doctor I'd seen running down the corridor was still there. I think he was one of the leading doctors. He stabilised Graham and some photos were taken of him. We knew from the outset that his lungs were just not strong enough. Sharon had been given various different drugs before the birth to help with the development of the baby's lungs. Her waters had broken at around 16-17 weeks so there was no fluid left. We spent the next few hours in the neo-natal ward with our son. Sharon then went back down to the ward and I went home.

"The following morning, I phoned the hospital to see how Sharon and Graham were," Terry continues. "I was told that I should go in. Sharon already had a daughter from a previous relationship; she was only five. Initially, I wasn't going to take her in, but I changed my mind and we both went in. I arrived at the hospital around 10am.

"Soon after this, the doctor told Sharon and I that the outlook for our son didn't look promising. It was the same doctor who had been there the day before. He hadn't been home all night. He must have done around 30 hours by that point. He was incredible, and he looked after our son so well.

"Just after 12.30pm, Graham passed away. We had been asked what religion we were. We said Catholic and then the priest came in to baptise Graham and give him his last rites. The priest had left Mass to come and do this for Graham. Our beautiful little boy's lungs had just not been strong enough for him to survive. He'd been on a ventilator since he was born.

"It was the first time I've seen anything like that on such a small scale. It was a bit of a shock as the tubes had been so tiny, so minuscule and Graham was only the size of my hand."

Terry continues: "We spent the next 22 hours in the SANDS' Family Room with Graham before he was taken to the mortuary. We eventually returned home on the Sunday. I knew I would then have the job of registering my son's birth and his death.

"When I arrived in the building, I was told to take a seat, and then I was aware of everyone else leaving the room. I began to get a bit stressed and irate as I was conscious that I'd left Sharon at home and I still had a lot to do. I remember thinking, please hurry up. It wasn't until a few years later that I realised when it comes to registering the birth and death of a child, they clear everyone out of the room so that the bereaved parent has some privacy.

"I registered Graham's birth and death. There must have been about three registrars there and they all took good care of me, offering their condolences. I almost felt like I was having an out-of-body experience. It was so hard to take in the events of the last few hours. I then had to go down to the Department of Work and Pensions to hand in the form for the birth and death. The person behind the counter asked me if I'd received any benefits. I was so taken aback, I said, 'No, he was born on Friday night and died on Saturday'. Again, I was asked if I had received anything. By this point, I was finding it hard to hold back, so I had to leave as soon as I could and walk away.

"I went home and picked up Sharon. We had been asked if we wanted a post-mortem but we decided not to have one as we felt our little boy had suffered enough and we already had a pretty good idea what was wrong with him, so we started to get on with arranging his funeral. We then went to Mortonhall and met the manager. We were shown the Rose Garden, the area they have for babies. However, we decided to get a plot for Graham which our family funeral director helped us arrange and they then guided us through the funeral arrangements which we booked for the Wednesday.

"The only thing that the funeral director charged us for was the plot and the opening fees that they were charged. Everything else was provided free of charge – the car, the coffin, taking Graham into their care. It was a huge help at such a difficult time."

Terry, a funeral coordinator himself, says: "I know most funeral directors don't charge for a child's funeral now but historically, they used to all charge. However, over time, it became apparent it was predominantly young parents that were affected and they couldn't afford funerals. So the decision was made by most funeral directors not to charge from that point on.

"Graham's funeral was held in the afternoon and it went as well as something so sad can go. We were picked up at the house and we were asked if I wanted to have Graham in the back of the car sitting on my knee. I said yes but I will never forget the feeling and the coldness I felt coming through from the coffin. I was a young man back then and it was a lot for me to cope with."

Terry recalls: "Even at such difficult times, it's sometimes hard to understand why people can make such thoughtless comments. I remember at one point someone asking me why I was as upset as I hadn't carried him for 6½ months. I almost couldn't believe what I was hearing. I was grieving for my son just as much, despite the fact I hadn't carried him.

"Sharon and I had married in 1997 so we were a newly married couple when Graham came along. Everything that happened put a huge strain on us. I felt I had to be strong for her and I almost wasn't allowed to grieve myself. Things became very fraught very quickly and tensions began to rise, so much so that we separated on the Thursday – the day after Graham's funeral.

"Looking back, things had been going wrong for a while. I think the split would have come eventually but perhaps all the grief over Graham brought things to a head. I was completely lost and didn't know which way to turn.

"Over the next few weeks, I spent a lot of time going up to the cemetery simply to sit by Graham. I was so devastated that I even contemplated suicide. There were so many thoughts going through my head: he was my son, I was meant to protect him and there was absolutely nothing I could have done. I wasn't coping well at all, but I was too stubborn to put my hands up and ask for help.

"Half way through November, I remember seeing a leaflet we had been given by the hospital about SANDS Lothians. I just remember thinking – I'm a guy – we don't do feelings! So I put it to one side and tried to carry on, bury my feelings and go back to work."

Terry goes on: "I'd had a meeting with Graham's doctor to go through everything that had happened to Graham and the treatment they had given him. At that point, the doctor asked me how I was and how I was coping. I just replied, 'Not bad, good days and bad days' and, quite simply, he then said, 'Talk to me, tell me about how you're feeling.'

That was the first time anyone had asked me how I was and how I was coping. I told him everything and he referred me to SANDS Lothians. It was the middle of November around a month after I'd lost Graham. I thought about the doctor's advice all night and, finally, it sank in. He was right, I needed help. I phoned the SANDS' office and made an appointment to go in the following week.

"It was so good to be able to talk, and I was told about the Christmas memorial service that was coming up in December and I was invited along. I let my then ex-wife know I'd been in touch with SANDS, and she came along too, although we didn't stand together.

"I always remember there was a lady at the service. I don't know to this day who she was but at one point during the service we were singing a carol and I was overcome by my emotions and I was about to start to cry. This lovely lady came over and put her arm around me and gave me a cuddle. To this day, I don't know who she was, but she brought me such comfort and with it came the realisation that I really did need help. The time had come for me to admit that to myself.

"I left my job in the bakery industry in April 1999. I started to have more one-to-one sessions at SANDS Lothians. I didn't feel the group meetings were for me. I guess there was still a part of me that felt I was this big tough guy who didn't need to do that sort of thing but of course, in hindsight, I'm sure it would have helped."

Terry bravely recalls: "one bleak Sunday night, in the April of 1999, I did try to take my own life by swallowing a load of pills. However, when I woke up in the morning and realised it hadn't worked, I was so annoyed with myself. So I walked into my kitchen, put the kettle on, decided I was going to take a shower and then I was going out to the Forth Road Bridge.

"From the December after losing Graham, to when I tried to end it all, I had gone across the bridge every other night and contemplated throwing myself off. I would stand there at 2 and 3 o'clock in the morning and think about jumping. The morning after my first serious suicide attempt hadn't worked I sat with my cup of tea and planned… I would go down to the bridge, park my car, I would be mid way across, a good point, no rocks and I'd be straight into the sea. Then all of a sudden, I don't know what came over me, but suddenly, I thought, 'What are you doing? That's not the answer. That is *not* the answer. The answer is, go and get help.

"I never finished my cup of tea. Instead, I got in the car and went straight round to my GP's surgery. I said to the receptionist that I needed an appointment to see my doctor. She said ok, but that it wouldn't be for a few days. Thankfully, at that point, my doctor came out, saw me and asked if I was all right. I simply told him that I had to see him and he took me through straight away. I honestly believe, if I'd walked out of the surgery that day and hadn't seen my doctor, I don't think I would be here today.

"When I spoke to my doctor, everything came out. I told him what had happened the night before, what I had done and what I was thinking. He immediately arranged blood tests for me and put me on antidepressants and arranged more counselling for me. I will be forever grateful to that doctor for the rest of my life.

"I continued to come to SANDS Lothians for around another year," Terry recalls, "and that, with the counselling my doctor offered me, gradually helped to turn me around.

"I took a break for three months and did absolutely nothing. Then I gradually got back into working and took a few driving jobs. I then spoke to a friend who was a manager at a local funeral directors and was told that there was a casual driver's job coming up, so I began helping them out on a Saturday. I was then asked if I was available during the week to help with driving, so I jumped at it.

"Then within a week of my starting, one of the other members of staff handed in their notice. I was then asked if I would be interested in a full-time job. I was so pleased to be given this opportunity and started full time from December 23rd, and I've been there ever since.

"I enjoy my job but it can be difficult at times," Terry says. "There have been times when I have had to do babies' funerals. For some reason, I can manage funerals where the baby's been stillborn, but neo-natal deaths I find very, very hard to cope with. My bosses know my background now, but I remember one time in the early days when they didn't. I was at the mortuary and had been asked to pick up from the hospital a child who had passed away in the neo-natal unit. We have a very strict identification policy and I remember opening up the sheet that the baby was wrapped in, and he was wearing exactly the same little outfit that Graham had been wearing. It was the same bed cover too and everything came flooding back. That completely knocked me for six and I was off work for about four and a half months after that with depression.

"Then again, earlier this year, we had to deal with another neo-natal death and had to bring the child into our care. When I went to the mortuary, the coffin lid was taken off and there again was this little baby with the exact same outfit as Graham. Again, the impact floored me. I have just finished eight counselling sessions arranged through my work to try and come to terms with that. After that, I had a long chat with my boss as I began to wonder if I was in the right job, but I do think I am. I am facing my worst fears head on."

Looking back, Terry says: "Perhaps, if I had been able to acknowledge that I needed help sooner, things may have been a bit less rocky for me. The advice I would give to other dads is don't be a stubborn male! Go and put your hands up and get the help you need. We all need it, we are only human, you have got feelings too and they are feelings that need to be talked about. Don't bottle them up, because it won't help in the long run."

Yuill Douglas Irvine 23 July 1991

Baby Yuill's father, also Yuill, begins: "My wife Jacqui and I married in 1989 and in 1990 we were delighted to find out that Jacqui was pregnant. We told all our friends and family and to this day, I still remember the excitement of telling my dad that he was going to be a grandfather.

"Jacqui was so careful throughout the pregnancy and was determined to do all the right things. She bought all the books and took great care over food and exercise and attended all the pregnancy classes and joined the local NCT group.

"Everything progressed well up until 28 weeks, when Jacqui had some bleeding. She was admitted overnight into hospital, where the baby was monitored and after a nervous wait, it was confirmed that all was well and Jacqui was discharged.

"The pregnancy continued normally, although Jacqui was retaining quite a lot of fluid; therefore, about six months into the pregnancy, we had to go in for tests to see if there was a reason for the extra fluid. Like many expectant parents, we started reading horror stories about why there may be too much fluid, which, of course, added to our concern. We were sent for a scan and the doctors found that our baby had small cysts in his kidneys. We were devastated. He was our first baby and we were so worried. However, the consultant did his best to reassure us and said they would monitor the baby closely. From that point on, Jacqui was booked in for weekly scans.

"The week until our next scan felt like an eternity. We tried so hard to hope for the best but we feared the worst. At last, the scan appointment finally came around. The cysts had completely gone. There were no other problems and everything had returned to normal. We couldn't have wished for better news.

"After all the worry, Jacqui went past her due date and we were given a day and date to go in for an induction on the 22nd July 1991. We eagerly anticipated our new arrival, excitement renewed, after getting the all clear from the scans. Little did we know what was to follow.

"Jacqui was induced at 10am and at 10pm was taken to the labour suite to have her waters broken. She was given an epidural for the pain and had a long labour that lasted through the night and culminated in the need for a caesarean section. Jacqui was fully awake when she gave birth to our beautiful son, Yuill, who appeared to be a very healthy baby boy. He was a good size too, weighing in at 8lb 1oz and scoring well on all the tests they carry out on newborns.

"I still remember my son's first cry. He was so beautiful and although one of his little eyes was still sticky he fought to open both eyes to look at his mummy and daddy. The nurses took our baby for a scan and within minutes were able to tell us that his kidneys were fine.

"The relief was overwhelming. After all the worry, our son was here, safe and sound. I called all the relatives to tell them the good news and everyone came to meet the new arrival. We had such a wonderful day with Yuill. We just drank in the moments with our beautiful baby, cuddling him and feeding him. I was so absorbed in the joy of being a new dad. I finally left the hospital at 10 o'clock that night with instructions as to things to buy and bring in the next day. I went home, walked the dogs and went to bed, the happiest person in the world.

"I was woken early the next morning by a call from the hospital with the news that Yuill hadn't been well during the night and that I should go in. This came as such a bolt from the blue as he had been happy and healthy when I'd left him the night before. I arrived at the hospital to find Yuill was in the intensive care unit and the doctors said they couldn't be certain what was wrong with him but they thought the problem may be with his heart. He'd had difficulty breathing and his heart-rate was erratic. They also said his spleen was enlarged so he may have an infection. He was transferred to Simpson's hospital for further checks.

"Around two hours later, a doctor came into the room and broke the devastating news that they thought our son had a major heart defect. They told us they still couldn't be certain but would like to operate that afternoon. Soon after this, a midwife took us up to Simpson's in a taxi. Jacqui was still in a lot of pain from the caesarean section so it wasn't an easy journey for her.

"When we arrived, we were taken to Special Care where we saw our son in an incubator. He almost filled it. He was linked up to so many monitors but was kicking about and even managed to pull a tube out of his nose. After a while the heart specialist took us to a room and explained that they no longer felt the problem was with his heart. Scans had shown it was fine. They had given him antibiotics and everything else they could possibly give him but, again, they still weren't sure what was wrong and needed to do more tests. Only hours earlier, we were ecstatic at the arrival of what we believed was our perfectly healthy son. Our poor little boy was really struggling and we had no answers as to why.

"We were then asked if we'd like to have Yuill christened. Our initial thoughts were yes, but we'll have all that done later when he's better. We hadn't allowed ourselves to take in what the consultant was trying to say. We had avoided letting the events since Yuill's birth sink in. Around the same time, we were told that the doctors didn't think it was fair to keep him on the ventilator. They suggested taking him off to see if he could keep going by himself. So our son was taken off the ventilator and christened while, all the time, having his little heart manually massaged to keep him alive.

"Our son Yuill Douglas Irvine was christened at 4.25pm on the 24th July 1991, 33½ hours after he was born. Five minutes later, we were told it would be cruel to let him suffer any more. He was brought out of the incubator, and he died, peacefully, in his mother's arms.

"For most of the short time we had our son, we had been blissfully unaware of just how unwell Yuill had been. It was only after we saw his notes that we realised he had suffered a heart attack.

"We were told he had fought extremely hard for his life, but had sadly been unable to recover. They still did not know why he had died and could give us no explanation.

"We were taken into a private room where we were allowed precious time with Yuill and were able to bath him, change him, look after him and take photos. Finally, the heart-wrenching time came when we had to say goodbye, and we left our beautiful son lying in his crib.

"Five days later, Yuill was buried at the Rose Garden at Mortonhall, and all our friends, family and neighbours joined us to say goodbye."

Yuill reflects: "The weeks and months after Yuill's death were agonising. Everything we had done up until Yuill's birth had revolved around his arrival and our getting ready for family life with our newborn. Jacqui had stopped working and the whole house had been done up for our new baby. When Yuill died, our world stopped turning. We struggled to function day to day. Everything we had planned and prepared for had gone in the blink of an eye. Jacqui and I were left with a myriad of unanswered questions.

"We had agreed to a post-mortem and around a month later got the results back. They showed that Yuill had a twist in his bowel. The food he had been ingesting had become blocked in his bowel which had then untwisted and the food had gone back into his system and poisoned him. If they had known about his condition, they could have operated. As it transpired, it was nothing to do with his heart, but his heart had struggled to deal with everything else that was going on in his body.

"At least the results gave us some answers as to why we'd lost our little boy, but we still had no clue as to how we possibly moved on from here.

"Thankfully, the hospital had given us some leaflets about SANDS Lothians. We began attending some monthly meetings and they became the one day of the month we looked forward to, where we were able to talk openly and get some release from the constant torment of our emotions. As time went on and we talked to more bereaved parents, we gradually realised how lucky we were to get some time with our baby and enjoy the simple pleasures of cuddling and caring for him, even for such a short while.

"I can quite honestly say, even all these years on, that I do not know how we would have coped without the SANDS meetings. We eventually tried to move on with our lives and return to some semblance of normality while all the time we were still in agony underneath our facades, but at the meetings we were able to talk frankly about the pain we still felt.

"As a father, one of the most difficult things for me was not only dealing with my own grief at the loss of my son, but it was also so hard to see Jacqui struggling so much – not only with her emotional pain but also with her physical pain from her caesarean section. She kept blaming herself for what had happened, feeling it must be something she had done wrong. She was so distraught at Yuill's funeral, and it was agonising to see someone I loved, so upset.

"I stayed off work for a while but I knew I'd have to go back eventually – after all, that's how life worked. I needed to try and carry on, try and get back to some sort of 'normal'.

"I underestimated how hard this would be. Before, I had been a successful businessman excelling in my field but now I found it hard to focus or concentrate as I was going through so many emotions. The 'old' me used to look at down and outs in Edinburgh and wonder how they could let their lives sink so low, but, after Yuill, I could see exactly how someone could feel so bad and so in the depths of despair that they would feel they couldn't go on and their life would spiral out of control.

"For a long time, I was just going through the motions, trying to make my way back to normality. Then almost like a lightning bolt, I decided, this was it. I could either sink lower and lower or I could start moving forward, a step at a time and a day at a time and start to make everything work again. Make sure I started to build a new future and make everything right for everyone again, and I would do all this in Yuill's memory. His short life would form the foundations of our new future, and I decided that everything I would do from this day on would be in my son's honour. I became determined that if I didn't get on with life and try and do well, it would almost be like I'd failed my son.

"Yuill had been so amazing, and he had given us an insight into how wonderful children are. Jacqui and I decided, fairly quickly, that we wanted more children, and we felt that would help us deal with our grief. A lot of people said to wait at least a year as that helps the mother's body recover and also allows you to grieve properly. We decided that approach wasn't for us. We wanted more children and didn't want to wait.

"Jacqui became pregnant again and we were then able to focus on there being a future for us as a family. However, what followed was a year of constant worry. We were petrified that something was going to go wrong throughout the pregnancy. Fortunately, our second son Matthew was born in 1992, a very healthy baby, but then came that hurdle of getting him through the first day of his life. It was like a mental and emotional milestone we had to pass. It took a while after he was born for us to settle down and relax a little, as every time there was something wrong with him, we thought he would die. We went on to have our third son, Edward, in 1996. I would then go on to have another son, Nathan, with my new partner after Jacqui and I split up, sadly.

"In hindsight, going on to have children fairly quickly after Yuill helped us hugely. It didn't stop us grieving but it made a massive difference. Yuill was, and still is, very much part of our lives and we talk to the boys about him. We still go up and visit his grave every year at Christmas time and birthdays. We have pictures of him around the house and we talk openly about him. Yuill showed us just how much we wanted to have children and just how amazing they were.

"Having gone through the tragedy of losing a baby, I have become acutely aware of how people can behave around someone who has suffered the death of a child or a stillbirth. People can be incredibly awkward and come out with the craziest things. I can accept that they probably mean well and may simply be a bit clumsy with their words, but with others, I often wonder how on earth they thought their comments were helpful.

"I remember shortly after Yuill died, one woman said to me, 'Well, he was only a day old, you didn't really know him.' Until you are in a position where you have lost a baby, you can't begin to know how hurtful comments like that are. You've not only lost your baby, but you've lost your future and all the memories you were hoping to create, and you are left with a gaping hole in your life."

Yuill continues: "I lost my mother when I was 11 and my father died shortly before Matthew's 1st birthday. Somehow, the loss of parents is slightly more bearable than the loss of a child. Although still devastating, it's the natural order of things. The loss of any young child and the loss of their future is a pain that is so hard to put into words.

"When Yuill was in Special Care we had a lovely consultant who looked after him. He went the extra mile for Yuill, Jacqui and I, and he wrote us a note after Yuill died, saying that the worst part of his job was that he couldn't give parents a healthy baby every time.

"Jacqui and I have stayed involved in the work of SANDS Lothians to this day. We'll do anything we can, from shaking collecting cans to putting a team in for the Edinburgh Marathon. I was chair of their committee for a while too and now continue to hold fundraising events within my workplace and try to spread the word about SANDS Lothians.

"Only recently at my work, a young girl aged just 17 came up to my room and told me that she'd lost a baby too, but up until that point, hadn't been able to tell anybody. It's amazing how all these things came from Yuill and they all help keep his memory alive.

"SANDS Lothians helped us both get through the bleakest time of our lives. As well as the group meetings, Jacqui got a great deal out of the counselling that they offered. There is no doubt that men and women deal with grief very differently. I chose not to opt for counselling. I've always felt, rightly or wrongly, that I'm reasonably in touch with my feelings. Granted, at times I'll crash on with things but I'll be aware that there may be issues in my head that I know I've not dealt with. I'm not ignoring that issue, I'm just not dealing with it at the moment but I will come back to it in my own time and deal with it in my own way.

"I've often found doing things, like giving a talk or writing things down, is as therapeutic for me as counselling may be for others. I was very close to my father when he was alive and remember so clearly one day we were talking about Yuill and my father quite simply said, 'It's an horrific thing that's happened, but you can't do anything about it. You can't get to a point when someone can give you reasons why you should lose your son, it's just happened. It's so horrific what you've gone through, but you've lost the wee soul and life goes on. Your future will be what you make of it.'

"I know it was so hard for my dad to watch me suffer, but in his own, gentle way, he taught me if Yuill's death was going to define my life from this point on, it should be in a good way."

Asked what advice he can give to other fathers, Yuill says: "A lot of dads find it hard to deal with the grief their wife goes through as well as the loss of their baby and deal with things differently. Men often bottle things up. Go to SANDS meetings – you will find it hugely helpful to listen to other people's stories and to know that there are other fathers going through what you are."

Yuill continues: "I remember feeling like such a failure – other people could have children and they were all fine, why did mine die? However, share your pain, your fears and your thoughts with others who understand. Sadly, stillbirth and neo-natal death is not uncommon. It happens and there is nothing you can do about it. When you think about a baby growing from a tiny little cell to a 9lb or 10lb baby, it's no wonder things go wrong sometimes.

"Losing my son was a horrific shock and a dreadful experience to have to endure. I remember at one point during his short life, I was walking down the hospital corridor, praying to God that he would make everything right. I wasn't particularly religious, but I pleaded with him, saying he could cut my arms and legs off and I'd do anything, if he could only save my son.

"I wish, more than anything, that Yuill was here, but his short life and death had a huge impact on me and have been a massive influence on everything I've done since. I hope telling my story can be another thing I do in Yuill's memory that will go some way to help others.

"I will never forget how dreadful losing Yuill felt, but a lot of the pain has eased now. I will never stop wishing things had been different, and I had four sons alive and well and with me now. Sadly, it wasn't to be, but Yuill taught me just how amazing children are and how much joy they bring, and, because of him, I have three other wonderful children, his brothers, who remember him every day and will continue to keep his memory alive."

Sean Kelly

Losing a child must be one of the most devastating things a mother has to endure. Very often there's another, often forgotten, broken heart that is suffered in silence, that of the father. This is Kevin's story.

At the young age of 22, fatherhood wasn't new to Kevin Kelly. He was already a dad to one child, and although he didn't know it at the time, he would go on to be a dad to seven children in total. Kevin had two step children, a boy and a girl, with Sean's mum but it was the birth of his second child, Sean, that would change his life dramatically.

On the 2nd January 1986, Sean Kelly was born. Sadly, Sean was born with a chromosome disorder and a story, tragically familiar to many bereaved parents, began to unfold.

"We knew something was wrong almost as soon as Sean was born," Kevin recalls. "He was kept in an incubator and the doctors and nurses tried to feed him for over a week, but he couldn't swallow. Eventually, it became clear that Sean's tube down to his tummy hadn't developed properly, so he wasn't getting any of the nutrition he needed. Because of the genetic abnormality, the long-term outlook for Sean wasn't good. He could have been tube fed, but he would remain on a life-support machine.

"Day after day, week after week, I visited the hospital," continues Kevin. "The sound of Sean's life-support machine stays with me to this day and, even now, visiting hospitals is incredibly hard for me.

"The doctors and medical staff did try to explain all the medical facts and implications, and it was clear that Sean wouldn't be able to have any quality of life. A dreadful decision was going to have to be made in the days to come. I will never forget one instance at the hospital, when I was almost on my knees with desperation, someone put their hand on my shoulder and I heard the words, 'Everything's going to be ok'. The words brought me so much comfort, but to this day, I have no idea who spoke them.

"Sean stayed with us for four and a half months until I was given the tortuous job of switching off his life-support machine, something no parent should ever have to do. The sound of the machines grinding to a halt and Sean's life ebbing away will stay with me forever. That single, terrible moment, changed me forever. I felt like I had murdered my son."

Reflecting for a moment on that painful time so many years ago, Kevin goes on: "I am 48 now and looking back over the last 26 years, hindsight is a wonderful thing. I can see so clearly now the extent to which I buried my pain over the loss of my son so deeply into my mind and my heart. Even if counselling had been available to me at the time, I don't think I would have been able to go through it. I couldn't face talking about anything, and I definitely couldn't express my feelings. I am a very deep thinker and a sensitive person, and I have been prone to a great deal of depression over the years.

"Although there have been a number of difficult events in my life during this time, I held on to so much pain over Sean, it would definitely have contributed to my bouts of depression. I felt like a constant failure. I felt I had let my son down. I couldn't allow myself to let go of the pain, as then, I felt, I would be letting go of Sean.

"I went on to have two more children with Sean's mum, even so over the years, I continued to punish myself as I felt I deserved to be in pain. But all the time, all the pain and distress over events all those years ago just got buried deeper and deeper and started to manifest itself as anger and frustration to all those around me. I didn't mean to be this way, I was just suppressing so much pain and anxiety, I didn't know how else to deal with it.

"Over the years, there were more events that just seemed to bring everything back and present me with more painful emotions that got added to the jumbled mess in my head and shoved back down a little deeper still. Although we had parted by this time, the death of Sean's mother brought everything back, as it almost symbolised the end of a shared history and another link to Sean gone.

"Then when my step-daughter suffered a stillbirth, it was like a recurring nightmare. Being around a little white coffin for a second time was just too much to bear.

"Through all the upsets since losing Sean, I felt it was my job to outwardly stay strong for everyone else. Inwardly was a very different matter. I was hurting so much and silently screaming out for help, and I just didn't know what to do. In 2007, I attempted suicide.

"By late 2011, I realised something had to change or my life would completely spiral out of control. It was then that I decided to approach SANDS Lothians. I booked my first counselling session and remember it well. My heart was pounding and I was clinging on to the arms of the chair, but I began to talk and tell my story and for the first time, someone listened.

"I missed my second session. However, the counsellor must have instinctively known how hard the first session was for me and how massive it was for me to open up after 26 years of keeping everything inside. She phoned me to see how I was and encouraged me to come to another session. I have now been seeing her for around four months and for the first time since Sean's death, I feel someone cares about me and what I've gone through.

"For years, I carried such incredibly painful memories of Sean. It was like every recollection of that time brought with it this monstrous memory of having to switch off his life-support machine and a flood of painful emotions that were too hard to handle. Amazingly, talking with the counsellor has helped me get past that and instead, remember the good things. I had a beautiful son with me for nearly five months. I held him, I changed his nappy and I enjoyed little cuddles with the wee lad. These are good things; they are precious, happy memories that I can begin to enjoy now.

"I will never forget my little boy, and equally, the pain will never leave me. But I can talk about him now, and now when I remember that time, it's good memories – it's memories I want to recall and cherish."

When asked what advice he could give to other bereaved fathers, Kevin says: "Fathers feel as much pain as mothers do at the loss of a child; we just feel it in a different way. The man always feels he has to stay strong for everyone else and must put all his feelings to one side, but that's not how it has to be. It's OK for men to show their feelings and it's completely understandable to be filled with a sense of despair and devastation at the loss of a child. It is so important that our feelings get dealt with too, and I don't mean that in any way to take away from the enormous, overwhelming feelings of loss a mother goes through too."

He continues: "It's never, ever too late to get help whether your loss is recent or long ago. Since the SANDS Lothians' counsellor, I now have an overwhelming sense of relief. For the first time in all these years, I feel, at long last, that I *do* matter, that someone is listening and my feelings *are* important."

Caitlin Emily Partridge

29 January 1998

"My partner Kerry and I were so excited about the pending arrival of our first child," Andrew Partridge begins. "I had a son, daughter and a step-daughter from my previous marriage, but this was my first child with Kerry and Kerry's first baby.

"At nine months and ten days, Kerry was admitted into hospital. The pregnancy had gone really well and the labour was progressing normally. Kerry and Caitlin were checked around 5.15am and all was well, then just after 6am they were checked again and they couldn't find a heartbeat for the baby. We were given the devastating news that Caitlin had died.

"I couldn't believe what I was hearing. Everything had been fine. How could it suddenly go so wrong? Kerry would have to continue to give birth naturally as the baby was so far down the birth canal, but we would have a stillborn.

"Later, the post-mortem would show that Caitlin had a blood clot and a heart attack coming down the birth canal. She had a very long umbilical cord – over 100 centimetres long and the average is around 50 centimetres. The cord was wrapped around her feet and her left hand, and she had somehow cut off her oxygen supply.

"After the trauma of Caitlin's birth, SANDS Lothians were amazing. I don't know how we would have got through without them. We were put up in their special family room and allowed to spend time with our daughter. We were able to use the room whenever we needed to. We had three full days and nights with her to begin with and then we had about an hour a day with her every day until her funeral. We would take photos with her, some happy, some sad. We would sing to her, sit and cuddle her and talk to her.

239

"Being able to do this was such a huge help with the grieving process. I was her dad; I wanted to do everything for her. I wanted to play the part of her father, if only for a little while. She was a beautiful, full term, perfect baby. My daughter.

"Briefly, my mind drifted back to when Caitlin was still safe and well in Kerry's womb. There were nights when Kerry would be sound asleep but I would be lying awake. Caitlin would be wide awake too. I would tickle her and tease her and I could see her moving all around inside Kerry. I would talk to her for hours. I'm sure she knew my voice and touch. Even before she was born, there was a special bond between us.

"My daughter bought Kerry and I a lovely little memory box and in it we put photos of Caitlin, her foot and hand prints, a lock of her hair and her little baby-gro. Also in it were her name tag and belly-button clip and a copy of her heart trace. We treasured everything in the box, but we wanted our baby.

"A thought then crossed my mind. My upbringing as a Catholic meant we always brought our dead family home. I asked Kerry how she would feel if we brought Caitlin home. She was initially against the idea, but I eventually persuaded her it was the right thing to do. We'd had Caitlin baptised in the hospital by a wonderful minister who'd told me, if there was anything he could do to help us, we were just to ask. So I asked him if we could take Caitlin home. Her nursery was all ready; we wanted to take our baby home and on the day of her funeral, we wanted to leave from the house.

"Initially, the minister said he didn't think it would be possible as he'd never heard of anyone doing that before. However, he got in touch with the funeral directors who agreed to our wishes, despite the fact that it was an unusual request.

"Kerry and I went home and the day before Caitlin's funeral, the funeral directors phoned to say they were downstairs with Caitlin – I was both nervous and excited. I told them I'd come down to meet them to pick up my daughter. The funeral director then told me that they were legally responsible for the deceased and that they wouldn't be able to let me do that. I'm afraid, I just insisted and said, 'I'm sorry, tell your driver to stay where he is. I'm coming down to pick up my daughter and I will be the one to carry her though the doors into her home.' The driver then agreed but did say that he would have to follow me up the stairs. I carried my daughter's little coffin up the steps and brought her home.

"I took her into the bedroom and laid her little white coffin on the bed. I asked the funeral director to open up the coffin. He warned me that she would be a bit discoloured, but I knew that. I'd seen her every day at the hospital. Caitlin had already been dressed in a beautiful baptismal robe that we had been given as a gift for her and we wanted her to be buried in this. If we had to be parted from her forever, we would send her away dressed like a princess.

"I put her in her cot – a little swinging Moses basket that would have been her bed. I wound up her musical toy above her crib. We had an hour alone with our daughter before all our family arrived. We wanted to give everyone a chance to meet her. It wasn't only Kerry and I who had lost a child, my mother and father had lost a granddaughter and my brothers had lost a niece. I wanted everyone who would have been a part of her life to be able to come to the house and see her before they said goodbye.

"People started arriving, and an old friend came with tea and sandwiches as everyone rallied round. Some people were surprised that Caitlin was at home but, after spending time with her, they were so emotional but happy. It really helped Kerry and me to be able to bring her home. When you go in to hospital to have your baby, you're all prepared for a healthy baby. You don't expect anything to go wrong; you don't have a 'plan B'. Nothing can prepare you for the loss of your baby. Your whole world is turned upside down. When Caitlin was stillborn, we had no idea what to do next or where to turn. If it wasn't for SANDS Lothians, I don't know how we would have coped.

"We kept Caitlin at home for one night before her funeral the next day. She lay in her little crib in her own home with her mum and dad. Our baby had come home.

"We had a big funeral for her and we were spared a bill. It was that particular funeral directors' policy not to charge for a child's funeral and, for that, we were extremely grateful. Caitlin left from her home and was laid to rest at Mortonhall. I remember when lowering the coffin, one of the cords got stuck and at the same time, there was the most beautiful ray of sunshine in the sky. I always felt that was a little message from Caitlin."

Andrew continues: "The year before we lost Caitlin, I lost my young brother to cancer, at 33. I'd also lost my job due to an accident at work and all this, including the loss of Caitlin, happened within a 12-month period.

"We'd been getting a huge amount of help and counselling from SANDS Lothians and, eventually, Kerry and I decided it was time to pull ourselves out of this black hole, so gradually, we began to piece our lives back together again. I went for a job interview and successfully got the position.

"With my very first wage, I went up to the place where we had registered Caitlin and I put in the wedding banns. I then went home to ask Kerry to marry me. She agreed and in the next breath told me that she was pregnant again and would have a big bump. I was over the moon and said, let's just do it - wedding dress, big bump and all! We have now been married over 14 years."

Andrew reflects: "I look on death very differently now. Once you've buried a baby, everyone else's death seems to pale into insignificance or at least, follows the natural order of things. Once you cope with the loss of a baby, everything else feels different. Having said that, only last year, I lost my eldest son, Tommy, and that is still very raw. I often wondered how on earth I would ever cope with burying another child, but Tommy had a lot of health problems. I remember one night I had this incredible dream that Tommy came to me and he was the picture of health and happiness and he told me he was fine.

"It brought me great comfort and has kept me strong ever since. It was almost as if he was telling me that when you pass over there's a healing process. I've buried two children now. I lost my future with Caitlin, but I was glad to be there for Tommy and be able to care for him to the end.

"After losing Caitlin, I felt that, although I was dealing with my own grief, I had to be strong for Kerry and Caitlin's brother and sisters. There is a 20 year age difference between Kerry and me but we have been together for 17 years. She's been my rock through losing two brothers, my mother and father, a son and Caitlin.

"I remember in the days after losing Caitlin, people would come to the house. They wouldn't know what to say but I would always tell them, 'Just come in. Come and sit with me, even if I can't speak to you, just your being here helps.' I often liken that feeling to an old coal fire with all the bits of coal burning away together, then one piece falls out and you sit and watch it cooling down and fading away. When you pick it up and put it back into the fire, slowly but surely, it starts to glow again.

"People just being there, helped me so much. I might not have been able to speak to them or hold a conversation but their company helped rebuild my strength. I know as long as I live, Caitlin will always be in my heart and in my thoughts. Bringing her home was one of the most important decisions in my life and she will always be my little angel."

Asked what advice he can pass on to other dads, Andrew says: "Often nobody ever asks the dads how they are and how they feel and they seldom have anyone they can talk to. Sometimes, they may find it easier to talk to a male counsellor or befriender and I know SANDS Lothians have a male befriender.

"Speaking to a group of dads helps, too, knowing you're sharing your experience with someone who really understands and who's been through this sort of loss themselves. Getting comfort from other dads and learning that it is possible to move on and that the raw grief won't last forever helps greatly. Talking is always good. I hope telling my story will help other dads. I would say to them, 'Don't bottle all your feelings up. Talk about your feelings and emotions or your grief may surface again, years down the line'."

Caitlin Poppy Ryce

"When my wife Natasha and I began trying to start a family, it happened very quickly for us. We were over the moon and on such a high," Dave Ryce begins. "We excitedly told everyone and with great anticipation. We had a big discussion about baby names. We eventually got down to a shortlist of seven which we then whittled down to three.

"My wife had a few health complications at the time, including diabetes, so because of these issues, she was getting a monthly scan. It was wonderful to see the little embryo on the scan. Natasha had to go to one of the scans on her own as I couldn't get time off work. She was so excited when she saw lots of movement. I stupidly thought there would be many more scans that I could go to.

"Our next scan was at 20 weeks. We had asked the midwife if we'd be able to tell the sex of the baby and we were told that we would. The scan was on the Tuesday and on the Thursday night before that, Tash hadn't felt quite right. Rather than take a chance, we went along to the hospital and they did an ultrasound. When the nurse initially said that she could hear a heartbeat, that put our minds at rest.

"We got the picture up on the screen and all of a sudden, I had a gut feeling that something wasn't right. There was a look on the midwife's face and she fell silent. I have snatched memories of those moments, but I remember, when we heard the words, 'I'm so sorry...' and we both started crying.

"In amongst my jumble of emotions, I remember feeling really sorry for the midwife. I don't think there could be any amount of training that could prepare you for telling someone their baby's died. The obstetrician we had been seeing then came in to speak to us and, shortly afterwards, we went along to the pregnancy assessment unit. We phoned our mums with the terrible news. It's strange what you recall – I remember on our darkest day, the sun was streaming through the windows.

"I also recall once seeing a film called *Sliding Doors,* which depicted the two different paths the film's lead character's life could take after simply missing her train and the rest of the film played out like a split screen. Suddenly, I had a split screen of my life running in my head. On one side, Tasha and I were skipping down the corridor excited about finding out if we were having a boy or a girl and on the other side was our current, bleak reality."

Dave continues: "We were then advised that the safest thing would be to deliver the baby rather than have a caesarean section. Tash was given the drugs to start the process and we were sent home. The hours after that were all a bit hazy. It was a day of nothingness.

"I tend to be one of life's optimists. I like to believe there is nothing in life that is a wasted experience. There is always something you can take from any situation, good or bad. One of the things I feel I can take from my whole experience is that I have a far greater understanding of grief. I had never before experienced the level of grief that came with the loss of my child.

"My main experience of death up until that point had been of elderly relatives who had lived to an age where their death wasn't unexpected. I had also lost some of my school friends but all had, at least, lived some of their life.

"For the first time in my life, I felt grief hitting me like a sledgehammer. I was amazed by how physical it was. I actually felt it throughout my body. It wasn't just a state of mind.

"We had been due to go back to the hospital in two days, but Tasha felt things start to happen on the Wednesday night so we got a taxi to the hospital.

"I don't think the nurse assigned to us was convinced it was labour as she felt the drugs wouldn't have had time to take effect. However, I always thought there was a chance that Tash could have gone into spontaneous labour anyway. Even I could tell it seemed like labour pains; they were coming in waves and getting closer together. However, the last thing I wanted to do was tell a medical professional her job or question her. A first-aid course was the extent of my medical training!

"I was left on my own a lot with Tash and that was a difficult thing to experience. It was so hard to watch her in so much pain. They had initially only given her a paracetamol, but they then gave her gas and air. I thought that was helping her, so I kept shoving it in her mouth. I really didn't know what to do; I was just trying to follow the nurse's lead.

"Tash then felt like she needed to go to the toilet and she was put on a commode as she was really struggling with the pain. Again, I just knew something wasn't right; it was a gut feeling once more. I just knew that she'd passed the baby.

"I pressed the help button and the nurse came back. She took the commode and the baby away. By that stage, we'd both been up all night and were exhausted and emotional. Tash fell asleep and I dozed on and off.

"The nurse returned and explained that we could meet the baby. At that point, they couldn't tell what sex it was. The prospect of seeing my child for the first time was really quite hard to face. There was part of me that thought maybe it would be easier if I didn't see her, but I then decided I would rather regret seeing her than regret not seeing her.

"Meeting her for the first time was wonderful. In the midst of all this grief and sadness, meeting and holding my child was such a peaceful, happy moment. We had created this life. I could see in her face, features from both Tash and I, and she looked like a beautiful little combination of the two of us. It was an incredible moment. We were able to spend some precious time with her and read her a story and take some photos."

Dave says: "After that, the days just passed, one by one. The following months and years brought a newfound understanding of grief. There's this heartbreaking event that changes your life. If you could draw a graph of your grief you would think it would be in a straight line that gradually inclined as things improved, but it's not like that. It's up and down, peaks and troughs. Sometimes, you feel fine and other times there's this spike of grief that just hits you without warning. Initially, others offer you sympathy and empathy and then, over time, your loss becomes yesterday's news.

"There's a kind of expectation with grief, that after a certain period of time you should just get over it. Even seven years down the line, something silly can remind me and I'm back again coping with another spike of grief. It's a strange beast grief – it's so unpredictable. Even now all these years later, my grief is still there. I'm not so comfortable expressing it, but it's still there. It can creep up unannounced when I least expect it.

"I don't really see myself as moving on from my grief. In a funny sort of way, it's comforting to still have it. If you lose someone who's lived their life, you have your memories but, with a stillborn child, you don't have that. Your grief is important to you, it is a huge part of the tiny memory of that time that you have and it makes it real. I actually associate my grief with my daughter. I need my grief.

"People deal with things in their own way. Men may often deal with things by blocking out their emotions by hitting the bottle. I went the other way. I never touched a drop of alcohol for six months because the last thing I wanted to do was block everything out. I wanted to feel the grief and the pain as that was one of the few things I had to remind me of my daughter.

"After the birth, we had a small family funeral and a burial. We buried Caitlin with all the other babies. It was lovely for them all to be together. Again, I remember with real clarity, the weather was terrible! It had been gloriously sunny when she was born and pouring when she was laid to rest.

"I carried the coffin and I remember thinking, a coffin shouldn't be this size. Tash and I held the ropes and lowered her into the ground. Tasha read a poem and we had a few minutes alone with our daughter at the graveside. I suppose that was it, that was the point where you're somehow meant to get on with the rest of your life.

"When we'd lost Caitlin, the obstetrician told us to give ourselves a break, to do our grieving and give ourselves a bit of time to come to terms with things. However, a couple of months later, Tasha was pregnant again. For us, trying again was the right thing to do. Sadly, that pregnancy ended in a miscarriage. Before the year was out, there was another miscarriage and then to round off a perfect year, Tasha's cat died. So 2005 was a miserable year.

"This time we decided we did need a break. I, for one, was sick of the sight of the inside of the hospital and basically, we'd reached the point of 'Oh no, not again'.

"Caitlin's post-mortem results had shown that she was a perfectly healthy baby. Tash had spent time on pregnancy forums. I think the forums were probably a bit wild! Pregnant women with hormones flying, all arguing and falling out with each other! However, Tash had got chatting to a lady in a similar position as her, who had suffered from Hughes syndrome and although the normal practice is not to test for this until you've lost your third pregnancy, but we managed to get tested for it. The tests came back positive.

"Again, I tried hard to see the positives of the results; they gave us an answer and, subsequently, a way forward. Tash went on heparin as soon as she found out she was pregnant. It may have been clutching at positives but we at least now had some knowledge that was helpful. Sadly, Tash found it hard to see it that way and she blamed herself.

"On a number of occasions, she said she'd killed our baby. I asked her to stop thinking like that and reassured her that wasn't how I felt and that I didn't blame her for one second. I told her how much it upset me that she would think that way and that no one else felt that way in the slightest. She had done everything possible to ensure a healthy pregnancy and protect the baby. It was so hard to hear her saying she thought she'd harmed the baby.

"She did stop speaking in that way but I knew she still thought that way. In the weeks, months and years that followed she turned things in on herself. I like to think I'm an understanding person but I found that really hard. Normally, she was such an outgoing person and I just couldn't read between the lines.

"Our relationship was under strain during the years that followed. I've since learned that people grieve at a different pace. Initially, our trauma brought us closer together but then our grief began to tear us apart as we were in different places. Gradually, I got back into life and a routine, but it took longer for Tash to feel functional again."

Dave goes on: "I then went through the anger stage. It was so strange for me as I'm not really someone who gets angry. Now I understand why they say anger is part of grief. Looking back, there is nothing wrong with that but at the time, you are walking around feeling furious about everything. It's all misdirected too – it comes from nowhere in particular, you just feel angry all the time.

"I think that's the hardest part of grief for others to understand. They can understand your being down and sad but when you're short and snappy with people, they're not so tolerant and they don't recognise that as part of grief. It's a stage I felt very keenly.

"Looking back, I can see clearly what was happening, but, at the time, I didn't have that perspective. Anger's not part of my character, so it was a very confusing time for me. It was an emotion alien to me, and I didn't like it.

"Tash and I were always able to talk and we had our own ways of sorting things out, but we had reached the point where we needed a little help. We eventually came along to the SANDS Lothians' meetings. We came to three or four group sessions. The group sessions helped Tasha but I didn't feel they were right for me. I was hearing such sad stories and taking comfort from someone else's loss didn't sit easily with me. I was making comparisons with other people's experiences and theirs were usually always worse than ours and, in a way, it made me feel I was moving further away from my own grief and my daughter and, because my grief was so important to me, I didn't want anything taking it away from me.

"However, SANDS Lothians offers a number of services, so I felt the individual chat might be better for me. I came along to see their counsellor and I got more out of that than the group. These sessions helped me so much in coming to terms with the anger stage of my grief. Just being able to sit and express it to someone else was such a good thing for me. It helped to talk through the problems we were having in our relationship and the gap that was growing between us. Tash and I worked through all our problems and grew closer again.

"We also went to the pregnancy support group, which was very good, in particular with regard to helping deal with anxiety in a subsequent pregnancy. There was a midwife at the meetings which was so helpful from a medical point of view. It helped me to rationalise things.

"As a bereaved father, I felt almost as if I had double grief – grief for my daughter and grief for my wife. I don't want to generalise between males and females, there is the human experience and all it brings. The instinct you have as a male is to be a protector. If Tasha is ever threatened or in danger, I want to protect her. There's something in the male psyche that makes you want to fix things, make them better but you can't tell someone how to grieve. You can't turn round and say, 'That's enough'.

"We live in a small village and news spread quickly. People were lovely but they always asked after my wife but not me. It didn't really bother me, she was more important, but sometimes, I feel the fathers get forgotten. We suffer too.

"I think Tasha's reaction to everything was almost more difficult than what actually happened. I wanted to make everything better, but there were some things that I just couldn't fix.

"My grief plays a big part for me, I associate it with my daughter, and it reminds me of her. I want to keep it. Talking about it helps, telling my story helps. It's a long time since I've spoken again in so much detail until today, but it's been so good to talk and very therapeutic.

"It's OK to dwell on things, reminisce and go back in time. I try to avoid the 'what ifs' but sometimes it's hard. Caitlin would have been at school now - all the first day at school photos were in the paper recently so I allowed myself to dream a little. It's that split screen again."

Asked what advice he could give to other fathers who may be struggling with the anger phase, Dave says: "Don't be afraid of the grief, don't fear it, embrace it and make it a part of your memories, accept it as part of the path you're on.

"For some people who are religious, which I'm not, there are events in their lives which will test their faith but losing Caitlin tested my *lack* of faith. Her dying and being buried in a box was no longer enough for me. I had to believe there was more. I had to feel she was somewhere. These were strange feelings to work through and, again, were all part of grieving.

"Blocking things out is a bad idea. You can discover a lot about yourself if you explore your grief. Your true character emerges when you have to weather the storm."

'I loved the Boy with the utmost love of

which my soul is capable, and he is taken

from me - yet in the agony of my spirit in

surrendering such a treasure I feel a

thousand times richer than if I had never

possessed it.'

William Wordsworth 1770-1850

MOTHERS AND FATHERS' STORIES

Ross Fraser Rhoderick Flannigan

"Despite nearly 15 years having passed, Mhairi Flannigan is often overwhelmed each November with a feeling of great sadness as a blanket of grief descends over her as she remembers the loss of her beloved son, Ross.

"It's not that I haven't been thinking about Ross," Mhairi says, "I'm just so busy all the time keeping family life ticking over and caring for my other four children. I used to always take time off work around the time of Ross's anniversary, but I haven't over the last few years and have regretted it. In amongst the hustle and bustle of everyday life, every year, around November, I often find myself in tears and struggling to deal with the inevitable build up of emotions and I realise that it's that time again."

Mhairi and her husband Stephen had two young sons, Andrew and Grant, when Mhairi fell pregnant with twins, Ross and Mhairi. The pregnancy had been progressing well when around 36 weeks, Mhairi began to feel tired and sick. She had been up through the night, and so in the afternoon she headed to bed to try and get a little sleep while her eldest son was at school.

Mhairi recalls: "When I woke up, I got up to go to the toilet and realised my amniotic sack was protruding from me. Although I didn't feel like I was in labour, I had no idea what I should do. I wasn't thinking straight with regard to what was happening. Eventually, it got bigger and bigger. I phoned the hospital who said they'd never heard of that happening before – it wasn't my baby's head, it was just clear fluid. I phoned for Stephen to come home and I phoned my mum and asked her to come too. They both came as quickly as they could from Edinburgh to Livingston. Mum arrived first and within a short space of time my waters broke, fortunately, all over the bathroom floor and not over the carpet!

"By this stage, excitement had taken over as we were about to have our twins. When Stephen got home, we all got in the car and rushed to the hospital. We abandoned the car in the car park; it wasn't even parked in a bay! We went in to the hospital, but it still didn't feel like I was in proper labour. I had no contractions but something was obviously happening with the amniotic fluid coming down.

"By the time they got me into a room, they could tell that Ross's head was very close. They then scanned me and it was at that point they realised that they couldn't get two heartbeats. They didn't tell us straight away as they were trying to find a consultant, but everyone was in meetings. When the consultant finally arrived we were given the devastating news that there was no heartbeat for Ross.

"We were then given the option of having the little clip put on his head that monitors the oxygen levels. From the outset, I had been advised to have a caesarean section and I was asked if I wanted a general anaesthetic or an epidural. Mhairi was lying across the way and Ross was obviously head down. The reason they'd offered to put the little clip on his head was to see if there was any sign of life in case they could revive him when he was born. I said no, as I just wanted him out as quickly as possible.

"They then prepared me for an epidural as I wanted to be awake and completely aware of what was going on. I couldn't bear the thought of just coming round after it was all over, I wanted to know what was happening as it was happening. Once that decision was made, everything happened so quickly and like clockwork. They had to get Ross out and then make sure they got Mhairi out quickly too.

"At this stage, Ross wasn't quite out but his head had crowned. However, they still delivered him by section and a minute or so later, they delivered Mhairi. They knew straight away that Ross couldn't be revived. Looking back, we almost had a sense of relief that he wasn't revivable because he could have been in a very bad state. So in a way, we were spared the agony of making the decision as to whether or not he should be revived. That option was out of our hands.

"The doctors thought that he'd only died about an hour before delivery. There was no meconium staining which often occurs in conjuction with other causes of fetal distress and there had been no sign of distress on his part. We decided that as there was no way he could have been revived. We didn't want a post-mortem done.

"Mhairi was fine," her mum continues. "She was 6lb 4oz and Ross 4lb 10oz." Reflecting on the heartbreaking outcome of the birth of her twins, Mhairi recalls: "Weeks before they were delivered, I'd gone in for a routine appointment. The night before that appointment, I'd been on my hands and knees in agony. I'd had a searing pain down my side. I'd had to crawl up the stairs to lie down on my bed until the pain passed. It came to light that from that point on, Ross hadn't grown. Being non-identical twins, each had their own placenta. I couldn't help but wonder if Ross's placenta had partially abrupted. The doctors couldn't or wouldn't say."

Mhairi continues: "I had every faith and still do in the consultant who delivered Ross and Mhairi. She was very open with us about everything that was happening and delivered them very quickly. After the birth, my dad came to the hospital. My dad is a minister and we asked him to christen Ross. Dad asked if he could have a white piece of cloth and a quaiche that he needed to christen him set up on a little trolley.

"At this point, we were distraught when the midwife said we couldn't christen him. Apparently, the rule is that they only christen live babies. Stillborn babies are not allowed to be christened. However, there is no law to stop this happening and nothing was going to stop my dad from christening his grandson. We wanted Ross to be christened, not just blessed. It was the only time there was a bit of contention between us and the hospital staff. Dad was a Church of Scotland minister and he christened Ross – that was all that mattered to us.

"Our beautiful boy was christened Ross Fraser Rhoderick Flannigan. We didn't have Mhairi christened at that time; we wanted to wait and have her christened in church at a later date. Mum arrived with Andrew and Grant not long after that, and we all had a bit of time together.

"After Ross was christened, we were moved up to the family room but this had not been an easy process! I was moved from theatre to the recovery room, then back to the room where we started off when we arrived that afternoon. After a bit of a wait – they wanted to wait till the corridors were quieter – we were transferred up to the family room.

"As I was still confined to bed, a nurse and porter pushed my bed. However, Stephen had to push the hospital cot with both Ross and Mhairi in it, through the corridors. It was a very hard thing for Stephen to do. Of course, there was no easy, private way to transport Ross. The ward staff had an old-fashioned Silver Cross-type pram, which they then used to take him to and bring him back from the mortuary when we requested to see him. They were superb at providing a member of staff to bring him to us when we requested.

"Despite all this trauma, it was lovely to have that time all together as a family in the family room. It was all so strange, though. Neither Stephen nor I were quite with it as we were experiencing such massive extremes of emotions. We were so happy and delighted to have Mhairi but the grief of losing Ross was equally overwhelming. It is hard to explain how it feels to experience such happiness and devastation at the same time. We wanted and needed to take photos and it was important that we took photos of Mhairi with her brother. One of the midwives took the photos, but I feel they're awful as I was crying so much!"

Mhairi continues: "Mhairi has only just been given the photos. We gave them to her on her 13th birthday. She was adamant that she wanted to see them, so Stephen and I sat down with her and bawled our heads off! Mhairi's has always known she was a twin. She was a very tactile baby; perhaps that came from close contact with Ross, but when they were born Ross was no longer there beside her. She craved skin to skin contact. Neither of us would put her down, she was a much cuddled baby! There was always someone hugging her."

Mhairi continues to reflect: "I think there's always been a connection with Mhairi and Ross. Mhairi was a late talker. We have a picture by our bed of Ross and Mhairi together in the crib at the hospital. Mhairi would always point to that picture and have a special look in her eye. Eventually, she was able to point to the picture and say, 'Ross', even though she didn't learn to talk until she was four and a half. She needed intense speech therapy all through primary one and now she never stops talking! Perhaps her late speech had something to do with the loss of her twin but I guess we'll never know. She's pretty well adjusted now. Understandably, she was a very cosseted baby. Our way of dealing with our own grief was to hold her and cuddle her so much."

The weeks that followed saw a very bittersweet time for Stephen and Mhairi. They both continue: "It was hard to balance all the emotions. We had to go on with day to day life with two young boys and a new baby daughter but in amongst that was our own, devastating grief. Looking back, we probably never gave ourselves time to deal with the grief properly. We had to care for the children and deal with their feelings of loss too.

"Andrew, who was only six at the time, needed a lot of reassurance and his way of dealing with things would be to confirm that Ross was dead and he kept saying over and over 'Ross is dead, Ross is dead'. It was so heartbreaking to listen to, but it was his way of coming to terms with why he didn't have two new babies at home. He had drawn a picture of the two babies when I went into hospital, and it was up on the fridge waiting for us to come home."

Stephen reflects: "Even now, all these years on, it's still really upsetting to think about losing Ross. I suppose at the time, I just tried to be rational, life goes on. We had Mhairi and the boys so I tried not to think about it too much. But all the pain's still there under the surface, and when I do think about it, it all boils over. We have our emotions about Ross shut away in a little compartment in our hearts and, occasionally, we bring them out, but not very often now, due simply to the pace of life, but it can still be very raw when we do."

Mhairi and Stephen continue: "In the early days, we went to Ross's grave on a weekly basis then, as time went on, on special occasions – Easter, birthdays and Christmas. If we ever went on holiday, we could hardly bear to go without him so always took him flowers. We have always kept a special box full of our precious memories of Ross and the little things that keep him close to us. My mum made lovely little flannelette gowns for Ross and Mhairi to wear when they were born. Ross is buried in one of them; it had a sailing boat on it as his great-grandpa was a sailor.

"We kept the one he wore in the box along with his blanket and the most precious lock of our little boy's hair." Mhairi continues: "We could never bear to leave the box alone if we ever went on holiday so it always went to my parents' house for safekeeping.

"Early in 2012, we went on holiday. We tried to be strong this time and didn't take the box to my parents. We then suffered one of the greatest violations anyone can endure. We were burgled. Our house was completely ransacked. We could barely get through the door into our bedroom. When we did, we saw utter chaos – every cupboard was emptied, ever drawer rifled through."

Mhairi painfully goes on: "I could see immediately all my three jewellery boxes were gone and then my heart completely sank, when, amidst the trauma, the most devastating thoughts dawned on me – Ross's box. The burglars had desecrated that too, strewing its contents across the room, tossing our most treasured mementos aside with utter disregard and indifference for the impact their actions would have.

"We never found the little lock of Ross's hair. It was the worst violation and the greatest loss – again. The police never caught the culprits and the insurance will never replace what we have lost, but the burglars will never touch the memories in our heart."

Stephen bravely continues: "When we first lost Ross, we both went to SANDS meetings in our area. I think the meetings helped Mhairi, but I found it hard. I needed to deal with things in my own way. I wanted to stay strong and support Mhairi, so at the time I focused on keeping everything in. In hindsight, that probably didn't help me, and now I would definitely encourage bereaved fathers to talk and share their feelings."

Mhairi adds: "My mum helped to promote a SANDS group for bereaved grandparents. She thought it was an excellent idea to provide support to grandparents. My mum and dad's lives were very hectic for a long time as they were Lord and Lady Provost, but they definitely wanted to help promote this aspect of SANDS' work and did an interview for a local paper. The grief and loss felt after the death of a baby affects every member of a family in different ways and it can happen to any member of society therefore it's so important to provide support for everyone.

"SANDS Lothians have specialised groups for almost everyone who could be affected following the death of a baby. They even have groups for parents and siblings of surviving twins. Knowing personally this side of a loss, I am sure that will be a much-needed group."

Mhairi continues: "Stephen and I went on to have an ectopic pregnancy a year to the day after Ross's death, so I was in hospital having surgery on Mhairi's first birthday. It was the same surgeon and she was wonderful. Then we were so moved when she came in from her annual leave to deliver our next child, Murray, and this meant so much to us.

"Murray knows all about his big brother. Ross is still very much part of the family. After the burglary, we had the whole house redecorated and some other things done to get the feeling of the burglars out of our house. The midwife who was on nightshift when Ross was delivered had made a beautiful cross-stitch for us but Mhairi commandeered this, announcing that it was her brother!

"We have a very special and precious picture of Mhairi and Ross together when they were born. She doesn't have it up yet in her room as we felt that if she had friends round, we would worry a bit about them looking at a picture that's so very personal for us. Steven and I both discussed the use of this picture when we'd previously done an article for the papers, and, at that time, decided we didn't want it included. We keep it by our bed; at the moment, it's still very private to us and treasured greatly."

Mhairi and Stephen continue to reflect: "When it's Mhairi's birthday, we would always go up to the grave on the 17th and then celebrate her birthday on the 18th. Once she'd started at school, just the two of us would go up to the grave. The first time she was aware of that, she was really annoyed with us and again exclaimed, 'But that's my brother!' After that, we would all go up at the weekends."

Mhairi poignantly recalls the sad time immediately after the birth: "I felt total numbness. It was as if the world had stopped. People talk about that and it was exactly how I felt. I remember so vividly at the funeral sitting in the car watching everyone carrying on their lives and just thinking, how can anything ever be the same again? It can't… ever.

"It was just a feeling of complete shock, numbness and disbelief; how can anyone smile? After Ross's small private funeral with our immediate family members and some of our closest friends, we went back to Mum and Dad's. I remember at one point, I had to run away and go and cry elsewhere. There were people just sitting, chatting away, which of course I understand is natural when people are all together, but I just couldn't cope with it at that time. Eventually, I came back out again and tried to put on a brave face and a smile.

"Then eventually, we started, very, very slowly, moving with the world again. We found the milestones very hard. Mhairi's christening was really difficult. We held it in the February, during the holiday week, so the church was very quiet, so thankfully, we didn't have to deal with too much. We lit a candle for Ross and we've still got that candle.

"The first day of school was also incredibly hard. Sometimes, it was so difficult explaining that Mhairi was a twin. On one hand, at these special milestones, we try to keep everything normal for Mhairi and, on the other hand, we do it with a very heavy heart.

"There is even a slight twinge of anxiety about the milestones that haven't even happened yet. Grant, our second son, has just left school and he was at his leavers' prom on Friday night. They all looked fabulous in their kilts, and the girls were beautiful in their dresses, and it struck me that this is going to be so weird when it's Mhairi's turn.

"There will still be that feeling that someone and something is missing, and, sadly, that will go on for life. It's hard not to think ahead to Mhairi's wedding. Her twin brother should be there with her."

Mhairi continues to reflect on the early days: "I used to make a point of avoiding anyone with twins. When Mhairi started nursery, there were two sets of twins in her group. I'm still very close to one of the mums, and it was quite strange when I admitted to her many, many years down the line that I had actively avoided her because she had twins and it was too hard for me to look at them!

"One of the first times I ventured out after Ross and Mhairi were born was to take the boys to the hairdressers. I remember sitting outside, I just couldn't bring myself to go in. Mum and Stephen took Grant and Andrew in while I stayed in the car. Then, unbelievably, a couple came wandering past as Stephen came out of the shop and they started talking to him. I heard them commenting on our people carrier and how did we like it as they had baby twins!! I found it so hard to believe that in the whole of Edinburgh, a couple should come past just at that time with twins and, to make it worse, they were exactly the same age as Mhairi."

When asked what advice they could give to other bereaved parents in a similar situation, Mhairi and Stephen provide these words of comfort: "Know you're not alone. Make use of the services offered at SANDS Lothians and talk to their befrienders and counsellors. Accept family support when it's offered. Let people help on a practical level and let friends and family do things for you as well as with you."

Mhairi and Stephen continue: "We're lucky to have friends that have stuck with us through thick and thin. We've had many traumatic life experiences but losing Ross was by far the hardest."

Mhairi goes on: "Having good friends who would simply cook us a meal, or come and scoop me up and take me to their house and help with the children was so greatly appreciated."

She advises: "Make sure you have time to acknowledge how you're feeling. I kept going to SANDS' meetings for as long as I needed to as it gave me a place of comfort to cry and let my feelings out. I felt I couldn't cry all over the place everywhere else.

"Sometimes, I would walk into the meetings and I would just be on the edge. I remember going into one meeting, sitting down, trying to remain calm and composed and then someone simply mentioned something, gently and calmly, about losing Ross and I just dissolved. I was almost just waiting for that moment to be able to cry and let everything out. The poor lady who mentioned him felt like she'd done something terrible, but I would have cried at anything at that point. I was trying so hard to carry on as normal at home and maintain home life as best as possible, yet I was in such turmoil inside."

Stephen adds that for grieving fathers: "Everyone's different but it's good to go to the meetings. It's not good to keep everything in and bottled up, it's exhausting and tiring – it's a relief to let it out. Fathers feel great loss too and should also get support from close family and friends. Even with a busy family life, it's important to take time to grieve."

Mhairi and Stephen agree: "We appreciate everything the SANDS team did for us; they were a lifeline."

Mhairi continues: "I came to meetings right up until Murray was born, apart from during my ectopic pregnancy. That was a devastating loss, too, and the year before that, I'd been in hospital with meningitis, so October and November are not great months for us! My pregnancy with Murray was very closely monitored then he was born in the January by way of an elective section. At last, some joy again in our lives."

Mhairi finally reflects: "My immediate fear when I lost Ross was, will there be a time I'll forget what he looks like? We said our goodbyes in the hospital and decided we wouldn't see him again but we changed our minds and went to see him at the undertakers the day before his funeral, which also happened to be our wedding anniversary. We sat with him at the undertakers and I'm so glad we did that, he looked so gorgeous.

"Keep every memento that you can – have a memory box, even if it's just a shoebox. Keep all the photographs. They are so precious. They're not macabre in any way, they are private and special. Take everything out and look at it, from time to time, treasure your memories. It makes it real when things feel so surreal – especially years on when the grief hits again, out of the blue. As the years pass and life goes on and as the memories may fade, as they inevitably do, your memory box will keep everything real and will help keep your precious baby close and always in your heart."

Our angel and our miracle

"We were so happy to find out I was pregnant. I couldn't imagine being any happier until we found out we were expecting twins at our 12-week scan. Towards the end of the scan, however, we noticed a change in the midwife's demeanour. After taking the usual measurements, she seemed concerned, explaining that there was a size difference in the babies. She immediately called the hospital and arranged for us to see a specialist consultant that day. We were very panicked by this turn of events. We had spent the weeks up to the scan simply hoping that the heartbeat would be strong. We didn't realise we could encounter complications at such an early stage.

"The doctors at the hospital were concerned and monitored our babies very closely over the next six weeks and diagnosed Intrauterine Growth Restriction (IUGR). They explained to us that this meant, at the time the egg split in the womb, that the placenta did not split evenly, leaving one baby with a lesser share than the other. We had broken the news to family and friends, who were all over the moon that we were expecting twins, asking lots of questions and celebrating. However, very few of them knew that we were living in constant worry about the health of the babies and how serious the problem was.

"The doctor had scheduled weekly growth scans to check the progress of the babies and each week we would hope and pray that the babies' hearts would be beating strongly and that they had grown enough to keep them alive.

"At our 18-week scan, the doctor gravely explained that while one twin was growing and progressing well, the smaller twin's growth was only just tracking the fifth percentile for his gestational age. The doctor explained that this was extremely serious and that we may need to consider our options. They suggested two ways forward for us to consider, firstly letting the pregnancy of both twins continue, hoping that the smaller twin could make it to

26 weeks to improve the chances for a viable but extremely premature delivery. The doctor explained that at 26 weeks there was very little hope for the smaller twin, but that the larger twin would have a chance of survival at this point. If the smaller twin were to die in utero before 26 weeks, there would be a significant risk of brain damage or death for the larger twin.

"The other option was selective reduction of the pregnancy which would mean losing the smaller baby with a greater chance of survival and reduced risk of brain damage for the larger twin. We were advised that it would be better to take any sort of action before 22 weeks to improve the chances for the larger twin.

"We decided to wait and see how the smaller twin progressed over the next few weeks, waiting for each growth scan to see whether his progress had picked up or not. At home, I was beside myself with worry, trying to stay calm despite the rollercoaster of emotions coursing through me. At times, I was hysterical, but most of the time I forced myself to remain in control, knowing that the upset was putting greater strain on the twins, the very last thing they needed.

"I struggled to contemplate the options we had been given. My husband and I both wanted the babies so badly and loved them with all our hearts. I kept thinking that mothers are supposed to protect their babies and it made me feel sick that I was even considering the pregnancy reduction. My helpless babies just needed me to look after them; how could I be letting them down so early?

"While our immediate families and a few friends were aware of the issues and were very supportive, there was no one we could speak to who knew what we were going through. I wanted someone to tell me what to do, to take the decision out of our hands, but obviously this was not possible.

"I trawled the internet looking for help, answers or shared experiences but each time I found something that would worry or upset me more in the unedited content. I eventually found the SANDS Lothians' website and sent a desperate email looking for someone to talk to. Thankfully, I got a reply quickly and I arranged to go in for a chat. I was surprised to meet two ladies who had both lost twins and had very similar experiences.

"It was a huge comfort to know that we weren't alone and to see that life does go on after these awful events and that you can go on to be happy without trying to erase the experience. It helped enormously to talk through my situation and to be told that the team at SANDS would always be there if I needed to talk and that I would be welcome to use their counselling services if required.

"For the next few weeks, the smaller baby clung to the fifth percentile line while the larger baby tracked the healthy 50th percentile line. By 21 weeks, the smaller twin had fallen and stayed below the fifth percentile line, and the doctors told us that if we were going to consider the pregnancy reduction option, we would have to act now. We had thought long and hard about the choices we were given and decided that it was our only option, but we went home to sleep on it overnight, one last time.

"I still don't know how we were able to make the decision. Faced with a lot of odds and statistics, we tried to reconcile the numbers with how we felt in our hearts. In the end, I realised that sometimes being a mum and protecting your babies means taking the most difficult of decisions for them and dealing with the consequences so that they don't have to.

"We decided to go ahead with the reduction in the hope that it would give the larger twin the best possible chance of survival and quality of life, and it would avoid a very short life of pain and struggle for the smaller twin. While we were desperate to give both babies a chance, the odds were now so stacked against the smaller baby that we wanted to minimise the pain and suffering for both twins. The next day, I called the doctor to tell her we would go ahead with the procedure and she made the arrangements for us to go to the Queen Charlotte Hospital in London for the specialised procedure.

"A couple of days later, we flew down to London where we met with a very specialised multiple births team. They made their own assessment and presented their findings, again explaining that the smaller twin was very likely to run into trouble soon and if they could not deliver in time, this would be highly risky for the larger twin.

"The outlook for the smaller baby was grim under both options. While there was hope for the larger twin if we reduced the pregnancy, with only a 10 per cent chance of co-twin death or brain damage. We took some time to consider everything again and agreed that our only option was the reduction.

"The procedure took only half an hour and did not hurt as much as I felt it should have. I wanted to experience an outward pain to reflect the pain I was feeling inside but I knew this was futile. Afterwards, we walked around London very slowly and with heavy hearts, praying that the larger twin was surviving the trauma and that the procedure had been quick and painless for our smaller twin. I didn't sleep at all the night before or after the procedure. I hugged my bump the whole time, wanting both babies to know how much we loved them and that we only wanted to do what was best for them.

"The next day, we returned to the hospital for a scan to check that the larger twin had survived and that the procedure had gone as planned. The doctors explained that the next 48 hours were critical for the surviving twin and that the risk of miscarriage would remain for the next month, and that an MRI should be conducted to ensure there was no damage to the baby. Thankfully, our surviving twin coped very well and continued to grow and thrive with no abnormalities on the MRI.

"It was heartbreaking having to tell all of our family and friends that we had lost one of the babies. We didn't tell many people the full circumstances of the loss. We could barely come to terms with the decision ourselves and couldn't cope with explaining it to others.

"People were very kind and supportive, but it's difficult for anyone to know how it feels to be carrying two babies, one living, the other not, and to prepare for the delivery of both. While I looked forward to the arrival of the surviving baby, it was difficult to contemplate finally letting go of our little twin.

"I visited the counsellor at SANDS several times after the loss of our twin. It was really helpful to talk through how I was feeling in order to prepare for the delivery of the twins and come to terms with what had happened.

"I was able to carry our surviving baby to full term, and he arrived safe and healthy by caesarean section. His twin was delivered one minute later, we know he kept his brother safe in there and that he will always be watching over him.

"We had a very small, private ceremony in the hospital, just my husband and I, together with our baby boys, where we welcomed our miracle baby to the world and said goodbye to our angel. I still can't believe it is possible to feel such joy and such sadness all at once, neither feeling diminishing the other. I think about our little angel every single day, and although no one is more aware than we are of how lucky we are to have a surviving baby, our little angel can never be replaced and he will always be in our hearts and thoughts."

Fraser Third 31 December 1988

Anne begins: "My husband Paul and I were delighted when we found out we were expecting our first child. Everything had been progressing well until we went for our 16-week scan. We were due to go on holiday up to Nairn shortly after this and, just as we were getting ready to leave, we got a phone call that would change everything.

"I had been busy packing, and Paul had nipped out for some chips for tea as we decided we weren't cooking the night before we left. Just as he was leaving, the phone rang and it was the hospital. I was told they had the results of my blood tests back, and they showed a lot of protein in my blood and my urine. I was told that could indicate one of two things – I could be carrying twins or there could be something wrong with my baby – good news or bad news!

"I was asked if I could go in on the Monday, so I told them I was just about to go away on holiday and that I would be away for two weeks. However, short, sharp and to the point, the lady on the phone told me that if there was something wrong with the baby that would lead me to opt for a termination, then we would have to move quickly. I was trying so hard to take all this in. I told them if it was a question of a termination, there wouldn't be one, simple as that. My spirits had just crashed down to my feet as it gradually sank in that there was a high likelihood there was something wrong with my baby.

"The hospital was pushing for us to move quickly; they were keen for us to have a scan on the Monday. They advised us that they would see if they could arrange the scan for the next day so that it could be done before we went on holiday.

"Just as I was trying to take everything in, Paul walked back in the door. He was happy as Larry, and then I had to rip his world apart. I hadn't realised that he had caught the end of the conversation so we were both left reeling from being so excited about our holiday and our future one minute, to our world falling apart the next."

Paul recalls: "The hospital told us that they could get us in for a scan on the Monday that we were due to return from holiday, but that would have meant we were nearly 20 weeks into the pregnancy."

Anne remembers: "They kept focusing on dates in relation to a termination and I just kept telling them that that aspect of all this was not up for debate – whatever happened, there was not going to be a termination."

Paul says: "In amongst all of this, at one point they had thought it may be Spina Bifida because of the amount of protein showing in Anne's blood tests."

Anne and Paul painfully recall: "We decided we would wait until we came back from our break for our scan, so we made an appointment for when we returned. We went away with this horrible dark cloud hanging over us. It was a difficult holiday, as you can imagine. We had been planning on buying baby things when we were away but, of course, we could no longer find it in our hearts to do that. We bought one little blanket, thinking that even if things didn't work out, at least our baby would still have a special blanket."

Anne continues: "We came back on the Monday and had the scan. It showed that there was no fluid around the baby. It wasn't twins, so that left us with the devastating reality that there was definitely something wrong with our baby. Our consultant was fantastic. He talked us through all eventualities, explaining everything carefully and putting us at ease. He told us how the pregnancy would progress, and he said that he thought the condition our baby had was Potter's syndrome. This meant that our baby had no kidneys and no renal system. Apparently, this is more likely to happen with boys and is common with the first baby. It's not genetic; it was just pure bad luck."

Paul says: "Anne's mum was really concerned too, so she also spoke to the consultant. She asked that, if Anne was to go to full term, would that affect her in any way. We were all so worried about the baby and Anne. We were told no, and if there was ever going to be any risk to Anne, they would do a termination. Although Anne felt so strongly against having a termination, if there had been any risk to her, she wouldn't put her family through any unnecessary suffering or worry. The months passed, and we had scans every few weeks. The doctors just wanted to be certain they'd made the right diagnosis, and, as the baby got bigger, they were able to see more clearly."

Anne continues: "The scans eventually showed that Fraser didn't have any kidneys so they didn't think he could survive past the stage of the placenta shutting down. It was the placenta that was keeping him alive. I remember at one point a junior doctor said to me that I should really consider a termination because my baby wouldn't look pretty.

"Quite firmly, I just said, it didn't matter what my baby looked like, he would be our baby and we would love him, no matter what. I was told he would have a little pixie face and a deformed head. I remained adamant – it was not our choice to end our baby's life. That decision would be out of our hands, we would let nature take its course and I would continue with the pregnancy."

Paul adds: "It was hard on us but it must have been hard on our consultant too. Every time we went to the hospital for each scan, there was always the chance that there could have been good news but there never was. Our baby was growing, but there was no improvement in his condition."

Anne says: "I ended up going to full term and even the medical staff were surprised at how big the baby got! They almost couldn't believe he wasn't healthy. He was even showing attempts to breathe in the womb. Nature is a marvellous thing; our son was trying so hard to live but we, heartbreakingly, had to accept that he wouldn't be able to breathe outside the womb. For our first-born son, it wasn't to be."

Anne goes on: "I went through a normal delivery although he was breach. My labour lasted around 12 hours and the whole medical team that were looking after us were fantastic. I was determined to go through labour even though I knew what the outcome would be – I wanted to do it for my baby. I wanted to see him and meet him, he was our son. We also wanted to bear in mind that we had been told there was still a chance he may have one kidney.

"The scans hadn't been able to show anything for absolute certain and it may still have been possible to treat him if he'd had one kidney. It would probably have meant a two-year stay in hospital but it would have meant he was alive and it was still a bit of hope. We had been on such a roller coaster of emotions, never able to be completely certain what the outcome would be. We had been so up and down throughout, trying to balance the agony that came with 'maybe he'll be fine, maybe not'".

Anne recalls: "The consultant had warned us that the Potter's syndrome babies that he had delivered before sometimes struggle for breath. Our beautiful baby wouldn't live but he may try to breathe. He warned us that we may find that distressing. The minute Fraser was born, they popped him on my shoulder for just a fraction of a second and I got a tiny brief feel of his cheek on my cheek. It is such a treasured memory. He was then taken away from me so quickly. I don't think they wanted us to see him if he was struggling."

Paul painfully recalls: "They took him away to the next room, bathed him and dressed him in a little babygro. They then brought him back and asked if I wanted to hold him. I chose not to. Whenever I'd held babies before, whether it was my nephews or my friends' babies, it would always take me a little while to get it right! Fraser was my first child and I was worried I would just get used to holding him correctly, then he would be taken away from me and I would have to say goodbye."

Anne and Paul continue: "We had about an hour with Fraser. One of the midwives on duty went to our church. She was fantastic. She took such great care of our little boy, putting him in his tiny basket, gently covering him with his blanket. His hair was still wet because he'd just been given a bath and, as it dried, each tiny strand started to stand on end, one by one – it was so sweet, he was so gorgeous.

"Because he'd been breach, it was a really difficult birth. At one point, one of the medical team must have been wearing surgical gloves and there was a little squeak. We thought it was our baby giving out a little cry but the team were quick to tell us it wasn't, so that we didn't get our hopes up. They think Fraser had passed away around three hours before he was born, so he was stillborn.

"All our families came in to see him in his little Moses basket. We didn't want him handled too much as we felt he'd been through enough already. We just wanted him to rest. It was such a special time, sharing our beautiful little boy with family."

Emotionally, Anne recalls: "My mother-in-law came to visit. She had actually already lost a grandson at nine months old, and I knew it must be so hard for her to lose another. She gently touched Fraser and held my hand and, for a special moment, we had a shared grief and understanding. I felt so sad for her too and everything she'd been through."

Paul says: "We had a funeral for Fraser and we were overwhelmed by the number of people who turned up. We had booked the small chapel, but we couldn't get everyone in. The flowers we had at Fraser's funeral, we sent back to the ward and the nurses all commented on how beautiful they were.

"We later found out that Fraser was born with no kidneys at all, and his condition had not been sustainable with life. It was only his renal system that was affected and it hadn't formed properly. He had no kidneys and no bladder and he couldn't produce urine. Everything else was fine, just his renal system didn't form. The consultant explained it further to us, saying that when all the cells come together, the cell for the renal system is missing. It's not about chromosomes or genetics; it's just sheer bad luck. Fraser also had a little pixie nose which is typical of Potter's syndrome babies."

Anne continues: "Fraser was stillborn on the morning of Hogmanay and we saw in the New Year in hospital. In the run up to the bells, the nurse asked me if I'd like a little sherry. In the background, I could hear babies crying on the ward. I just thought to myself, I have to go and look at these babies or I will never look at another baby in my life. So I picked up my sherry and walked to the nursery with the midwife. I went in and had a little look at the other babies, some were tiny and some huge! Simply walking round the nursery really helped me.

"I was discharged on New Year's Day and, understandably, Hogmanay was difficult for us in the years after that, and we tended to shut ourselves away. However, when our other children, Louise and Euan, came along, we tried to do a bit more. The first anniversary of Fraser's death was the hardest."

Anne continues: "The months following Fraser's death were very difficult. I went back to work in the March but Paul went back only about a week after Fraser's funeral and that was quite hard for me. No-one knew what to say to me, and it was harder when they said nothing.

"We'd been given lovely gifts in the run-up to Fraser's being born and that was hard too because we hadn't really told anyone of the problems with the pregnancy. So we were left in the difficult situation where we had to put on a brave face and tell people what had happened. We had originally decided not to tell anyone what was going on because we were never certain ourselves. We knew doctors sometimes get things wrong and we had always hung on to the tiny bit of hope that we had, but, of course, that left us having to try to explain everything all over again to people we hadn't told, when the worst happened."

Paul recalls: "It turns out that two of the men I worked with had been through similar experiences and they came to chat with me and share what they had been through. I'd hardly spoken to these people before, and I took great comfort from them coming to talk to me.

"Looking back, if I could recommend anything to newly bereaved parents, it would be to take longer than a week off work. I tried to go back to work far too soon and didn't give myself long enough to grieve."

Anne adds: "Some people can really say the daftest things, though. I remember one person said to me, 'Don't worry, you're young, you can have another one.'

"When you lose a baby, you don't want another one at the time, you just want the one you've lost. My son was lying in a cold mortuary, I couldn't even think about having another baby. That's another thing I found hard – I hated the fact that the mortuary was so cold; I fretted such a lot about that. It was the little things that often got to me and that I found so hard to cope with. I'd kept my son safe and warm for nine months, then I felt he was ripped away from me and put in a cold mortuary. I know, of course, mortuaries have to be cold, but it broke my heart at the time.

"You go through a whole range of emotions and grief. One day you can be sitting crying all day and feeling really angry, then that changes and drifts into another emotion."

Paul says: "Even hearing songs bring back memories, there is one song in particular that every time I hear it, I remember the day we were told Anne had too much protein in her blood and there might be something wrong with the baby."

Anne adds: "There is a Status Quo song called 'Burning Bridges' that we now call Fraser's song as one of the days I was very big with Fraser I was dancing around the room and we were having such fun one afternoon in amongst all the sadness and uncertainty we were having to live with. It's a happy memory for us.

"We decided to try for another baby and if something went wrong again, we would give up. In 1989 I became pregnant again. I had a threatened miscarriage at 10 weeks, but, thankfully, all progressed normally and we had our daughter Louise in October 1990, and it was the most joyous occasion. We then had our second son Euan in 1995 and they are both such a gift. My every breath is for them."

Paul says: "We had been married 2½ years before Fraser was born. Losing him did put a strain on our relationship and we knew our grief may pull us one way or the other. In the beginning, it brought us closer but, as the months passed, we had some difficult times. However, I remember we had a good chat one day about our emotions and how we could work to save our marriage and, gradually, we became stronger again. We booked a holiday in Somerset to help start rebuilding our relationship and, slowly but surely, we reconnected.

"We first heard about SANDS Lothians when we were given leaflets at the hospital and we went to one of the memorial services. We also wrote Fraser's name on one of the little wooden hearts that they put on the bay trees in the office. We had Fraser cremated at Warriston, but we got a little plaque with his name on it at Mortonhall Rose Garden.

"Fraser has always been part of our lives and always will be. Louise and Euan grew up knowing they had a big brother."

Asked what advice they could give to other long ago bereaved parents, Anne and Paul say: "Do what is right for you. Sometimes, opening up old wounds isn't a good thing, but do what feels best for you. If you need to talk, talk, connect with others, don't feel isolated but listen to your heart and do what's right for you. It's about the person and their circumstances; there is no right or wrong in the way you grieve. We had four or five months to prepare for our baby not making it and that was bad enough, but for it to happen with no warning must be awful.

"We always feel there is a reason for everything and, if even now, twenty years down the line, telling our story helps others, then that has to be a good thing. This is for him, this is for Fraser."

INFORMATION

Up to the 1600s, it was against common law in Ireland to kill a white butterfly because they were believed to hold the souls of dead children.

Feileacain Stillbirth and Neonatal Death Association of Ireland

BIRTH AND DEATH CERTIFICATES and STILLBIRTH EXTRACTS

If a baby is born alive **before** 24 weeks but dies soon after, the legal requirement is that a birth and death certificate must be issued.

If a baby is born alive **after** 24 weeks but dies thereafter, again, the legal requirement is that a birth and death certificate must be issued.

If a baby is stillborn **after** 24 weeks, a stillbirth extract is issued.

If a baby is stillborn **before** 24 weeks, it is classed as a miscarriage and no certificates are issued or required. However, the practice in some hospitals is that the hospital or their chaplain may issue some form of certificate to acknowledge the birth of the baby. However, this does not happen everywhere.

In the late 1980s, SANDS Lothians entered into discussions with the Registrar General as to why parents who suffered a stillbirth did not automatically get a stillbirth extract and why they could not have a First name on the extract. The normal practice, at that time, had required the parents to apply to the Registrar General for permission to have a stillbirth extract and to have their baby's name added.

Thanks to SANDS Lothians' influence, this practice has changed and parents are now automatically offered an extract and are encouraged to have a First name put on the certificate.

(This information is correct as of September 2013)

COLD COTS

A Cold Cot is a special piece of equipment which can be used following the death or loss of a baby, through a miscarriage, stillbirth or shortly after the baby has been born.

The little time parents get to spend with their baby after their death is so precious to them and many wish to extend that time for as long as they can. It helps greatly with the grieving process and the difficult times that lie ahead.

The Cold Cot keeps the baby cool and can slow down any deterioration that may occur in the baby once it has passed away. It can help preserve the baby's condition and appearance and make the whole experience a little less traumatic.

Bereaved parents' time with their babies is often all too brief. A Cold Cot can help them have more time to create their precious memories and to say their goodbyes.

The cost of one Cold Cot is £3000 and they cost around £200 a year to maintain. A Cold Cot can also warm a baby up again, so that a final kiss and cuddle with Mummy and Daddy is a warm and comforting one.